Face the Storm

C D Kreger

Copyright

The events in this book are true as remembered by the author. Some names and identifying details have been changed or omitted to protect the privacy of individuals.

Cover design by: C D Kreger

Regestration Number: TXu 2-365-168

Effective Date: March 15, 2023

Library of Congress Control Number:

Printed in the United States of America

Dedication

To all my fellow survivors. To everyone who has ever walked this path and to everyone who loves them.

It is time. We have lived in darkness for far too long.

It is time.

Time to break the silence.

Time to step out from the shadows.

Time to reach out and join with one another.

Time to hold hands and walk into the light.

We can do this.

Individually you are stronger than you know.

Together we can change the world.

We can be heard.

We can provide care and comfort.

We can prevent future harm.

All we have to do is come together and tell our stories.

All we have to do is talk about it.

All we have to do is Face the Storm and Tell the Truth.

Trust me. It will be okay.

Watch and listen.

I will even go first.

Contents

Prologue

How do you tell a story that no one wants to hear?

Those of us who have lived the nightmare of sexual violence know the world is full of perfectly decent, caring people who reflexively block the pleas of survivors and who have no idea of the compound damage they cause by shutting out our cries for help.

The average person does not want to be the cause of more pain. This average person genuinely believes there is a time and place to address our spiritual, emotional and physical wounds. This persons' conscious remains clear as long as they can also believe they are helping us; they are teaching us to protect ourselves by limiting our outcries to appropriate settings. This person has not yet learned, seen, or accepted the reality that for most of us there is no safe space, no trusted confidant, no support group. Crises hotlines rarely have the resources to provide long term support. Few therapists specialize in traumatic response to sexual violence and fewer survivors have the resources to afford their services.

As a lifetime survivor I have learned that the cost of reaching out is almost always rejection, increased loneliness, isolation, and more pain. I have been dismissed in medical, religious, and educational settings. I have been laughed at, called liar and worse, I have been labeled emotionally unstable and outrightly dismissed, often with the hated phrase, "You have to understand..." None of these experiences lessened my hunger to simply be heard. I continue to reach out because the need to be heard, the need to be seen, the need to matter, is always greater than the pain of one more rejection. Slowly, gradually, painfully, I have learned how to reach out from a place of strength. I have learned how to project confidence and self-assurance despite my internal feelings of vulnerability, anxiety and weakness.

Don’t be fooled by this outward projection of confidence. I have lived a lifetime of pain and trauma. I have lived a lifetime of feeling unworthy and believing that I was the cause of all the dysfunction in the world around me. I think I have learned to stand strong in the face of those who continue to tell me I have “no right” to share this story.

Sadly, my journey to self-assurance took far too long. Maybe, by publishing this book I can help someone else get there sooner.

Reader; are you ready?

Join me.

Let’s Face the Storm and tell the truth!

A Beginning, in Three Parts

I was born in the early 1960's in the rural upper peninsula of Michigan. I was the first child of married, white, middle class, college educated, Christian parents. We looked good on paper.

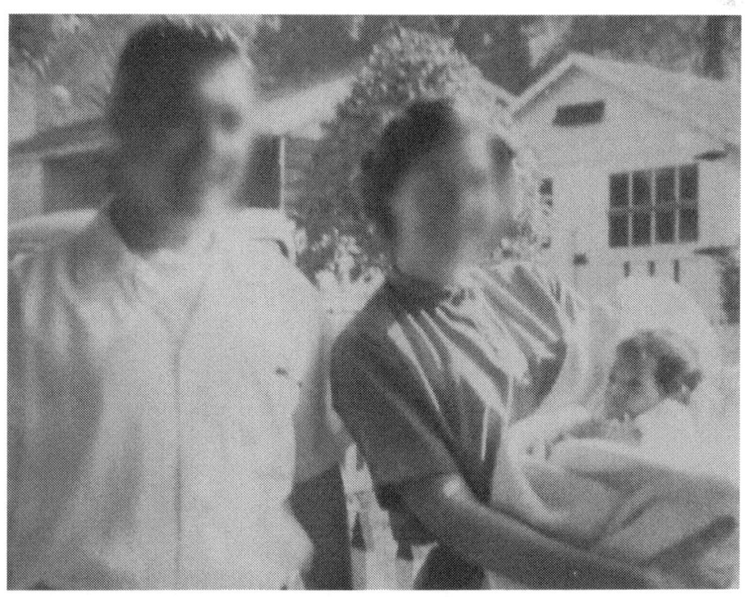

A very young me with proud parents.

Part 1: Memories

One of my earliest memories takes place a few days after the assassination of JFK.

We were gathered with extended family in my mother's childhood home. Everyone was anxious and upset. I was confused. I was witnessing words and emotions I didn't know. All I could understand was that all of the grown-ups were sad. They were sad about the President. "President" was a new word. I asked what it meant and was told that the President was a person; a very important person but this answer didn't explain why people were sad and I didn't know the other words they were talking about; words, like "death," "killed," "assassination," "United States," or even "country."

My inner dialogue gravitated to what I could understand. Something very bad had happened. People were very sad. All of the grown-ups were so sad it seemed like they couldn't pay attention to anything else. They weren't quiet sad or crying sad. They were pacing back and forth sad, talking angrily to each other sad, and sometimes sitting down and looking stunned sad. I hadn't ever seen people sad this way, and I hadn't ever seen so many people sad at the same time.

Even "Sad" was new to me. It seemed kind of like mad. I knew about mad. People in my family got mad a lot. They got mad at each other. They got loud and threw the mad back and forth between each other; like tossing a hot potato except that the game didn't end with just one person holding the potato, it ended up with everyone being mad.

I didn't like it when all the grown-ups were mad, but I was familiar with it, I knew what to expect. I knew fights usually didn't last more than part of a day. There were a lot of fights but if there were fights more than once a day, or multiple days in a row, they were usually different fights and in between there was talking, or maybe crying; some kind of interaction that was not fighting. I hadn't ever seen sad or mad go on and on like this, day after day.

This big sad frightened me. I wanted to find a quiet corner and hide, but the big sad also compelled me. I wanted to understand. I was witnessing a whole new sea of emotion, and I knew it was important for me to learn how to swim safely through it.

We were at Grandma and Grandpa's house in northern Michigan. It was late afternoon, and the sun was sending long, warm, bright rays through the big living room window. Grandpa and Uncle Ron were standing in front of that window, one on each side of the boxy console TV. They were shouting and waving their fists at each other; father and son locked in endless battle, each striving to exert their place of dominance in the family. I couldn't make out their faces because the bright sunlight placed them in silhouette, but I could tell by his voice that Uncle Ron's face was red with rage. Grandpa's voice was booming but he held his body still and firm, unyielding like the brick and stone walls that, as a mason, were his life's work.

I had been standing in the dining room, one hand gripping the edge of a chair for balance. It was at least four steps from there to the sofa; difficult steps because there was nothing to hold on to. I had to focus on each one. Walking was hard work. My view of the room swayed as I waddled from the dining table to the sofa. I was happy to reach out my right hand to the soft vertical wall that was the end of the couch. It was a good place to stop, catch my balance, watch, and try to understand.

The sunlight was warm on the back of my hand. I looked at it for a minute. I looked at the line where the sun met the shadow. I focused on the physical sensations; the texture of the woven material on the side of the sofa; the warmth of the sun on the back of my thumb and first two fingers, warmth that didn't extend to the other fingers still in shadow.

I can still see all of this in my mind today. My pudgy child's hand splayed against the yielding fabric of the couch. Grandpa and Uncle Ron in glowing silhouettes. They looked like pictures of Angels with the sunlight radiating all around them. But in all the stories I heard about Angels they were never mad or sad and they certainly did not shake their fists and yell at each other.

By peeking around the sofa, I could see the feet and ankles of Mother, Aunt Marie, and Grandma. Mother and Aunt Marie, seated on the sofa, were stylish women in fashionable pumps with shapely ankles and calves. Grandma was in the armchair; her shoes were older and her ankles were wider. I didn't have a view of the women other than shoes, ankles and calves but I knew who was where. I rarely saw people's faces at that age. I knew all the grown-ups in my life by their shoes, pantlegs, and stockinged ankles.

For most of my life I thought this was my earliest memory. JFK was assassinated in November of 1963. I was fifteen months old.

This is one of many, very early memories but this one is significant because I can date it. Most early memories do not have such anchors to a specific moment in time. How do you sift through your very early memories? How do you establish a timeline when you don't yet understand the basic concepts of days, weeks and months; or even before and after?

My family never helped. They were the sort that talked at children, not with them. When I tried to talk about the things I remembered, especially if I asked for help to understand what was happening and why, my parents, especially mother, would only laugh and tell me that I could not possibly remember any of the things I asked about. She always responded this way, even in later childhood and adolescence. If she wasn't laughing at me for making up the most outrageous stories, she was angry at me and would tell me I had no right to say or even believe such things. I learned to keep my memories to myself.

It was a long time before I understood that Mother never validated any of my memories because so many parts of my childhood were secrets she didn't want me to remember and stories she didn't want me to tell.

Thirty years later, as the nation recognized the milestone anniversary of the Kennedy assassination, I asked Mother about the scene in her parents' home. How did it relate to the assassination? Her first reaction was, of course, to insist that I made it all up. I ignored her dismissal and described the scene. I described the room and who was in it, then detailed the argument between Grandpa and Uncle Ron in front of the television. I asked what it all had to do with the assassination.

Eventually Mother explained. She said JFK was killed on Friday, but people were upset and frightened for days. There were rumors and fears of a plot to overthrow the entire government. No one knew what might be coming next. She also explained that in her parents' home the rule was no television on Sunday. The scene I described took place on Sunday. Her brother Ron wanted to see the evening news. He wanted to know if anything else had happened. He needed to know if his country was stable.

Mother still refused to acknowledge that I remembered the event, but she explained everything I described. Her explanation validated my memories. We were in Grandma and Grandpa's home. Grandpa and Uncle Ron had fought in front of the TV. The argument took place in time for the evening news, after Sunday dinner, when the table was cleared and the dishes put away, when the adults (male and female) were all gathered in the living room and the late autumn sun's rays would have angled through the front window casting my Uncle and Grandfather in silhouette before reaching further into the room and warming the end of the sofa. All the parts fit together. This wasn't something I just made up.

Another early memory centers around a child's wooden chair.

One day Mother came home with a horribly ugly child-sized wooden chair. She was beaming with pride as she showed it to me. She said it was a present for me. She obviously thought this was wonderful and I was supposed to be delighted with the gift, but the chair was so ugly. It was scary ugly! It must have been painted several times and then all the different layers and colors had been stripped with solvent. The result was dead, grey wood with streaks and strains of various blended shades. It looked like something that had been formed from a pool of dried, crusty vomit! Just looking at it made me want to cry and yet Mommie insisted that it was special, it was for me, and I was going to love it!

A day or two later I watched as Mother spread newspaper on the cement floor at the bottom of the basement stairs. Then she opened a can of paint. She told me the color was 'peach.' I didn't think the color looked like peaches at all, certainly not the yellow-orange canned peaches I loved, but the light coral shade was beautiful, like the delicate color at the base of an apple blossom petal. I sat across from her on the floor and watched as that ugly, evil, chair transformed with each stroke of her brush. I didn't understand that the paint was covering the ugliness. To my eyes it looked as if she was brushing away the ugliness, carefully erasing it with every stroke of her brush to make way for the beauty underneath.

My memory of that peach chair is rich and layered. I feel revulsion and anxiety. "Don't make me look at it. Please don't make me touch it. It is so ugly it hurts!" In my memory I also feel miracle and wonder. "How can something that evil and ugly become so beautiful? Is this magic?"

Because the memory is so strong. I assumed it must have taken place when I was two or three. I assumed this because between two and three was when I learned to trust myself and the thoughts in my head. It was the age when I began to use memories and experiences to build an understanding of my world. It was also when I began to understand myself as a unique being, separate from other people in my life. These were simple basic understandings built on simple experiences. If Mother told me to come with her to the grocery store, I knew to put my shoes on. I knew we would walk to the end of the block and then turn left and cross the street. I knew these things because we had done the same before. I remembered them.

Then there is the matter of language. I understood everything Mother told me about the chair. It was for me. It was a present. Yes, it was ugly, but she was going to fix that. She was going to make it beautiful. Because I understood what she explained to me I assumed I must have been old enough to talk. When did I learn the meanings of all these words? I must have been at least two, if not older. Based on those assumptions I believed she gave me the chair while we were living in Detroit. I believed this even though I knew that the physical surroundings of my memory did not fit the Detroit house. The basement where I sat on the cement floor and watched Mother magically heal that awful, ugly chair, wasn't right for the house in Detroit. The stair rail was on the wrong side. The light was wrong. Maybe Mother was right. Maybe I did make things up in my head. Maybe I didn't ever know what was true and what was just my imagination, after all I was still practically a baby, how could I possibly remember all these things?

My memory of the chair wasn't something I shared. It was mine. It was a personal, private thing, a happy experience from early childhood. I didn't want to share it. If I did, I would only be told how often I made up the strangest stories. Why would I share a happy memory just to have someone take it from me and ruin it?

One day, more than 55 years later, and after I started writing this book, I sorted through a stack of old photos looking for ones that would be suitable to include in this memoir. The stack contained a handful of black and white snapshots taken on my first birthday. There I was, a chubby baby, with an intimidating piece of over-frosted cake, sitting in the freshly painted peach chair, on my first birthday!

My memory of the ugly chair and the miraculous peach paint occurred before my first birthday! I remembered it, and I remembered it correctly. All these years I had wondered why the configuration of the stair rail was backwards in my head, but it wasn't backwards at all. I had just been trying to place it in the wrong house.

The events in my head were real. I just had to trust myself!

Me on my first birthday in the chair Mother painted.

Part 2: Peanut Butter

For most of my life I could not eat peanut butter. I am not saying that I did not like peanut butter, I am specifically saying that I could not eat it.

I don't particularly like Brussels Sprouts but when my favorite aunt proudly set them on the table for Sunday dinner I smiled and told her they were very nice. (Okay, so internally I carefully considered the minimum helping size and how to express appreciation without encouraging her to serve them again, but I ate them. They didn't hurt me. I didn't even make a face.)

Peanut butter is a whole different thing. I have choked it down once or twice, but it was a real challenge, one of those situations where you have to force it down, you have to keep it down, and in order to do this you have to find something else, anything, to clear the flavor.

And yet I have known for years that there is no rational explanation for my absolute, inflexible, soul deep, intolerance of peanut butter.

I am an adventurous eater. I like food in all its many flavors, tastes, and textures. Sure, I like some foods more than others, but nothing comes close to my all-out inability to tolerate peanut butter.

Another thing that doesn't make sense about my inability to eat peanut butter is that I was *allowed* to reject it. My parents never ever challenged me or pushed me to eat peanut butter. Both my parents were born during the Depression. Food was not plentiful in their childhoods. The very real possibility of going hungry shaped their attitudes for life. No one in our home was allowed to be a picky eater. We were expected to eat what was given to us and be grateful for what we got, Brussels Sprouts and all. These were strict rules, consistently enforced. The only exception was peanut butter and the only person the exception applied to was me.

My father loved peanut butter. His favorite way to eat it was on pancakes. He would smear a whole stack of them with a thick gooey layer of peanut butter between each one; like frosting a cake. Just watching him was enough to turn my stomach. If I raised an eyebrow or looked away, I would have to listen (again) to the story of how I loved peanut butter as a baby and then one day I simply refused to eat it ever again. How I was in the church nursery and Mother had to be called to come get me; how I was too disruptive to handle and how I had absolutely refused to eat the peanut butter sandwiches that were the only thing on the menu that day.

So, there was the mystery. My father loved peanut butter, apparently, I did too, until one day I just didn't; in fact, I couldn't even stand to see it or smell it. My parents treated picky eaters like they were sinners. They would talk endlessly and derisively about the family that casually served their child a hot dog because he wouldn't eat any of the other food on the table or even the family who didn't force their child to clean her plate. "Can you believe they let their child get away with that? No child of mine will ever get away with such behavior..."

And yet no one ever challenged me on my refusal to eat peanut butter, they just laughed nervously and told the story of how odd I was for one day deciding I would never eat it again.

Interestingly, Mother never ate peanut butter either. I didn't notice this until decades later. No one ever said a word about our sharing the same aversion. It was just an unspoken rule of the household.

I have other memories from that era. These are less specific, more general and repetitive. Most of them take place in the fellowship hall of our church, in Mother's hometown congregation.

Our denomination, Community of Christ is very social. Our congregations consist of small, tight-knit groups. Many include multiple generations of one or a few families. As a rule, we like each other, we enjoy each other's company. Time spent after Church, to include hanging with friends and sharing lunch, often lasts longer than the Service itself.

In my early Church memories, I am small. I am working my way through a room crowded with adults. To me the room looks like a forest of knees. No one is looking at me or for me. If I want to be noticed by an adult I have to reach up and pull on the hem of a skirt or the knee of a pantleg.

These memories take place after church service, when all the grown-ups are standing around, when the children have been released from age-appropriate activities and have nothing specific to do. I wander through the crowd of ankles and knees with the swaying gait of a toddler. When I find my mother's skirt, I reach up and tug on the hem to tell her I am there. Her response is always the same. She will point to an older man in the crowd and ask me if I have been to see him. She will tell me that I should go visit with him. I should be nice to him. Often, she will say that he likes to spend time with me and that he and I have a "special relationship." Then she will say he probably has candy for me and nudge me toward the person indicated.

I don't remember the name of the man. He isn't someone who squats down to greet me as I head his way. He doesn't have any special treats waiting just for me. But I have been told what to do so I dutifully head toward the intended target. I make my way across the room and tug on his pantleg to get his attention. I explain that my mother told me to ask him for candy, so he is supposed to give me something.

This is the mid 1960's and we are a non-smoking denomination. The men my mother indicates are always near the edge of the room. They are the ones who attend but don't fully fit in. Since they are men in the 1960's they naturally smoke. They try to hide this when they are at church. They use mints or gum to mask the smell of smoke on their breath and ease the need for a cigarette.

I tug on a pant leg and ask for candy, as I was told to. The target looks embarrassed and says he doesn't know if he has any. Then he searches his pockets to see if there is anything left. If there is nothing in the pocket, he may pull out the inner lining to show me that it is empty. I have to tip my head way back to see the empty pocket above me. I don't want to fall over so I keep a good grip on the pantleg as I look up at the limp white flag of a pocket liner. Sometimes a little lint falls from the inverted pocket towards me, at least once I can see that the white pocket has been poorly mended with dark colored thread.

If he has "candy" it is probably some kind of mint. There are Pep-o-mint lifesavers, Wint-o-green lifesavers, the pink wintergreen candies that can be bought loose... At this point in my life the only candies I know are various forms of mint.

One time there is only gum. The man tells me that gum isn't really candy and I probably won't like it, but I don't buy his excuse. If gum is kinda like candy and gum is the only candy he has, then I want the gum. He reluctantly passes down a rectangle of shiny silver foil and explains that I need to chew it but not eat it.

He has given me a stick of Doublemint gum. It is old, stale, and brittle. I only have two tiny front teeth. I have been learning that I can use them to bite but I do not understand chewing. I carefully nibble off a tiny corner and taste the powerful flavor. It is so stale that it breaks like a hard candy but it is sweet and minty, so I slowly eat the whole thing.

When I get back to Mother she asks if I visited the man and if he gave me candy. I earnestly explain about the gum and how it is not candy. My disclosure produces a lot of excitement. She tells me I am too young for gum and insists I give it to her. I tell her I can't. It is gone. I ate it; and it kinda seemed like candy... She responds with the ridiculous request that I spit it out and give it to her. I just stare up at her wondering how on earth I am supposed to do that? When I don't produce the gum she picks me up, turns me upside down, and prods around in my mouth to find the gum she is sure I am hiding from her. When she is finally satisfied that there is no gum to give up, she puts me back down and sends me off to go bother another target while she continues on with her adult conversation like absolutely nothing happened.

As an aside. I never liked Doublemint gum. I find it overpowering. The only time I enjoyed it was that first time when it was so stale I could break it into tiny itty bitty bits and swallow them like candy. I spent half of my childhood trying to find another appropriately brittle piece of Doublemint but never got it exactly right.

This is where I was the day I stopped eating peanut butter. I was at church in my mother's hometown, surrounded by her family, lifelong friends, and acquaintances. I can't tell you exactly what happened. I don't have any memories of that day, only the carefully edited stories of my parents. It was apparently a conference Sunday which means that in addition to the Worship Service there also business meetings of some sort. In our tradition such meetings take place once or twice a year. They involve things like budget discussions, or task assignments, such as who will teach which Sunday school class for the next year...it is a longer day than usual, so the little children are gathered in age-appropriate groups, and in this case the nursery children were served a lunch of peanut butter sandwiches.

This was the day that I told the world I would not eat peanut butter again, ever! I must have made a pretty big fuss. I have been told I was crying and fussy for no obvious reason. I absolutely refused to eat. Any and all attempts to elicit interest in the peanut butter sandwiches only made things worse. Eventually my parents were called. They were obviously embarrassed by this unprecedented temper tantrum. When they couldn't calm me down they put me in the car and took me home.

Part 3: Impact

And then we moved.

Me on our farm with our Siberian Huskies Nanook and Tabuk in the background.

Our home was a 40-acre farm on a spit of land jutting out into the north shore of Lake Michigan. We owned this farm. My parents bought it shortly after I was born. It was the first home they ever bought, and we had only lived there for a little more than a year.

The farm was about 10 miles outside Mother's hometown. Father's family lived in Montana so we couldn't be close to both sets of parents and location didn't matter to him. He worked as an auditor for State of Michigan, Social Services programs. Since his job had him traveling to a different part of the state every week, any town in Michigan was as good as any other.

We didn't grow crops other than a vegetable garden and a long-neglected apple orchard. Mother made extra money by breeding rabbits (for food) in the chicken coop and breeding our pair of Siberian huskies Nanook and Tabuk.

With all their money tied up in the farm and nothing to draw us out to another community we just moved. One day I threw a fit at church and refused to eat peanut butter. A week or two later we packed our stuff, sold all the rabbits, found a new home for Nanook and Tabuk and walked away, leaving a farm we owned, the first property they ever bought, sitting empty for the next four years.

I have never been given any explanation for leaving the farm, but I know that they didn't leave for me. They didn't pack up and leave their home to protect me. They left because of me. They left to protect themselves.

Mother had been a sexually abused child. She was abused at Church events and in her hometown. At this point in her life, she had not acknowledged that the friendly man from church who met her at the movie theatre, who bought her candy and liked to sit with her in the back row, so she could let him put his hand up her skirt; was a pedophile. She had also not told anyone about the man at the summer church sponsored family camp we call Reunion; the man who noticed her and made her feel special, the man who had invited her into his tent and given her candy in exchange for being allowed to kiss her secret, private places.

I do not know if these were two different men or just one, but it hardly matters. She was living with her own unresolved trauma. When she entered puberty, her abuser rejected her and his rejection cut so deeply she never got over it. When I was born, she saw an opportunity to vicariously renew her "Special Relationship." Her behavior wasn't rational, but it fits common patterns of abusive interaction, reaction and attempts to normalize trauma.

Mr. "Special Relationship," the man she regularly sent me to and told me to ask for candy, was Grandpa aged. He had been part of our congregational life since before Mother was born. I am convinced that he was her abuser, and mine.

True pedophiles lose interest as their targets grow into adolescence and adulthood. The secret friend who made her feel special as a child rejected her as she approached puberty and she was reminded of the pain of that rejection every week. She needed his attention and approval, longed for it. Is it any wonder she saw me as a vicarious lure, an opportunity to renew the secret friendship that had made her feel special, loved, and important?

I don't know how he managed to get me alone. I've only recently recovered the shadowy recollections of a huge adult hand, a hand large enough to cover the back of my head, my neck and most of my back, pushing, forcing my face down, towards the peanut butter smeared thing rising up from his lap.

That day changed everything. Mother wasn't ready to face the challenge of dealing with her own abuse. I was too traumatized to take back to church, and there was no easy way to explain any of this to friends or family, so we moved away. We packed our stuff and moved into a rented house in Bellaire, a town in

Michigan's lower peninsula, about 100 miles southwest of the Mackinac bridge.

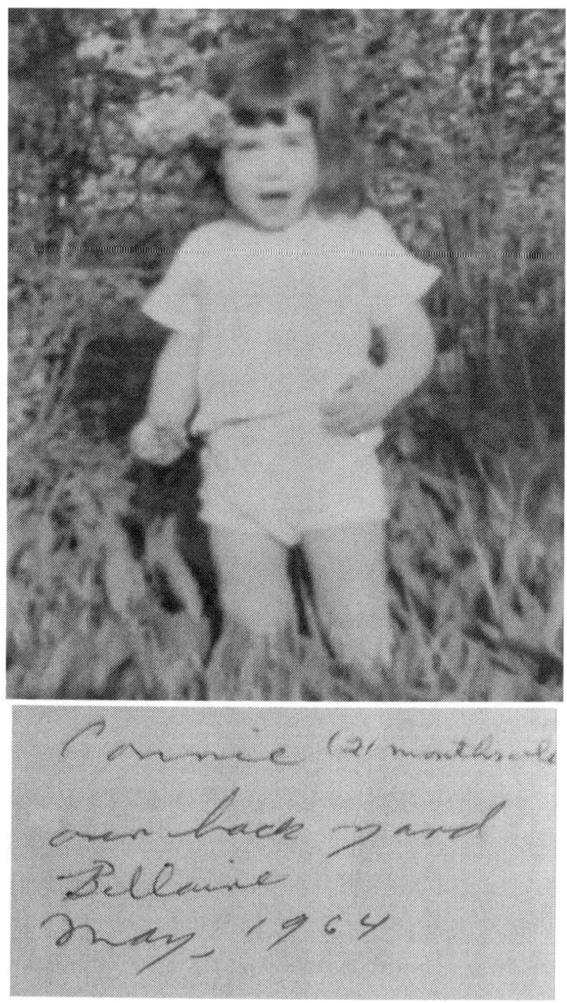

Me in front of a lilac bush outside our new home in Bellaire MI. The date and location were written on the back of the photo by Mother

Three months later, my father would enroll in a work-study graduate school program at Wayne State university in Detroit, and we would move again.

Peanut butter and our sudden move away from Mothers hometown remained mysteries to me for a very long time. Even after I began talking and writing about the abuse, including sexual abuse, of my childhood. I couldn't make all the pieces fit.

Eventually, I learned some of Mothers' background. I learned that her abuser was a member of her home congregation. I began to understand how victims of abuse often try to recreate circumstances of abusive events in an attempt to normalize those experiences.

One day, more than fifty years later, I had an experience that triggered a flash back. I was at a church retreat where I had been talking to a group of people about sexual abuse; it's prevalence everywhere (including our denomination) and how by acknowledging its presence we can do a better job of preventing such abuse and caring for the people affected by it.

As I rushed to the next event, I passed my husband going the opposite way on the same path. He leaned in for a quick kiss and as his lips touched mine, I was overpowered by the taste and smell of peanut butter. I physically jumped back as a single image flashed through my mind. In that instant, rushing between activities, dealing with the hurt and confused look on my husband's face and the impact of my own traumatic past, I knew!

I saw the peanut butter. I felt the unyielding pressure of a massive hand at my back, pushing my face down and into it. I knew that somehow; I had ended up alone with this man; the man who had abused Mother as a child. For just an instant the real world around me disappeared and my knees threatened to let go and drop me to the sidewalk. I knew what he had done to me and why I was so traumatized that I could not eat peanut butter for the next 50 plus years. All the pieces fell perfectly into place, and yet I was in the middle of a busy retreat with little time or opportunity to pause and take in the sudden rush of new information.

Wesley, my husband, said he had eaten a Reese's Peanut Butter cup. This should not have bothered me. I should have tasted more chocolate than Peanut butter on his breath. But on that day, a simple peck on the lips, a dry kiss from my loving spouse of over 20 years, produced an explosion of peanut butter, fear, revulsion, an indescribable sound of agony, and vivid images.

He looked at me with understandable hurt and confusion. How could I explain? I couldn't even catch my breath. My head was suddenly full of new knowledge with no time to process any of it. I looked back at him and lamely explained that all I tasted was peanut butter, there wasn't any chocolate at all, not even a hint.

How do I explain that moment of revelation? I was a woman in my 50's. I knew I was a survivor of sexual abuse. I knew my life had been shaped by layer upon layer of secrets, most of which I would never learn. I knew that my life, my own history, was full of questions I could never answer. I was coming to understand a deep personal calling to stand up and speak out; to stop carrying and covering for other people's secret sins. Now there I was, in a public place, on a hectic, sunny, summer day; seeing, hearing, and feeling events that had been locked in my memory for more than half a century.

I wasn't ready. I couldn't accept this knowledge at that moment. I did what I am good at. I pushed it back below the surface and resolved to deal with it some other time.

When we returned home a couple of days later Wesley walked into the house hungry. As soon as the car was unloaded, he made one of his favorite snacks, toast with peanut butter, then took his plate out to the family room.

I walked into the kitchen a few minutes later and stared at my nemesis, a Costco sized jar of Jiff, sitting on the chopping block. My husband was in the next room, focused on his laptop. I was effectively alone with a lifelong foe. Now was the time to challenge it.

I removed the lid, took a deep breath, stood up straight and mentally recited the phrase I had been working on. "The peanut butter isn't the problem. It never was. The taste you can't handle is just a memory. You know that now. You can choose to separate the memory from the present. You can choose to taste only the peanut butter." Then I dipped my finger directly into the jar and for the first time in over 50 years, I actually tasted peanut butter.

Peanut butter doesn't taste at all like the muscle memory that overwhelmed my brain and psyche for so long. The aversion was gone!

Today, peanut butter is a food I like. Even peanuts taste different than they did. Apples and peanut butter are a favorite snack. Yes, I gained a traumatic memory, but I also gained an understanding of myself. I have control!

Peanut butter is triumph! Peanut butter is power! I don't just tolerate it. I like it!

At least most of the time.

On the day I first wrote this passage Wesley prepped his snack of peanut butter toast (with thinly sliced bananas). When he sat down at the table next to me the smell as so overpowering, I had to get up and leave. In all the years when I couldn't eat peanut butter at all, the smell of it on someone else's plate never bothered me enough to force me away from the table. Now, just writing about the experience brought back the aversion, and it was stronger than ever.

I was crushed! I had won. I had scaled that mountain. Now, even though I knew that what I was tasting and smelling wasn't real, I couldn't make it stop!

I wasn't willing to let the past take control of me again. I tried to force the issue. I got up, walked to the jar and dipped in my finger and sucked off a tiny glob of brown ickiness. Sadly, I had to force the tiny dab of peanut butter down then hold my stomach and close my eyes waiting for the revulsion to pass. I tried but failed to remind myself that what I was tasting wasn't real. But in that moment, it was real. It was visceral and no mere logic could make it otherwise. I had to close the jar, move away from the kitchen, away from the table, and away from my husband, then find some other taste to try and cleanse my palate.

It was three days before I could eat peanut butter again. Three days later I was fine. I happily enjoyed my apple and peanut butter snack.

A week after that the aversion was back. My poor husband sat down on the sofa with a simple piece of peanut butter toast, and I had to ask him to go to another room. I was in a chair, four feet away but I could not tolerate the smell.

A day or two after that I was fine, again, and hoping to stay that way.

Months later, I edited this passage while snacking on a yummy plate of peanut butter and sliced apple! I would like to say this was the end of the story. I would like to claim the final triumph of editing this section with a crispy apple and an open jar of peanut butter, proving to myself that I can overcome all things…

Sadly, peanut butter has become an unpredictable boomerang. One moment I love it, a day later just the scent of it pushes me out of the room.

I complained to my therapist. I told her how frustrated I felt at thinking I had overcome this challenge only to learn that it could sneak back into my psyche at any time. She literally raised an eyebrow to say I was being terribly unrealistic and asked, "What did you think would happen?"

There is a lesson here. Sometimes we can control our mind-body responses. But not always. Pretending to be whole is not enough. I know I need to respect my physical body and take care in allowing it to heal from disease and injury, but I still struggle to apply the same care and respect to injuries of psyche and spirit.

Becoming

The years in Detroit were wonderful!

I say this despite recognition that many readers will be confused by this assertion. My father was rarely home. He was attending graduate school, working internships, and pastoring a congregation across town. My mother was at best an indifferent parent. Many would see her as guilty of child neglect. But I was two. The world was new and exciting. Unexpected wonders were revealed every day.

I had lots of freedom to roam. There were very few rules. "Stay on the sidewalk. Don't cross the street. Come when you are called."

I was free to travel two houses to the right, far enough to visit the little boy my age who lived there but not past his house as he lived on the corner of a busy road. To the left I could venture further. There was a large boulder in the yard about four houses up. I could wander as far as the big rock. This distance gave me access to a family with multiple children. The oldest, Debbie ,was just a little older than me.

Debbie was loud and brash. Mother insisted she was a bad influence. I loved her dearly. She had three younger siblings. Her home was chaotic, child centered, and always exciting. They had an above ground pool, which to a two- or three-year-old is just a pool, a real pool! They ate and played outside all summer. They had all kinds of child friendly foods, toys, activities… They practiced risky behavior like a five second rule which prevented all kinds of unhappiness when a morsel of something tasty hit the ground. As a small child used to spending all my time with only my mother in a home that was always clean, tidy and sterile, Debbie's house was a little slice of heaven.

One particular memory occurred on a day Mother told me I was sick and had to stay home. She claimed I had gotten a case of swimmers' ear from Debbie's pool. At midday Debbie knocked on our door and gifted me with a plastic sandwich bag filled with six large, triangular, golden yellow chips. My first taste of Dorito's! (I have verified this. According to Wikipedia Dorito's were first introduced in 1964.) Thank you Debbie!

Our house had a large back yard, just a flat patch of weedy grass surrounded by a chain link fence. The fence meant nothing to me. It was an easily climbed ladder, a stile, leading into the untamed empty lot behind it. Maybe Mother didn't think it necessary to explain the purpose of the fence or maybe she just didn't care. In either case I was never forbidden from climbing over the fence and exploring beyond its perimeter. I was young enough and small enough to fit my sneakered feet inside the chain link openings and hearty enough to scramble up and over the top with ease. Scaling that fence took only seconds. I did it every day.

I was not a disobedient or willful child. I have always had a mild temperament. I wanted and needed much more attention than I received so I was careful to be a "good little girl" and do things I hoped would earn me love and affection. But in the innocence of childhood there are no implied rules. I didn't yet have the experience or context to reason things out. I followed the rules I was given. I washed my hands before coming to the table. I didn't go past the big rock...

When I was told to go out and play, I was free to be on my own. No one ever told me not to climb the back fence so I had no reason to believe it was off limits. If one of my parents came outside and called for me, I would run towards the house and climb back into the yard. If they noticed that I had been outside the fence they never complained.

I suspect I had some sense of the rhythm of the days. I had an idea of how much time passed between breakfast, lunch and dinner and subconsciously knew when it was safe to venture further and when I should stay closer to home. And so, I roamed. I became my own person. I had my own experiences. I developed my own sense of self-awareness and made the most of my stimulating and unique environment. While I don't recommend this mode of parenting, I believe I owe much of my emotional resilience to those early, unsupervised years.

There were so many wonderful things on the other side of the fence! The house backed onto a landlocked, unused urban space. It was a few acres of undeveloped land with no street access. There was a stream just the other side. I was too small to jump across the stream, but some former visitor had spanned it with a wooden plank; a perfect bridge for someone my size. Beyond the stream was a riot of tall grass, trees, weeds, and wildflowers. There should have been thorny blackberry and raspberry brambles, but I don't remember any problem with thorns.

Further back and to the right were the basketball courts outside the local the high school. They were surrounded by a very high chain link fence; too high for me to climb. To get past that fence I had to squeeze through a gap at ground level. Of course, it was just a basketball court. It was paved, uninteresting, and populated by big boys who never invited me to join their game. I didn't visit very often.

Off to the left and a bit further still was the "Hippie" house. It was an old wood frame farmhouse that faced the main road. The Hippie house had a long porch down one side, next to a dirt drive with a turn-around circle at the end. There were always people, young adults, about. Both the men and women had long hair. The women wore colorful long skirts and flowing blouses. There was an actual spinning wheel on the porch and a metal barrel that always had a fire in it in the circle of the driveway.

Someone was always playing guitar and singing. I really wanted to be a part of the hippie house.

The first time I was spotted hanging out near the edge of the woods a young woman came over to say hello. She squatted down to my level (a kindness I rarely received). She asked my name. She said she was happy to meet me. She asked where I lived, if I knew my way home and then, just as I was hoping for an invitation to join the singing, she told me I should turn around and go back home. I didn't understand! For a moment I had felt so welcome, but now she wanted me to go away.

A few days later I came back. When I stepped out of the woods I heard a voice say, "Hey everybody it's Connie!" For another moment I felt warm and welcome, until I was told again that I should go home. Eventually I stopped visiting. I couldn't understand why people who always seemed so happy to see me would then tell me to leave, but it was pretty clear that I would never be allowed to sit on the porch and join the singing. Watching from the woods just made me feel lonely so I stopped going there.

The hippie house lives in my heart to this day, a beautiful Shangri-La that is always just out of reach. I sometimes wonder if my entrance to Heaven will feel like being welcomed into the Hippie house.

The one happy thing I enjoyed with Mother was her piano. She was a decent pianist and frequently played for church services. She had an old, upright piano. I loved listening to her practice hymns, but my favorite was when she sang and played funny, childish songs. I would sit next to her on the piano bench and try to keep up as she sang, "Cockles and Muscles" or "Yankee Doodle Dandy." The music was magic, and I wanted to be able to make my own.

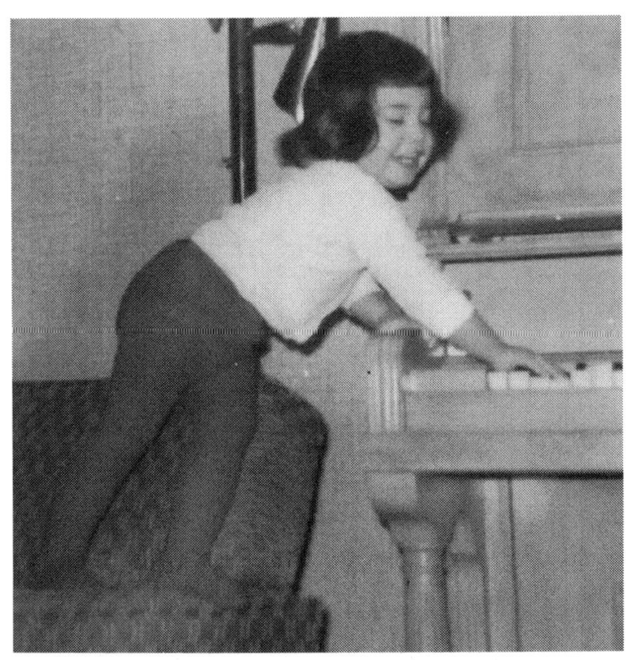

Me at Mother's piano. About age two.

I have one particular memory of that year that effectively outlines the family dynamic. I had been playing outside by myself and came back to the house at about lunch time. Mother was sitting at the kitchen table with her head in her hands, crying about how sick she felt. She didn't look up or acknowledge my presence, she just kept her head down crying and moaning, "I'm so sick I can't even feed my child."

I tried to tell her that I would be okay, but she didn't answer or even look at me. Eventually I said, "don't worry Mommy. I can get my own food." Even then she did not respond to me.

Since the problem seemed to be all about feeding me, I decided to just go ahead and show her that I could take care of myself. I moved one of the chairs from the table and placed it in front of the refrigerator, then I brought my child sized stool out from the bathroom and placed it next to the kitchen chair. The stool was low enough that I could climb onto it and from there I could climb onto the chair. Standing tippy toed on the chair I could just barely reach up and open the freezer compartment of the refrigerator.

It was the first time I had ever looked or reached into the freezer, and it wasn't what I expected. The inside of the refrigerator was lit. It was bright and the air that came out of the refrigerator was cool, dry, and reasonably fresh. The freezer was unlit, dark, and musty. There was thick dry frost around the edges of the compartment and despite being colder, the air felt damp. I wrinkled my nose, just barely even with the bottom of the freezer compartment, at the funky, stale odor.

My target was a box of popsicles. It was there in the front, partly open. The cardboard box sagged from the moisture. Little bits of frost clung to the outside of the white popsicle wrappers. To my relief there was a half popsicle available and within reach. I was concerned about this because whole popsicles (two sticks) were more than I could finish and wasting food was not tolerated. Mother usually banged popsicles on the edge of the counter to break them in half but I knew that I was not strong enough to do that for myself.

Goal achieved, I climbed down from the chair and stool and proudly waved my trophy. “See Mommy. I got my own lunch.”

I was hoping for a bit of praise. I thought I was clever, brave, and helpful. Sadly, Mother's response was only more self-pity. When I pushed back to say that really, I had just gotten my own food and I would be okay she became angry. She told me I couldn't possibly understand her problem and I should leave her alone, so I took my popsicle and my hurt feelings and went back outside and over the fence.

A Visitor

One morning we had a visit from a stranger. It was a weekday so only my mother and I were at home. I was seated on the living room floor watching Romper Room when the strange man came to the kitchen door.

Mother seemed very happy to see this person. She brought him into the living room to meet me. He squatted down and balanced on the balls of his feet, so we were almost eye level. (Still a curtesy that I rarely received.) He was wearing an overcoat (maybe a raincoat?) and a broad brimmed hat. He seemed genuinely pleased to meet me, as if just seeing me made him happy. He had brought me a gift, a hollow formed red plastic train engine. It was about the size and shape of a loaf of Wonder bread. It was kind of a cheap throw away toy, but it was an unexpected gift from a new person in my life, someone who really seemed to see me.

The strange man told me that I had had a birthday and that I was not two anymore. I was three! This was a revelation. I did not know that people's ages changed or that the change was marked by celebration and presents. What an amazing experience!

Mother told me the man was a friend from Church, but I didn't think this was true because we went to church all the time and I had never met this man before. As it turned out I never saw him again either, so I wondered, if he was from Church, where did he go? Would my mother tell me something that wasn't true? Why would she do that?

A little while later (days or maybe a week) my mother said she was going to go away and I would have to stay at home by myself. I was not to worry because she would be back later in the day. This was another new thing. I had never been left home alone before. I started wondering what would I like to do if I had the house all to myself?

I feel the need to point out that there is an innocence in being three. I understood the difference between right and wrong. I understood explicit rules but not the logic or reasons behind the rules and I didn't have enough foundational knowledge to recognize implied rules. Planning what to do with my home alone time was an innocent act, no different than cooking my favorite "I love this, but my husband doesn't" meal when he is out of town. It was like climbing over the back fence. It was there. It was climbable. There were interesting things on the other side. No one ever told me I could not climb the fence so why wouldn't I?

Now I had most of a day with the whole house to myself. What would I like to do? I gave this a lot of thought and finally decided on cough syrup.

Cough syrup was yummy. It was something Mommy gave me when she was being nice and paying attention to me. But for some reason I only ever got one little spoonful of it, and I didn't get any at all unless she thought I was sick. I knew we had a whole bottle. It was behind the mirror over the bathroom sink, the hidden cupboard called the medicine cabinet. I could climb onto the sink from the toilet and reach the mirror. No one had ever told me not to get into the medicine chest. Yes! If I had the house to myself, I would have a party with the cough syrup. I guess it was my version of a tea party.

As promised, after my father said goodbye the next morning mother picked up her bag and said goodbye too. I was supposed to stay inside the house but there weren't any other rules.

I had a wooden bathroom stool with a piece that flipped up or down. With the piece in the down position, it was a two-step stool. With it flipped up the stool became a bench with the mobile piece as its back. As soon as Mother left the house I went to the bathroom and placed the stool in front of the toilet, then I climbed from my stool to the toilet, and from the toilet to the sink. From there I could reach into the medicine cabinet and get the cough syrup. Cough syrup in hand, I moved the stool into the kitchen and used it along with a kitchen chair to reach the silverware drawer to get the necessary spoon. Finally, I took the bottle and the stool to the hallway. I flipped the step down so that it looked like half of a tiny picnic table and set up my "tea party."

With everything in place, I tried using the spoon to properly serve myself multiple helpings of sweet sticky cough syrup. The thing is, this was harder than I thought it would be. I was spilling more than I was getting. I felt bad that I couldn't serve it the right way, but I was also sad to see the yummy syrup wasted when it landed on the floor, so I gave up on the spoon and drank the rest straight from the bottle.

That's where I was when mother came home. Sitting on the floor in the hallway, next to my little picnic table, with a spoon, an empty bottle of cough syrup, and a big sticky mess.

As a rule, Mother did not deal well with anger, or messes. She was prone to explosive temper tantrums which could be set off at any time by the smallest, most insignificant thing. But for some reason that didn't happen this time. She did not get angry at all. She just seemed anxious to get everything cleaned up before my father got home and for some reason didn't seem to notice that I was the one who had caused the mess, or that I was drunk on cough syrup.

Because Mother left me home alone once and didn't even get upset about cleaning sticky cough syrup off the floor, I thought I must be a big girl. I thought this was the new rule. If Mother, or

Mother and Father, wanted to leave the house why should I have to go with them every time?

The next time my day was interrupted by the requirement to put my things away and accompany them on an outing or errand I said they should go without me. As I understood it, this was okay now. I did not expect to be laughed at. I did not expect to hear Mother nervously say to Father, "Where does she get these ideas?" or to be told that I should stop making up stories and lies.

I tried to stand up for myself. I tried to say, "But you left me alone before. Remember?" I rarely got to complete the statement. She would grab my arm or simply pick me up and head for the door. I lost the battle every time, but I never stopped trying. It made me angry that she could just pretend the one day that she left me home alone, all by myself, never happened. Why was it okay for her to tell lies like that?

I was six the day I finally won. We lived in a different house in a different part of the state. It was a glorious summer day. I had been playing in the side yard all morning. The side yard was past the garage, which was past the carport. No one could see or hear me when I was playing there.

Mother had to walk out of the house and around the garage just to tell me to get in the car for a trip to the store. I looked at her and asked why, "Why is it okay for me to be anywhere in the neighborhood as long as you are in the house. Why can I be out of sight and out of hearing and you never care, but it is not okay if you drive to the store? You almost never know where I am or what I am doing when I am outside so why do I have to stop and come with you any time you leave the house?" Mother started in with the hated statement that I was just a little girl. I reminded her that the first time she left me home alone was years ago! She was about to accuse me, yet again, of telling stories and coming up with crazy ideas, but on this day, Father stepped in and took my side. He said, "Just leave her alone" and "We won't be gone that long." A few minutes later I watched as they drove away. I can still feel the joy and triumph of that win.

Changes

Me, with Mother, in the child's seat on the back of her bicycle.

I was three, and an only child. The word 'pregnant' meant nothing to me. I knew that families came in different shapes and sizes, I did not know that families could, and did, change, or that little children became bigger children, and new children were born. I certainly didn't have any idea how babies were made, or any reason to be suspicious of a visit from a male stranger shortly before announcing a pregnancy.

The first change that had meaning for me was Mother's new bicycle. Since we were a one car family, she opted to buy a bicycle with a child seat on the back for transportation to and from medical appointments. I found this to be an exciting way to travel. I thoroughly enjoyed the trips to the Doctor's office as well as the Doctor herself. Of course, I had no idea why we were there or how our lives were going to change.

Sometime later we took a family trip to a local hardware store. I was walked to the back of the store where rolls of brightly colored linoleum stood on-end, leaning against the wall. Then I was asked to pick the one that I liked best! I chose a roll with yellow bouncing balls and Teddy Bears on a reddish-purple background. We threaded it through the back windows of the car and drove home with it sticking out on both sides. I had no idea what was happening or why, but it was still great fun.

The pretty linoleum was rolled out in an empty corner of the basement. My parents laid it flat on the floor then carried all of my toys down from my bedroom. I was told that this was my new space, and I could set it up any way I wanted. For a couple days I had fun setting all my things just so, around the perimeter of the Teddy Bear linoleum, but then I got tired of being in a cold, damp, windowless basement and fell back into my old routine of spending mornings in front of the TV with Romper

Room and Captain Kangaroo, followed by afternoons in the wild, wide outside.

Me, with my kitty Butterschotch. Fall 1965.

The next surprise was even better, a whole lot better! We drove to a strange place where I was shown a playpen full of kittens and told I could pick one of them to take home! I selected a beautiful white and yellow-orange tabby and named him Butterscotch. I was enthralled.

Allowing an animal in the house was very out of character for Mother. I can only guess that it was someone else's idea. I can easily imagine an older woman at church, or even her Dr, pushing the idea of giving me a pet so I wouldn't feel displaced by a new baby. Mother was always firmly against the idea of animals in the house, any house, even other people's houses, but she may have given in to pressure. Sadly, once the kitten was acquired and the pressure was off, she would have felt growing resentment at being pushed outside of her comfort zone. I was over-the-moon with my, all mine, forever, furry companion but this story was never going to end well.

Only a week or two later there was a day when I could not find Butterscotch. I looked in all the usual places, but he was nowhere to be found. When I finally asked Mother if she had seen him, she responded, “I took him back to the pound.” I asked what the pound was and why he had to go back.

Mother explained about the pound; an animal shelter and justified her action by claiming that Butterscotch had turned mean. She vividly described seeing him reach through the bars of the crib, where I still slept, trying to rake me across the face with his claws.

I knew this couldn’t be true. He hadn’t scratched or bit me ever. He was still a small kitten. Why would he have to reach through the bars of the crib when he could walk right between them. For that matter, reaching up from the floor didn’t make any sense. He was too small to stand on the floor and touch the bottom of the crib, let alone reach up and through the bars.

My forever special friend was gone. My mother had taken him away from me and was lying about it. I would never see my kitty again and there was nothing I could do. I was three and she was judge, jury, and executioner.

It took a day or two to absorb the loss of Butterscotch and reconcile my feelings. I was in the back of the car with both Mother and Father when I announced that I was okay. I was very sad that Butterscotch had to go back to the pound, but the pound was where I had first found him and I was sure some other little girl would find him there too. As long as I knew he had a little girl to love him and take care of him I could be okay with that.

Mother chose to disagree. She carefully explained that he was too old. Even though he was still a kitten he was too big and people only ever adopted kittens when they were little so no, no one else would adopt him. She said that the people at the pound would just put him to sleep.

This didn't sound too bad to me. I figured a good nap might be just the thing to get him ready for the daunting task of picking out a new little girl to adopt him. I explained this three-year-old logic to my mother. Of course, I was wrong again. I didn't understand the euphemism "put-to-sleep," so Mother very deliberately and specifically explained. Butterscotch was dead. She had knowingly given him back to the people at the pound so they could kill him. Simply taking away the kitten I loved wasn't enough for her. She wanted me to know that he was dead and that he was dead because she decided he should be killed, because she said so.

To this day I believe she was wrong. Mother might have wanted me to know that she could, and would, kill the things I loved, but she didn't actually understand the power of love. In my heart I still believe Butterscotch found a happy home and lived a long and well-loved life.

There is a follow-on to this story. An event from Mother's past that she shared several years later. I think I was about ten when she told me about her kitten as a child. She said she was about seven and had a kitten who was very small. The kitten had been poisoned. She did not explain the who or the how, or if she even knew these answers. She told me how she stayed awake all night long, holding and caring for her trembling, shivering kitten until it died. She claimed nothing I had experienced or could even imagine could be as awful as it was for her watching her kitten die.

She only shared this story once. At the time I didn't relate her experience to Butterscotch, but as an adult I cannot help but wonder how a person who claimed to be so affected by the death of a pet could deliberately inflict the same heartache on her own small child.

A Sister

My parents were friends with another couple from our church. Andy and June were several years older. Their one, late in life child, Amy, was a year younger than me. I loved them all. Time spent with Amy and her family was comfortable; easy. Amy was a well-loved only child. She had all the best toys and when I was at Amy's house, I didn't experience the constant undercurrent of anxiety that was always present in our home.

Me, with my friend Amy. Spring 1967.

When it was time for the new baby to arrive, I was taken to Amy's house and introduced to a nice young woman called a babysitter. Andy and June, and my Mom and Dad, were going to a place called a hospital while Amy and I spent the night with the babysitter. My first slumber party!

The next day Andy took me for a ride to the hospital. It was a big red brick building with an even bigger parking lot. Andy explained that children couldn't go inside but he had a way to let me see my mother and new sister. We walked around the building on a grassy lawn and up to one of the ground floor windows. Mom and Dad were on the other side. They came up to the window and waved. Mother held up a bundle in a pink blanket. Andy told me her name was Donna, but my sister would later choose to change her name to Heather.

Heather looked just like a swaddled-up baby doll. I understood that I was supposed to be excited about the new baby but truthfully, I was much more impressed by the novelty of a night away from home, with a favorite friend and in the care of other adults.

My birthday, also the day I met Mother's friend John, had been in August. Heather was born the following May.

Heather was born with flaming red hair. As she grew older it would soften into a beautiful strawberry blond but as a baby her hair was so red, I was afraid that it would burn me if I touched it.

Mother fell into the habit of always telling people that my paternal grandfather, of Swedish stock, had red hair. This was a true statement, but I never understood why she took such effort to explain. For years she would introduce us by saying, "This is my daughter Connie, and this is my daughter Heather. Bills father had red hair." Of course, Mother's friend John also had red hair.

A baby sister didn't change my life much. I had never gotten much attention from my mother. If she was too busy taking care of a baby to notice me then I had a little more freedom to do my own thing. I still enjoyed Romper Room and Captain Kangaroo in the mornings and roaming the wooded lot over the back fence in the afternoons.

Actually, a baby sister meant more time with Mother, not less. There were more medical visits, and two children were too many for the bicycle seat. Since we still had only one car, we all had to ride together in the morning (cutting into my Captain Kangaroo time) to drop my father off at the university and I had to tag along for all the medical appointments. I didn't mind the rides or waiting rooms. The rides took me through new and interesting territory and the waiting rooms always had toys. When we saw the doctor, I would go with Mother and Heather into the exam room. Because I was quiet and well behaved, I think sometimes I blended into the background where no one really noticed me or considered whether or not I should be present.

Heather was not a healthy baby. She suffered jaundice and endured visit after visit where they took her blood again and again. She was small and yellow and didn't easily give up blood for testing. When the doctor had to stick her multiple times, Mother would focus on holding the screaming child and no one gave any thought to me, not quite four years old, standing wide eyed and silent in the corner. I have etched into my brain the image of Mother holding my screaming, squiggling sister. She is upside down; the doctor is trying to get blood by stabbing her heel but the heel is refusing to bleed so the doctor takes a little bitty leg in both hands and squeezes from thigh to foot in an attempt to force out a single drop of blood. Even today I can feel my heart pounding in my chest with fear and anxiety at the thought of that scene.

When I was about 20 months old, I had become ill with a very high fever. I am told my temperature maxed out the mercury thermometer at 107 degrees. My father, who worked as an

Auditor for the State of Michigan, had to be called home from whatever site he was auditing that week. He once told me that he spent all of the six-hour drive home expecting that I would be dead before he got there and preparing to comfort his grieving wife.

I was hospitalized for about a week and treated with the medicine of the day, basically aspirin and ice baths to keep the fever as low as possible.

It was a traumatic experience for everyone involved. When Heather developed a similar fever, Mother insisted she did not want to go through the same ordeal again and refused to hospitalize her, so the doctor gave instructions for treating her at home. The nights that followed were eternal. The basin on the changing table was filled with ice water for wetting towels. Heather would be wrapped in a sodden, ice-cold towel, screaming the whole time. Her body was so hot that it only took a few minutes for the towel to literally start to steam. Then the now warm towel would be replaced by another fresh from the ice bath.

I sat in the corner of the room night after night watching the same scene play out again and again. I have no memory of my own experience with ice baths and fever, but I will never forget my sister's. I understand my parents not wanting her to go through such a thing at the hands of strange people and in a strange place but keeping her home might have been worse. It violated her sense of home and safety and took place in the hands of people she should have loved and trusted.

Another early memory of becoming a big sister took place on a walk to the grocery store. It was an easy two block walk to the store. Mother and I had walked to this store many times. When it was just the two of us, she held my hand as we walked along the busy street and into the store but now, with a new family member it was different.

Mother had a stroller that held Heather plus room for a couple of grocery bags. I was similarly equipped with a toy baby buggy and a doll. We set off on our walk with Mother in front and me trailing behind. I knew to stay close and 'not dawdle.' I actually felt quite grown-up strutting along behind with my own buggy and 'baby.' Of course, because I was pushing a buggy, I had to stay two or three feet further back. Mother would not have been forgiving if I had rammed her heel or the back of her calf.

The 1960's automatic doors operated on a pressure pad. When someone stepped on the pad the glass double door would open from the middle with the right and left panels sliding apart like barn doors. As we left the store Mother walked across the pad and the doors opened. Then I stepped on the pad, but I didn't weigh enough to stop the doors from closing. In one of those freakish moments of perfect timing the doors slid shut and caught me perfectly in the middle.

I was trapped! I wasn't hurt, but I was trapped, one door pressed firmly against each hipbone. No amount of tugging and wriggling was sufficient to set me free. Mother, who hadn't seen and didn't know, was rapidly disappearing across the parking lot. I tugged, and I squirmed. I called for help. Eventually I hollered loud enough to be heard. She turned and saw me stuck between the automatic doors and immediately began to scold me for not keeping up, as though all I had to do was pick up the pace and catch up to her. I had to interrupt her tirade, to explain, "I can't. It's got me. It won't let me go. Please come help me!" After a few such requests she reluctantly walked back to the door and stepped on the pressure pad releasing me. Then she turned her back and headed for home, scolding me all the way, blaming me for causing the accident by my laziness and lagging behind. I followed dutifully behind still careful not to follow so close that I hit the back of her heel with my buggy.

Getting Bigger

One day Mother said she wanted to go for a walk with me. I cannot say if it was the weekend and my father was home to watch my sister, or how this was arranged, but I am certain that it was just she and I who left the house. We headed down the street, in the opposite direction than the grocery store, right past Debbie's house and even on beyond the big rock. When our street ended at a 'T' intersection we crossed over and continued right on the new road, then there was a left. By this time, I had no idea where I was. Finally, we stopped at a fenced in lot with a playground. Mother sat on a bench for a few minutes and told me I could play on the swings and slide. Wow! What an unexpected treat! I thoroughly enjoyed myself for ten or fifteen minutes until Mother decided it was time to head home.

A couple of days later we took the walk again, and then again. On the third or fourth trip she started asking me to lead the way. I remembered where to make the first turn. But I was anxious. I was on new territory. I didn't know what features to focus on. Simple things like choosing permanent landmarks, such as a building rather than a car, were new skills for me.

I liked the walks. I liked the opportunity to expand my territory, but the task of learning the route was hard and I didn't understand the purpose. Eventually Mother explained. She told me I was going to be five soon and that after I turned five, I would go to school. She said the building behind the playground was going to be my school and that I needed to learn the way so I could walk there by myself, every day.

If I had understood what school was, I would have been excited, but I didn't know anything about school. I didn't have any bigger brothers or sisters to tell me about school. My friends, Debbie and Amy, didn't have any bigger brothers or sisters. I didn't know what school meant. I did understand that I was going to have to learn the way because I was going to have to walk there, every day, all by myself. It was a big, daunting task. I wanted to succeed but I was afraid. I was afraid of getting lost on the way. I was also afraid of going all by myself into that red brick building that looked like the hospital where my sister had been born. It did not occur to me that Mother would probably go with me on my first day or that I would have a teacher and eventually classmates and friends. All I saw was a big, scary building. I did not want to tell Mother that I was afraid because I thought she would be angry, so I kept trying to learn the route. But I didn't enjoy the playground much because I couldn't get past my anxiety.

New Places, New Experiences

As it turned out, I never did make the long walk all by myself to that Detroit Kindergarten. It was spring of 1967. My father was newly graduated with an MSW and looking for a permanent position. He found work in Michigan's Upper Peninsula (UP), closer to Mother's hometown, so we packed up and moved back north.

Our first stop was a rental home in the tiny town of Trenary an unincorporated township in the Central UP. US census data does not even list Ternary, it records a total population of the surrounding county at less than 600 people in both 2000 and 2010.

What the Trenary had to offer was location. It is right in the center of the UP, halfway between my mother's hometown, on the lake Michigan shore, and my father's new job on the Lake Superior shore.

The house was ramshackle cabin at the end of a very long driveway (if you can call a two-rut path a driveway) which was itself at the end of a dirt road. There were outbuildings, including a small barn with a barrel for burning trash, and a guest house. The 'yard' consisted of several wild acres including an old apple orchard with all the trees well past their years of productivity.

A large and densely packed patch of Canadian Thistles, covered in fuzzy purple blossoms, attracted scores of orange and yellow butterflies and were an endless source of both fascination and frustration. The thistle bushes were as tall as I was. I sooo wanted to catch the pretty butterflies but they always stayed safely out of reach, protected by the prickly thistles.

The open areas around the house were surrounded by dense woods. There were no neighbors in sight. For a half-wild four-year-old with a love of the outdoors and exploring new places, it was paradise.

My new toy was a slingshot, a single piece of wood carved into a 'Y' with a heavy rubber band secured between the tines. Father showed me how to shoot acorns and small rocks. He claimed he could use it to shoot squirrels and birds out of trees. I wasn't quite as skilled. I managed to snap myself with the rubber band several times and occasionally fling a small rock three or four feet, but never in the direction I intended.

Some weeks after moving in I turned five. There was a small celebration attended by the four of us and an older couple from the small church in our new Northern UP community. The couple brought me a present of a red plaid dress and reminded me that I would be going to school soon. The dress was pretty and nicer than anything else I owned but I was disappointed. I didn't appreciate a gift of clothes. I had plenty of clothes and didn't much care what I wore. Gifts were supposed to be toys!

The first day of school finally came. It was half-day, afternoon kindergarten so I spent the morning restless and anxious. At about 10am Mother walked me to the end of the rutted drive where it met up with the rutted, sandy, turn-around circle at the end of the dirt road. I was surprised to be greeted by a neighbor. A ragged man was standing at the entrance to a dirt path that led into the woods from the end of the road. He had long shaggy hair and beard, homemade rope sandals on gnarly feet, and wore a long, tattered coat that could have been made from either deer hide or yellowed canvas. To me he looked more like a fairytale creature of the forest than an ordinary human. Today we would describe him as 'living off the grid.' Mother called him a hermit. How cool! It was my first day of school and my neighbor was a bonafide, no kidding, honest-to-goodness hermit!

We waited ten or fifteen minutes for the bus while mother stood there and chatted with the hermit, easy as you please, just like they had been neighbors and friends all their lives.

Eventually a totally empty, large yellow school bus arrived. Mother greeted the driver and urged me onto the bus which turned around in the dirt circle and trundled away.

The ride to school took about 90 minutes. We zig-zagged our way across the county until all the kindergarten bus students were collected. There were only four or five of us. I did not mind the ride. I had no problem with long drives. I enjoyed looking out the window at all the new places. I was a self-sufficient, well-behaved child but I was also social and outgoing. I might have been the new kid in town, but this was the first day of kindergarten for all of us and since I was the first child on the bus, I was the leader of the bunch. I greeted each new child as they boarded the bus and started getting to know my new friends.

The school was a squat, cube shaped, gray brick building. There were eight classrooms, four to a floor, one each for grades one through eight. We five or six kindergartners shared a room with the first grade. We had a low, round table at the back if the room. In the middle of the table was a beautiful carousel of brand-new crayons. They looked so pretty in their tiered container, with their perfectly shaped cone tips pointing up, like a brightly colored wedding cake. Sadly, they were a cheap, waxy, knock-off brand, not at all good at transferring their bright shiny colors to the equally cheap waxy paper we were given.

First graders were learning rudimentary math and reading. We kindergarteners had stacks of ‘educational’ coloring pages. These were mimeographed images of block letters and numbers such as a capital ‘A’ next to a drawing of an apple, and so on. Aside from joining the first graders for story time our only task was to sit there with crayons that didn’t draw well and paper that was too slick to hold the color. I would have enjoyed getting to know the nice little girl next to me but talking was not allowed and since we didn't arrive until after lunch, we did not have any recess or other time to greet or interact with our classmates.

At the end of the day, I got onto the same bus but now it was packed full with children from all the grades. A large boy put himself in my path and explained that it was the big kids who were in charge and I had better remember that.

As it turned out I didn't have much opportunity to get on his bad side. I had been the first child picked up by the bus earlier in the day. On the way home I was the first child off. This was confusing. The driver stopped the bus and told me it was time to get off. How had he gotten me home so fast? I hadn't been able to see when we turned onto my road because the big kids occupied all the window seats. Actually, they occupied all the seats. Most of the small kids, including me, were left standing in the aisle. When I stepped down from the bus, thinking there was no way I could possibly be home, there I was, in the dusty turn-around circle, looking at the end of our long, two-rut drive.

School wasn't bad. It was just boring, and long, and it was hard to stay inside all day, and sit still, and be quiet. The days resolved into a routine. The hermit came to the end of the road every morning and he and my mother chatted while I waited for the bus then I took the long ride in on an empty bus and the short ride home on a full one.

Once or twice, I walked to the head of the hermit's path and peered into the dark woods hoping to get some glimpse of his world. Sadly, I couldn't see anything. The path was narrow and dark with thickets on either side. The ground was damp with standing water in the low places. I was curious about hermits and how they lived. Did he have a house, or did he live in a cave, maybe a hollow log? I wanted to know more but both he and the path were scary. It felt a bit like the story of Hansel and Gretel, so I only looked, and never walked down the path.

One day Mother told me not to get on the bus after school. She needed to go into town and would pick me up on her way home. I asked if she would have the car, but she said "No," she was going to walk and she would pull my sister along in our wagon. This didn't seem like a good idea. I asked if she understood that the school was a really long way away. I didn't believe she could walk that far. Did she understand that my morning bus ride practically took hours? She insisted she knew what she was doing. I knew better than to argue so I promised to wait for her and not get on the bus.

When school let out, she was there waiting. My year-old sister was bundled in the back of our red wagon with the slatted wood sides, along with a couple of packages. We started off on what I expected to be the longest walk of my life. We turned right out of the school drive and right again at the first corner. After about a block the pavement ended, and we continued along a dirt road. A few hundred feet later as we rounded a bend, I recognized the abandoned khaki yellow house that was the last building on our road before the entrance to the rutted lane that was our drive.

What kind of magic was this? Years later I read a fantasy novel in which the characters navigated alternate worlds by knowing how to step around blind corners and into a different reality. This was exactly how I felt as a child, on that magical, ten-minute walk home from a school that was 90 minutes away by bus.

A New Home

About a month into the school year, we moved into our permanent home closer to Father's new office and only about half a mile from the Lake Superior shore. A new home meant transferring to a new real kindergarten. It was sooo much better!

There is a particular frustration and fatigue that comes with having to pretend to be active and engaged when there is nothing to do. It is the same fatigue I encountered later in life during the first few weeks of new office jobs. It is a challenge trying to appear industrious through too much down-time, time spent waiting for system access, credentials... The days of just sitting around with nothing more to do than read and re-read an outdated training manual are more draining to me than the busiest, most stress filled days of any job I have ever worked. This was how I felt in those first weeks as a kindergartener sitting in the back corner of a room full of first graders. The stress of being 'on' but simultaneously idle took a hefty toll and left me mentally, emotionally, and physically fatigued by the end of each day.

Real kindergarten! Now, that was a different story.

I wasn't queen of the school bus anymore but that was okay because I got the best bus with the best driver. His name was "Baldy." He was one of those adults that you wouldn't ever think of disobeying, but he wasn't cold, or too strict. When you were on his bus you felt like you belonged. You felt safe. We knew to sit in our seats and not cause trouble, but we were free to enjoy each other's company and absolutely free from any kind of bullying or harassment. He created a much-appreciated safe space. I owe Baldy a debt of gratitude. He is on my list of souls I must find and thank in the afterlife. I was a newcomer but on his bus the rules were simple; every one of us belonged and we were all valued and sheltered by his care.

My new school was a rich, engaging environment. There was learning time when we focused on recognizing letters and numbers and reciting the alphabet. There was story time, nap time, snack time, outdoor time, and inside free time with a wide array of activities; all kinds of toys, stand up easels for fingerpainting, a sand table, a water table with toy boats, puzzles, games… It was amazing how much activity could be packed into a half day.

And, there were all the other children, all of them just my age. I had never known so many of us existed!

On my first day I looked around the room, picked out the cutest little girl and decided she would be my best friend. When I went home that night and told my mother how I had selected my new best friend she sanctimoniously suggested I might want to look for attributes that were more than skin deep. It was a reasonable suggestion but totally wasted on me.

My friend's name was Lisa. She lived a few blocks away. Lisa was a little younger than me and she had a sister, Cindy, who was exactly a year older than Lisa. With two children sharing the same birthday their family threw the very best birthday parties!

I didn't have to ask Lisa to be my best friend or work at getting to know her. She simply was my best friend from the moment I declared it so. Cindy was my second-best friend. The three of us meshed like we had been together from the day we were born. Even years later, after they moved to a different town, we still managed occasional play dates. I may have thought I chose Lisa because she was cute, but I am pretty sure (smugly) the connection was more than skin deep.

Me, with my friend Lisa on the hill behind our house.

Our teacher was an older, thin, cranky woman who reeked of cigarettes. She was close to retirement and did not find any joy in her profession. My specific complaint was that she never added me to her list of children who got to hold the flag during the Pledge of Allegiance. Flag duty was supposed to rotate around the class with each child having a turn. Some weeks in I realized we had looped the class and I had been left out. I asked if she had skipped me. She assured me that everyone had a turn. I just had to wait for mine. After another rotation of the class, I asked if she would please check the list to be sure I was on it. I knew I hadn't started the school year with everybody else and was pretty sure she just hadn't updated her list when I arrived. It seemed like a simple request and an easy fix. She, however, knew her job and was not about to let any child tell her she didn't. Eventually I quit asking. By the end of the year, I was the only child who had never had a turn holding the flag.

Interestingly, I wasn't bitter or horribly hurt by this. I somehow found the emotional space to roll my eyes and think "Yeah, yeah. Sure lady. You are the always right teacher. Don't let the whiney child confuse you."

This might have been the most important lesson of the year. Yes, I was left out, but it didn't have anything to do with me. It didn't mean I was unwanted or undeserving. Yes, I tried to explain the problem and have it corrected. I did my part. I wasn't responsible for her failure. Yes, I was denied a privilege given to all the other children, but I wasn't harmed by that loss. She didn't have that much power over me. This powerful lesson likely helped me survive many crushing experiences to come.

Room for More

My father's new job was as a social work, case worker for the state of Michigan. His office was above the local hardware store on the main downtown street. The upper peninsula of Michigan is rural and poor. The regional Social Services office was staffed by only three personnel, a supervisor, a clerk, and a case worker (my father). They were responsible for a large part of the UP. In essence, my father was the only case worker supporting child protective services in our part of the state.

Not long after we settled in our new home, Father became involved with the very sad case of five Native American children abandoned by their mother. My father, who was himself 25% Chippewa, was also young and in his first professional position. He was profoundly affected by the plight of these children. Their mother had loaded her family into an old car, driven some distance from known places and people, then pulled over on the side of the road and walked away. She told her children she had to go and do something and asked them to wait in the car, then she just walked away and never came back.

The oldest child was an eight-year-old girl. The youngest a baby. They were five in total, and they were all each other had. No one foster home could handle all five of them. They would be split up and sent to multiple facilities. My father was heartbroken for them. He wanted a way to keep them together. He decided our family should adopt them.

Obviously, I do not know all of this story, but I can speak to the events that involved me. First there was the farm, the home my parents bought when I was a baby. We had moved away before I was even two, but we still owned it and did not have a current tenant. The farm was on the lake Michigan shore, nearly a two-hour drive from our current home so not an option for expanding our family, but it was an asset, so they sold it.

The next step was to find a home large enough to handle a five-person addition to our four-person family, as our snug three-bedroom ranch would not suffice for a family of nine. My parents identified a suitable old farmhouse a few miles out of town. The house looked like a Norman Rockwell painting. It was hidden from view of the main road by a long drive that curved around the side of a hill. It had brick-red siding, white trim, and a gracious front porch. A tire swing hung from a stunning, large, old oak and further back was a big red barn.

The house wasn't large enough to handle a family of nine but was deemed suitable with minor renovations. The three existing bedrooms would be parceled out with one for my parents, one to serve as my father's study (he always insisted on maintaining a dedicated room for church work) and one for the six-year-old twin boys. An enclosed sun porch would be converted into a nursery for the baby. This left four girls. In age order the two oldest adopted children, me, and my sister. For us the walk-up attic would be converted into one large room.

I loved the house. I loved the sight of it. I loved the tire swing under that beautiful oak. I liked the attic space. My friend Amy (from Detroit) had a converted attic as her room. It was big but the slanted walls made it feel cozy, like a tree house. When we played up there, we felt like we were in our own private place, away from the prying eyes of adults. But Amy was my friend. We liked each other. We never fought. I was safe with her.

I didn't think I would be safe in this new attic room with two new big sisters. I hadn't met either yet, but I had overheard Father expressing concerns. The eight-year-old was protective of her family. She looked out for her siblings. This might not go well for two natural born children in a blended family. My father openly admitted that she was a bully; she had a history of getting into fights and had hurt other children. He told me she would be hard on me. This was not a comforting thought. I wouldn't have any allies in that third-floor room. It was too far from the main floor kitchen and living room. What if I was in trouble and no one heard me cry for help? I was afraid, lonesome and anxious, and there was no one I could talk to about how I felt.

In the end none of this happened. I am sure there would have been many adventures and many challenges in that expanded family, but all of our lives took a different path.

There is one more story to tell about the first year in the UP. My mother's old piano had been left behind in Detroit so part of the money from selling the farm went towards purchasing a new one. She bought a shiny new Yamaha upright in the summer of 1968. As soon as it was in the house, I renewed my campaign for lessons.

Mother insists to this day that she searched diligently for a teacher but was absolutely unable to find anyone who would accept a five-year-old. Of course, by now, I was only a month or two shy of six, and I would have been perfectly happy if allowed to play "Chopsticks" and/or "Mary had a Little Lamb" until the start of the new school year and real lessons. Unfortunately, in our house things had to be all the way or not at all. Mother decided she would teach me herself.

She purchased a John Thompson's piano book and outlined her expectations. I was to master one song each week. The first week was simple. It only took two or three times through before I had it down cold, but I still had to wait a full week before I could try the next one. The second piece was just as easy as the first. Number three was a different story. Songs one and two used only four fingers and one hand. Song number three used all five fingers. My hand was too small to reach the fifth note without breaking tempo. The stretch was wide enough that it was physically painful. I couldn't play it well and didn't want to play it at all because it hurt. And I thought the tune was awful. Couldn't I just skip the bad song and try the next one instead?

The answer was, "No!" When I failed to master the song in one week, I was told I had to keep playing it for a second week. When I didn't master it after the second week, Mother told stories of how she learned piano, including a nasty old woman for a teacher. If Mother didn't play well the woman would hit her knuckles with a ruler, sometimes until they were bloody. Her story and threats left me stunned. How could something as beautiful as music be an excuse for such harsh punishment? And why couldn't she understand my problem with the song. It wasn't because I didn't try or didn't practice, even though I didn't like the song. No amount of effort was going to make up for the fact that my pinky finger just couldn't reach that one key. Couldn't we overlook this one song, at least until I grew a little bigger?

The argument escalated. We both yelled and screamed. I was in tears. Finally, I was given three choices. I could stop complaining and work until I got the song right. I could take a knuckle rapping and then work on the song until I got it right, or I could just quit. It was outrageous! Why did we end up in such a horrific fight over a single song? After a prolonged argument I screamed through my tears that if I had to do piano her way, I never wanted to touch it again!

This was the end of the argument. Mother stopped yelling, looked at me and said if that was what I wanted that was the way it would be. I was not going to learn the piano. At first, I was relieved. I certainly didn't want her to teach me ever again. It took a few years for me to realize that when she said I was not going to learn piano ever, she really meant ever.

Rape

Please understand that this section is hard to write. The experience was traumatic and there are a number of large holes in my memory. The era is also complicated by other significant family dynamics and by the fact that as a child I was not included in all the discussions and decisions that impacted me. I am not sure of the order of some events. I have strung them together in the way that makes the most sense. Please bear with me and I will do the best I can.

First there was pain. The space between my legs, including the place I urinated from, was raw and sore. It hurt all the time. It ached and it burned. I couldn't help but rub and hold it, as all humans do whenever any part of our body is wounded.

Mother and Father were angry at me. I had misbehaved in some way that I did not understand and every time I touched the places that hurt, I was apparently doing something very bad.

I didn't have any idea what I had done wrong or where or when, and it didn't occur to me to wonder about these questions. The pain and my parents' anger were just there, like they had always been a fact of life.

Mother and Father were also angry with each other, they were angry at me and about me and they didn't agree about how to treat me. Father said that it was not uncommon for children my age to "masturbate", maybe they should just establish some rules. Mother did not want to discuss the issue.

I had no idea what the word masturbate meant nor the context to understand it even if it was explained to me. I just wanted the pain to go away.

Eventually, we had a very uncomfortable and confusing conversation. Mother explained that I shouldn't touch myself all the time but if I only did it sometimes, like if I was particularly sad or lonely, it could be okay.

This did not help at all! Exactly what was I doing wrong? What did she mean by "touching myself?" Don't we all touch ourselves, all the time? How can we not touch our own selves? We wash ourselves. We dress ourselves. We touch our faces. We fold our hands when we say Grace…

I was left on my own to figure out what touching was okay and what was "bad." Lying on my stomach with my hands protectively over the sore parts was the only way I could sleep. It was also "bad." I tried to sleep in a kneeling, prone position that let me use my heel to protect the sore places, but that was still "bad." Pretty much anything I did to ease the pain was apparently "bad."

One day I was sitting cross legged on the floor and my father pointed to me and explained to Mother that this too was a "masturbation" position. He went on to describe female patients in a mental hospital who would spend large parts of the day sitting cross legged and how by rocking back and forth they could experience multiple orgasms an hour. I didn't know what the word orgasm meant. I was just sitting on the floor watching TV like I always had. In fact, this was a rare moment when the pain was quiet and I could focus on other things. I had been relaxed and enjoying the TV program, but somehow, I was still "bad."

Around the same time Mother took me to visit my pediatrician. He was a warm, friendly, jovial, older man who had removed my tonsils a few months earlier.

On this visit somehow, he and I ended up in the exam room by ourselves. This was different. I was used to Mother and or the Dr's nurse always being in the room. I do not know how he managed to get me into the exam room without Mother, it would have required perception, planning, and likely a coordinated effort between him and his nurse. He is another person on my list of souls to find and thank in my afterlife.

Dr H was particularly grave, careful, and gentil with me. This was different from his normal warm, fun-loving behavior. He set me up on the table rolled his wheeled stool close so we could be face to face.

He asked me questions, but I couldn't answer them. I mumbled that my mouth was very sore, and it hurt to talk. I had canker sores. A lot of canker sores. The inside of my mouth and down my throat was one big mass of sores, they overlapped each other so that there was almost no healthy tissue left. Moving any part of my mouth was horribly painful.

Dr. H said he could help with the sores. He took a long handled swab and dipped it into a solution he called silver #####?. I tried to understand and remember the second word, but it was a new word, one I had never heard before, and my mind was fuzzy. I really wanted to learn the word, but I couldn't hold the sound of it in my head. Dr H slowly and gently applied his solution to every sore spot in my mouth. It was like magic. As he passed from spot to spot the pain eased. By the time he finished I could talk again and even swallow.

All this time he kept asking me questions. I could hear his words, but they didn't make any sense. He asked again and again. He spoke slowly, softly, carefully, like he was trying to coax a wild deer to eat from his hand. "Did anyone… ########? Can you tell me #########? …" I tried hard to listen. I tried to pay attention. I wanted to answer, but every sentence somehow devolved into gibberish.

It was like listening to the teacher's voice in Charlie Brown cartoons except that with Charlie Brown the teachers voice is just a silly part of the story.

I knew Dr. H was trying to ask me something important. I knew he was using real words, simple words, words that a five-year-old could understand. He wasn't like Father, deliberately choosing big confusing words like "masturbate" and "orgasm." Dr H wanted me to understand what he was asking. He wanted me to be able to answer. I tried. I leaned towards him. I concentrated and I tried to hear his words. But the harder I tried the worse it got. It was as if his words drifted away in the air, like smoke. There was a roaring sound in my head, the edges of my vision filled in with fuzzy blackness and I felt like I was falling.

Later in life a friend asked if the solution was silver nitrate. She pointed out that silver nitrate is used to treat gonorrhea. She really wanted me to agree that Dr H had treated me with silver nitrate. I think she hoped that if she said it enough times I would remember and agree that the solution must have been silver nitrate, but my brain; my brain that remembers clearly the visit and conversation with Dr H; my brain that was so traumatized it refused to translate the sounds of his questions into language, my brain cannot recall those sounds because it never processed them in the first place.

My friend believed that if I could claim to have been given a compound used to treat gonorrhea, I would have evidence of sexual abuse. My psyche doesn't work like that. All I can claim is that some traumatic event left me in so much genital pain that I still struggle with it to this day. This event also left me with a mouth covered in canker sores and unable to mentally process simple words when carefully, sensitively, questioned about what had happened. Isn't this evidence enough?

Shortly after my visit to Dr. H, maybe a few days or a week later, we went on an outing to the annual State Fair. Attending the State Fair was a bit of a family tradition but this time we took my father's supervisor and the supervisor's ex-wife along for the trip. This was a very strange thing for us to do.

I had met Ex-Mrs. Supervisor once when my father first started his job. We had visited his supervisor and ex-wife in their home, where they lived together even though they were no longer married.

Sometimes, if we were downtown during the week, Mother would stop us by my father's office, and we would greet everyone there, the supervisor, the clerk, and my father, as part of our visit. We never interacted with my father's colleagues in any other setting. They were not the right kind of people according to my family's standards.

It was bad enough for Father that he had to work with such a disreputable supervisor. Divorced and living together out of wedlock! Plus, they smoked! A Saturday trip to the State Fair with this couple was very much out of character.

As we drove to the fair, I listened to Mother obsessively listing all the things she (and apparently by extension, the rest of us) didn't like about these people and why we shouldn't be expected to go on outings with them. As soon as we arrived, and everyone said their hello's, the ex-wife took hold of my hand and said she wanted the two of us to have some time alone. Before I could catch Mother's attention and ask if it was alright to go off with this disreputable, disliked, almost stranger, I had been dragged halfway across the parking lot.

What followed was an awkward and confusing afternoon. She bought me a whole cotton candy on a stick. (Our family tradition was limited to a single cotton candy, in a bag, and shared, hygienically, between my mother, my sister, and I. Eating directly off the stick was not proper behavior at all!)

Ex-Mrs. Supervisor also bought me a helium balloon and took me to the game booths; another thing I was never allowed to do. Mother described carnival games as "just people trying to steal your money." Playing them was like gambling. Only bad people gambled. It was both a sin and “bad stewardship”. Ex-Mrs. Supervisor insisted I try my hand at several of these games.

I won a prize for picking up a little yellow duck and tried to shoot a rotating target; all while juggling a balloon and a huge stick of cotton candy. None of this relaxed me or made me comfortable with this pushy, smelly, disliked stranger. I wanted to be a good little girl. I knew to respect the adults in my life but what was I supposed to do when the adults told me to do sinful things?

On top of all this, ex-Mrs. Supervisor started asking me strange questions. Just like when I was with Dr. H, some of the questions did not make any sense and some of the words dissolved into unintelligible sounds. The harder I tried to listen the more the words morphed into nothing. Concentrating and asking her to repeat the questions didn’t help. I felt like I could physically feel her words slipping through and out the back of my brain despite my best attempts to pay attention. Just like with Dr H, if I tried really hard it just got worse. The effort of trying to hear her words created a buzzing in my ears, and inky black spots around the edges of my vision.

She did not have the kindness or patience of Dr. H. She wanted something from me that I couldn’t provide, and she was clearly irritated at me for failing. Unlike Dr H, she got louder as her frustration grew. She crouched down low so her face was closer to mine; so close that I could feel and smell the stale cigarettes on her breath. I was relieved when she finally gave up and deposited me back with my parents.

There wasn’t any other group time. Once ex-Mrs. Supervisor finished interrogating me the four of us got into the car and headed home. My parents seemed colder and angrier than usual, but no one bothered to explain anything.

There were other changes that likely went unnoticed by anyone other than me.

When I was with playmates the only game I wanted to play was "Kidnap." It didn't matter if we were outside role playing or inside playing with our Barbie dolls, all plots revolved around being tied up and kidnapped. We had never played "Kidnap" before and none of my friends were very interested in it now, but it was the only story line I could think of to act out.

One time I made my friends tie me to a lawn chair with a jump rope then I got mad at them because they didn't do it right and I was able to wriggle out without help.

I also suffered chronic insomnia, nightmares, and headaches. Some of the nightmares even occurred while I was awake. Once after getting up in the middle of the night to use the bathroom, I had a horrible waking vision of Satan and hell. I was inside the bathroom with the door closed but when I looked towards the door, I realized I could see right through it and into a portal from hell. It was an incredibly realistic vision of a fire and brimstone pathway winding its way through dark, sooty, ashy boulders with occasional spouts of flame and glowing embers. Standing in the middle of the path was a full-sized six-foot plus, red skinned, cloven hoofed, forked tail, horned devil. I was trapped. There was no way out. He grinned at me, he laughed, he licked his lips.

I tried not to cry. I didn't want him to hear me, but I couldn't help but shake and whimper. There was only one way out of the bathroom, and he was standing just outside the door waiting for me. After several minutes my crying woke Mother who came to investigate. Of course, in order to check on me she had to open the door. In that moment, as the door swung open, I knew the Devil was reaching out to catch me. Just the thought of it still raises my heart rate today.

Somewhere in the middle of all this I passed my sixth birthday. I had a party with all the friends I had made in my part year of kindergarten and my new neighborhood. I wore an orange dress with large yellow polka dots. It was good.

My sixth birthday. I am in the middle, wearing the polka dot dress. My sister, Heather, is at the back left. The girl at front right is Denise, older sister of my friends Lisa and Cindy. Lisa and Cindy are behind her looking towards me.

The only place where I could be alone with my pain was the bathroom. I would stay there for hours. I could let my guard down. No one ever checked up on me. I could relax the tense, spasming, pelvic muscles that I would learn, decades later, were the cause of all the pain.

One day when I was sitting in our half-bath, just off the kitchen, I heard Mother answer the phone and enter a loud, long, aggravated conversation with my father.

Some of what she said included:

> *She (Mother) didn't care what the doctors said. She knew what a kidney infection was and that (a kidney infection) was the only thing wrong with me (Connie).*
>
> *She (Mother) didn't care that I was only five. Obviously a five-year-old could get a kidney infection, after all, I had one. What more proof did they need?*
>
> *No. There was no other reason for so much blood. The only possible explanation for my bleeding into the toilet was, again, a kidney infection. Who did these doctors think they were? They obviously had no idea what they were doing.*
>
> *Something was said about Reunion, a woman who found me in the ladies' bathroom. More blood. The doctors at the hospital…*
>
> *It was still a kidney infection. That is all there was to it. Everyone else was wrong. It didn't matter who they were, what they had seen or what they said.*
>
> *Anyone who didn't believe it was a kidney infection was just wrong! It was ridiculous! Who did these people think they were to say such things about us?*

I knew better than to let my mother know that I was overhearing this phone call, but I listened. This was information. I was finally hearing some of the conversation I had been left out of. These were the things my parents had been talking about when I was not around, the whispered conversations from late at night that I knew were about me but could never quite hear from behind their closed door.

Blood? Kidney infection? Reunion? Hospital? ***Five***?! I was ***six!*** How could she not know how old I was? When was I in the hospital? When had we gone to Reunion? I didn't remember Reunion. I didn't remember any blood. I didn't remember going to a hospital. Surely I would know if I had gone to the hospital. *Why couldn't I remember any of this?*

I tried to think backwards. What had I been doing earlier in the day before I came inside to use the bathroom. I was in the half-bath by the kitchen door not the full bath down the hall from my bedroom. This meant I must have been outside. Why couldn't I remember? What happened earlier today? What happened yesterday? What had we done last weekend? How could I not remember? Why did trying to remember make my head buzz and my vision blur? ***What was wrong with me?!***

I cannot explain the feeling of loss and helplessness of that moment. I couldn't even try to think about all the questions in my head. It was like trying to catch a live fish with your bare hands. My own thoughts were far too slippery to hold. Every attempt was less successful than the one before it. I felt like I was falling, drowning.

I knew better than to ask Mother. I didn't dare. Not knowing was frightening enough but asking her was too scary to even consider. Mother and Father were both angry with me but they wouldn't admit it and they certainly wouldn't explain. I knew better than to push her for information. She would just get angrier and tell me that I was the one who was evil and that I made the bad things happen. She liked to yell at me and tell me these things.

That moment was the beginning of a sort of unholy bargain with my family. It was the moment I began to believe that somehow something about me made other people do evil things. I didn't know why or how I was evil or what I did to cause it, but it was true that other people, people who were otherwise good and Godly, became evil around me.

I didn't understand why I always made Mother angry. I didn't know what I had done to make Mother and Father, and Doctors (Doctors? The only Dr I knew was Dr H. Who were these other Doctors?) angry but everything seem to revolve around me. Somehow evil was a part of me. After all, hadn't I literally summoned the Devil?

Mother was affected the most. When she became angry, even if it wasn't at or about me, it was still my fault. She would say that I "pushed" her, that I liked to make her lose control, that if I was really honest with myself I would see that I made the bad things happen. I could make her rail obsessively for hours on end.

But if I caused all the bad things, maybe that meant I could also fix them. I had to try really hard to find the evil part of me and fix it because then, maybe, I could make the bad things stop. Maybe, if I tried really, really hard to be good, even though I knew there was too much evil in me for me to ever truly be good, but I could pretend to be good, if I pretended so well I could believe it myself; maybe I could hide the evil parts of me and maybe then we could be a normal family.

If I never brought up the bad stuff maybe Mother would go along with my act and not tell other people about the evil in me. I just had to forget all the stuff about blood and pain and causing people to do monstrous things that they would never have done if not influenced by my evil, then we would all be better. Mother and Father would stop fighting all the time, I would stop hurting and everything would be better.

In practice this meant that I could never complain, I could never ask questions about the holes in my memory, or tell anyone about the pain. I didn't forget. I just accepted that people did bad things around me because the evil in me made them do so. But as long as I tried to keep the evil to myself and pretended that everything was good, I could still live with my family, and be fed, and clothed, and safe.

I was barely six. Sane or no, these were the thoughts in my head. They were the closest I could come to making sense of the world around me and my place in it.

Fallout

Shortly after the overheard phone call I was told that we would not be adopting any new brothers and sisters after all. Mother said we were not going to be able to buy the pretty farmhouse. It was an estate sale and the son had decided he just wasn't ready to sell the old family house yet. Nobody suggested maybe we could look for a different house or explore other options so we could still adopt the children we had promised to welcome into our family. One might think that if we really wanted to welcome all these children into our family, we wouldn't let a little thing like missing out on one house get in the way, but according to Mother that one house was the only option and without it there was just nothing more we could do.

Sometime later Mother told me that all five children had found homes. They had been split into three groups. The two girls went to one home together, and the twin boys stayed together too. The baby was the only child that went to a home alone. Mother thought this was probably okay as the baby was small and not so attached to his or her (I honestly don't know if the baby was a boy or a girl) siblings.

In the end I only ever met one of the children, one time. My parents took me to see the twin boys at a group home not far from where we lived. It was a big, old, Victorian house that looked kind of sad and romantic from the outside. Inside was dark and cold. My parents asked to see the boys and we waited in the big, empty, dark, front room. The walls were dark wood and there wasn't a single piece of furniture. The winter sun coming in the windows cast the interior in dark gloomy shadows.

After a few minutes a dark-haired boy, only one, a little larger than me, came most of the way down the wooden staircase. He said "Hi." I said "Hi." We looked at each other for a couple of minutes and shifted from one foot to another. I mostly looked down at our feet and the bottom of the staircase. The steps were worn through the finish on the banister side, and visibly dusty and dirty along the wall. There were bits of broken toys mixed in with the dust and grime. It was so sad and lonely. I felt like I couldn't breathe.

A year or so later my school bus route changed so we could pick up a child from that home. She was older than me. Her coat and knit hat were worn and shabby and smelled kind of old and stale. I used to watch her as she got on the bus and wonder how she ended up in that house and where she would go from there. The bus picked her up every day for about three weeks and then we stopped going by the house. I never saw the girl again. I still think about her sometimes. As an adult I wonder why my school bus never collected any other children from that house. Why didn't all the children go to school?

After overhearing my mother's conversation about Drs. and bleeding and kidney infections. I tried to put together the bits and pieces of what had happened to me. I had been hurt, bad. I didn't know how I had been hurt or what I had done that was so bad that no one would even tell me what it was. Whatever I had done, it was related to Mother and Father being mad at me. I had been taken to the hospital where Mother told the Drs. I had a kidney infection but apparently the Drs. didn't believe her. What did the Drs say? Why couldn't I remember being hurt or going to the hospital? Going to a hospital is a big thing. How could I not remember?

Mother also talked about being at Reunion. I didn't remember Reunion either. How was that possible? Reunion lasted from Saturday through the following Sunday. How could I not remember anything for a whole week or longer? Going to Reunion was a big deal, it was a trip, with new places, activities, and people. It made no sense that I would go on a trip, go to the hospital, be away for a whole week and not remember anything, but trying to remember made my head hurt, and my stomach too. It felt like buzzing and other, scary, intelligible sounds. I wanted to close my eyes because it felt like the room was closing in on me and the floor was swaying back and forth. This had never happened to me before. Why did my head hurt when I tried to remember things?

I figured out that the visit with Dr. H and the ex-Mrs. Supervisor happened because they were trying to get me to tell them about how I was hurt. But I didn't know how I was hurt, and Mother and Father didn't want me to know what had happened, so how could I tell anyone else? When I tried to ask questions, they got angry and gruff. They acted like these were grown up things and I should know better than to ask about them.

How could I be hurt and not remember how it happened? Why would my parents take me to my Dr but not want me to tell him how I was hurt? Why didn't they help explain what happened? Did they not know either? Except it seemed to me like they did know. They just didn't want me to know. How could my parents want me to forget I was hurt, but Dr's and strangers wanted me to tell them all about it? Why did my parents take me to see these people but then get angry because I talked to the people they took me to see?

Why couldn't I understand people's words when they asked me questions? It made no sense! How come I couldn't even hear the words they used? I never had trouble understanding other people but when Dr. H and ex-Mrs. Supervisor asked questions the words warped into nothing but nonsense syllables. What was wrong with me? What if it kept happening? What if it got worse?

And what was all this stuff about "touching myself" and "masturbation" and "orgasms?" I didn't know what any of these things were, but clearly the whole issue revolved around something that I was doing. It was all me. It was all my fault. I was the cause of all that was evil and wrong. Since, whatever it was, I was the one doing it, then I was the only person who could fix it. If I could only figure out what it was.

Our lives changed after that day. Being a small child, I wasn't fully aware of this. My life, the place where we lived, my school and all my friends stayed the same, so I didn't feel the earth-shattering changes. I am sure the dynamics between Mother and Father became more strained than ever, but we were never a close or functional family so that wasn't very apparent to me either.

We stopped visiting Fathers office on the days we drove into town for groceries and errands. I was surprised the first time we skipped what had been our regular visit, but Mother didn't want to explain and while I was disappointed it wasn't something to get upset over.

I noticed when Father came home in a new powder blue sedan. Now this was exciting! I hadn't known we were going to get a second car. When would I get to ride in it?

The answer was never. This wasn't our car at all. It was a work car so that Father could take it on out-of-town business trips. For some reason he was going to spend time on the road again, like he had when I was little and we lived on the farm; before he had gone to graduate school; before he had completed his MSW and been promoted to Case Worker and before we had moved back to the UP and into this nice house and neighborhood.

Had he been demoted? Was he back to being an auditor? Had he been transferred to a position where he wouldn't have direct interaction with or influence on the lives of children who passed through Social Services?

I didn't understand that in the fallout from my rape, and as a result of my parents attempts to hide what happened to me, my father's professional reputation and the willingness of his superiors to trust him as a case worker in situations of child abuse and neglect was severely damaged. I don't know that they found a way to re-assign his case load. I cannot verify that they sent him back out to do the auditing work he had done earlier in his career. I cannot even tell you how many days a week he was out of town. I can only tell you that he got a "State" car; that he hated it; he didn't like to drive it or even talk about it; he expressed anger and bitterness every time it was mentioned.

The car didn't come home on weeknights. The garage that housed it remained a sheltered, not in the house, play area. I seemed to be more aware of the cars absence than I was of Father not coming home at night.

And then there was the soap. Hotel soaps were little "single use" bars, maybe 2" by 1.25" by .25". They were perfect for my small child-sized hands. Every weekend when Father came home, he would bring me a handful of child sized bars of soap. I kept them in the medicine cabinet of the half bath. I stacked up as many as would fit on the bottom shelf and then I started another stack, and another…

The State car didn't stay too long, maybe just a year or so, by then I had all the child's size soaps I would ever need. I outgrew the little bars long before I depleted the supply.

I never saw ex-Mrs. Supervisor again and only saw Dr H one more time and then it was only by accident. We ran into Dr. H and his nurse at a local fast-food restaurant. I saw them and happily tugged on Mother's sleeve before running over to say hello. I just wanted to say "Hi". I liked them and was happy to see them, but Mother grabbed me by the arm and physically dragged me back. Dr H looked up. We made eye contact, but he didn't wave or call out to me as Mother dragged me away. I was hurt that he didn't seem happy to see me.

Mother still had me by the arm. She hissed at me, “You don’t know what they did to us!”

How could I? She would never explain.

First Grade

I don't have as many stories to tell about first grade, and I am not sure why. One possibility is that not very much happened. We didn't move. I didn't start school for the first time and then transfer to a new school just a few weeks later. I didn't have to find all new friends. These are the nice things that might explain why I have fewer stories to tell. Of course, there are also some not so nice reasons for having fewer stories. My emotional response to the trauma of rape was to block weeks of memories. I may have remained in a sort of dissociative fugue for a good part of the year.

What I do remember is the joy of real school. First grade taught me sooo many things. Kindergarten academics had taught us to recite the alphabet and recognize our letters and numbers. The flash cards we practiced with included pictures, like a picture of an apple on the 'A' card, and a baseball bat on the 'B' card... Each picture had a string of letters below it. I knew these letters made up the word for the item in the picture, but we never talked about the letters or the words. I wanted to understand them. I wanted to be able to read. It was soooo frustrating when my teachers and my parents told me to be patient, that I wasn't ready yet.

In first grade we were issued Dick and Jane readers. If you have never seen a Dick and Jane reader, consider yourself lucky. They teach reading through gradual, repetitive exposure to simple words and sentences of no more than three or four words. Early dialog is something like this.

> See Dick.
>
> See Jane.
>
> See Dick run.

See Jane run.

See Spot.

See Dick run.

See Jane run.

See Spot run. (Are you bored yet?)

We would sit in a reading circle and pass the book around giving each child a page to read. The other children in my reading circle found this difficult. A child would stumble over the word 'See' in "See Dick." And then stumble over the same word again in 'See Jane." When the word 'run' was added the child would stumble over it with every repetition. I wasn't allowed to help. I had to be patient and let them work it out for themselves. I couldn't say, "It's the same word you just read two seconds ago!" I wasn't very good at being patient. I knew there was so much more to learn and couldn't contain my impatience to get there.

When the book finally got to me, I said with impatience and bored emphasis. "See Spot run. See Spot run, huh!?" Look at that! It's a new word! I don't know this word. I have never seen this word before. How am I supposed to deal with this new word?

My teacher, another wise and caring person to touch my life, walked me through it.

What is the first letter?

"A."

What sound does 'A' make?

"Ah."

What is the second latter?

"W"

What sound does ‘W’ make?

"wha"

What is the next letter?

"A." What sound does ‘A’ make?

"ah."

What other sound does ‘A’ make?

"Aye"

What is the next letter?

"Y"

What happens when you sound the ‘A’ and ‘Y’ together?

"A-ee?" "a-ee?" "Aye?"

Now start with the first letter.

"A-wha-aye?" "A-way." "AWAY!" “See Spot run AWAY!”

Until that moment, reading was just a matter of recognizing and repeating familiar words. We talked about phonetics. I understood that ‘A’ was for apple, ‘B’ was for bat, and so on but hadn’t realized that the other letters in the word could be sounded out, that if you sounded out each of the letters, they all worked together to create the word. Now it all clicked! I understood the secret code! I knew how to do it! I could read!

Mother was dubious, that afternoon, when I announced that I had done it, that I could read! Nobody learns to read in a single moment, but I had unlocked the code. By the end of the week, I had been reassigned to a different reading group. I had permission to borrow any of the ‘advanced’ books at the back of the room and I was devouring them at warp speed.

We didn't have any children's books at home. Mother read to us as children but the only book I remember as mine was a copy of "The Cat in the Hat" by Dr Suess and it has always been my least favorite of all the Dr Suess books. I was the child of a woman with a temper as volatile as nitroglycerine. Our home was always tidy and sterile; any deviation in her environment could set off an uncontrolled explosion. How could I possibly enjoy a story about children left alone and visited by a stranger who then destroys the house?

Mother believed in libraries and took us there frequently. She tried to time our visits to "Story Time," when someone from the library would read to the group of gathered children but we didn't always have time to browse the library shelves, so we didn't always get new books to bring home.

When I didn't have age-appropriate books I made do with newspapers (the Sunday comics worked well) and magazines. I started with the advertisements. They were easy, bold pictures, big letters... Then I worked my way down to the fine print at the bottom of the advertisements. I wasn't reading for context. I was just de-coding words. The fine print was a treasure trove of complicated letter strings. Even if I didn't understand the meaning of a word, I could sound it out. Then, once I could say it, I could ask for the definition.

Packaging was even better. I once took the box from a tube of toothpaste to bed and spent the next hour carefully sounding out all the names of the ingredients.

Books, when I could get them, were still the most interesting. On our next trip to the library, I checked out every Dr. Suess book available. After a week or two the librarian started setting new titles aside for me. (The list of angels who touched my life keeps getting longer.)

At some point, in this phase of reading everything I could find, I saw my first Playboy centerfold. I entered our one full bathroom and there was a magazine setting on the floor in front of the toilet. It was open to a page that folded out into one long photo of a very pretty woman. I didn't really notice that she was naked. To my literal mind she wasn't actually naked. She had on some pretty, white, filmy, see-through clothing, trimmed with white rabbit fur. The fact that this clothing only served to enhance her private parts was wholly lost on me. She looked relaxed and happy. On the right side was an image made to look like a page of lined, yellow, school paper. The paper had a list of printed questions and "handwritten" answers. She shared her name and age, her measurements, her favorite authors and musicians, her "turn-ons" and "turn-offs."

I had no idea that this was proof of my father, knowingly and deliberately, engaging in the sinful act of masturbation; the same act he had repeatedly accused me of as I recovered from the pain and injuries of rape, but at some level I did know that this magazine was not for me. I never told either of my parents about the foldout page with the pretty lady. They never knew that my early readers included Playboy magazine, or that for years to come my role model was that pretty Playboy Bunny. I wanted to be like her. I wanted to be a pretty lady that people paid attention to. I needed to learn more about books and music so I could have favorite authors and artists. I wanted people to care about what I liked and what I didn't like. I wanted people to be interested in me.

First grade was also the year I developed an unusual but happy fantasy. I imagined myself orphaned. I imagined getting off the school bus and turning toward the house only to find that it had burned to the ground.

The farm, where we had lived when I was small, had in fact, burned. I knew this but it shouldn't have affected me much. We hadn't lived there for years, and we didn't own it anymore. I hadn't seen it burn or visited the site afterwards. The only reason I knew it had burned was because I heard my parents talking about it.

I don't think I had ever seen a burnt-out property but I did a pretty good job of imagining what it would look like. I imagined a smoldering pile of ashes where the house had been with blackened, twisted remnants of the appliances and thin trails of smoke still drifting up to the air. The only thing my imagination missed was the smell.

In my fantasy I stood in front of the remains of our house for a few minutes, all by myself, taking in the revelation that home was gone. After a little while, adults entered the scene; responsible, authoritative adults. There was a fireman, a teacher and a social worker. The adults treated me kindly as they explained that my parents and sister had all died in the fire, so I didn't have a family or a place to live any more.

The social worker said she would try and find a good foster home for me, but I asked her not to. I knew that foster parents were given stipends to cover the cost of housing and feeding the children. I asked if I could get the stipend instead. I explained that I would rather be left alone to take care of myself. I explained that I knew how to feed myself. I knew how to cook canned soup, SpaghettiOs', and butterscotch pudding.

In my fantasy the adults agreed. They helped me find a small apartment. The apartment looked a lot like the front two rooms of our house, but it was sunnier and had more happy green plants. The responsible adults came to check on me every few weeks but I was always clean and well fed, and I still showed up at school and did well, so they decided I really could take care of myself and they let me keep my happy little apartment.

Over the years this fantasy changed from time to time. In the summer, when the leaves were on the trees, I would build my fantasy home hidden under the drape of a large and beautiful weeping willow. After seeing a movie about Pippi Longstocking I imagined a beautifully bohemian home in broken down cars in a junk yard. In adolescence I dreamed of being taken in by a wealthy relative who allowed me to stay in a vacant servants' apartment and left me alone to manage my own life and affairs.

What all of these fantasies had in common was liberation from family. It wasn't liberation from all people. In my fantasies I had friends and supportive, though generally distant, adults. It wasn't a world of infinite candy and no rules. I continued to go to school, to learn and grow and make plans for the future. The only thing that had no place in my fantasy was family.

Putting the Pieces Together

In August of 1969 we went back to Reunion at the Park of the Pines campground near Petoskey Michigan. What I remember of the trip down is how agitated Mother was. We spent hours in the car listening to her obsess over how things would be different than the year before. As she railed on I learned that the campground had been built on a terraced hillside leading down to lake Charlevoix. That the highest terrace was reserved for trailers and RV's while tent spaces were on the lowest level. Apparently, all of the problems the year before occurred because our tent, on the lower terrace, flooded during heavy rain.

Also, according to Mother, it was totally unacceptable that "They" reserved all the good sites for people who could afford nice RVs and trailers while people who only had tents were relegated to the older section at the bottom of the hill. (Mother was always complaining about a mysterious "They" who controlled all kinds of things and made all kinds of rules with no purpose other than to make life hard for the rest of us.) It was discrimination! It was absolutely unfair. We were not going to put up with it!

This was all very confusing to me as I still had no memory of the previous year's visit. My head was full of questions. "What are you talking about? We have never been here before. How come I don't remember any of the things you keep going on about? Why does my head hurt whenever I try?"

I knew better than to ask any of my questions. Mother was highly agitated. She was close to what my father called "blowing up." When Mother blew up, she devolved into a screaming rage that encompassed everyone and everything around her. She would hit, slap, and throw things. She would scream hateful accusations at anyone in her path. Her rage could last for hours, sometimes even into the next day. Her hatred and vitriol eclipsed the real world. Nothing could stop it. Blame for the blow-up went to the last person to speak to her before she lost control. Most of the time that person was me.

As soon as we arrived at the campgrounds and pulled into a "reserved for campers or trailers" camp site I made myself scarce. Even if Mother hadn't been agitated before I knew better than to hang around while Mother and Father were setting up our tent. I do not think they ever set up the tent without a major blow up and I didn't want to be available to take the blame. I needed to get as far away from Mother as possible. No one would complain if they could not find me, no one would bother to look for me. Alone, I was safe. Staying close to camp was the riskier act.

I took the opportunity to explore this place, a place I had been to a year before but somehow couldn't remember. It was a strange feeling, wandering around the campgrounds looking for anything that seemed familiar.

The upper terrace held nothing for me. It was graded and level with a new brick bathhouse and smooth gravel pads for RVs. The road continued down to the lower terraces. Even to my child's eyes I could see the logic of leaving the RV's up-top rather than risk having one or more stuck on the steep, narrow, rutted tracks.

For pedestrians there was a long staircase leading to the middle terrace, the heart of the camp. There was a dining hall, two chapels, some smaller buildings for classes, more bathhouses, and a playground. I explored each space. What about those swings? Hadn't someone taught me a new song? I can feel myself sitting on that swing, over there on the right, singing and liking the pretty sounding song. Can I find anything else familiar?

The lower terrace was the tent level. By the end of the week, I had worked out where we pitched our tent the year before. I remembered the rain and the sound of the tent zipper opening and closing as Mother went out after putting my sister and me to bed. I remembered Mother pointing to someone else's tent and explaining how all their things got wet and they had to find someplace else to sleep because their tent flooded.

One site had a slatted wooden base, like a large wooden palette or a slightly raised stage. This supposedly helped with the flooding, but it wouldn't have mattered to the people in the tent that did flood, they got swamped because they kept touching the roof and walls of the tent until it couldn't hold the rain out any longer. She also explained that this was their own fault. If they had been careful their tent would not have flooded, but they were bad, sinful, careless people and so all their stuff was ruined, and they had nowhere to sleep.

This was an odd bit of information (aside from the "bad things happen to people because they are sinners" part). I was used to the sinner's refrain, but "only bad people touch tent walls?" Huh? So, the tent keeps the rain out as long as we don't touch the walls? What kind of logic was this? I was used to hearing that God made bad things happen to sinful people and that when the bad things happened it was important to figure out what the person did that was sinful. But why would God care? Why would God treat a person like a sinner if all they did was touch the walls of their tent?

I am sure what Mother meant was that pressure on the inside of the canvas can stretch wet fibers and provide a conduit for water to seep through, but as a five-year-old my logic wasn't that good, and Mother never explained anything.

Obviously, I had to test this theory about tent walls and flooding. That. That! I remembered that! I remembered lying on my back on a cot with the sound of rain drumming on the tent all around me. I remembered reaching my hand out to the damp canvas wall, applying just enough pressure so I could feel dampness on the inside from the wet on the outside. I wondered how hard I would have to press before the water came through, but I didn't dare try because I didn't want to have to face mother if we got swamped out of our tent and it was all my fault.

It didn't matter. The rain that year was enough to overwhelm the best tents available. Eventually all the tent dwellers had to relocate to buildings. I have one or two images in my head of sodden clothes hanging to dry in one of the chapels, and sleeping bags spread out on the pews.

I found just a couple of other memories from the first year at Park of the Pines. Most significantly a pine snake. A big pine snake, as long as I was tall. (My apologies to those of you who dislike snakes. I was never taught to fear them, but I was taught how to catch them. I was low to the ground, fast, skilled, and proud. And in this case the snake plays an important part in my story.)

I came across the pine snake in an unused corner of the park, down by the lake. I stalked it for two or three days before finally catching it. Once I caught it, I trapped it in a shoe box so I could keep it as a pet and show off my great hunting skills.

When dinner time came, I was heartbroken to learn that I could not take my snake with me into the dining hall. I was afraid to leave it alone outside. Someone might take the lid off the shoebox and my snake could get out and get lost! I had worked so hard to catch it. This was an end of the world event for five-year-old me.

Mother had an idea. She knew the person who was working in the ticket shed outside the dining hall. His name was ??? ??????. (I can hear her voice in my head but not his name. I can hear the cadence of it. One syllable for the first name, two for the last. Accent on the second syllable, but nothing more.)

Mother reminded me that ??? ?????? and I had a Special Relationship. He would be happy to watch my snake.

Mr. Special Relationship! Mr. Special Relationship was there! Mr. Special Relationship of the “Go ask ??? ?????? for candy.” Mr. Special Relationship of the “??? ?????? likes to spend time with you.” Mr. Special Relationship who is somehow the reason that at the age of two peanut butter became the grossest thing in the world; the reason even smelling it could make me want to puke. He was there at Reunion the year I came home injured with a big black hole in my memories and the inability to even hear questions about why! What did he have to do with trauma so deep I was unable to hear or understand words whenever anyone tried to ask me how I was hurt? He was there! He had to be part of the story!

What Happened

Here is what I have been able to put together.

My mother, my sister Heather, and I went to the Park of the Pines Reunion in August of 1968. (I have been told that Father was unable to come with us. This is consistent with my not having any memories of his being there, but I couldn't have said for sure that he wasn't there.)

We pitched our old canvas tent with several others on the lower terrace. Heavy rains flooded most of the tents and people had to look for dry places to sleep. I believe Mr. Special Relationship was staying by himself in a trailer and offered to let me stay with him.

Mother was happy to let me sleep in his trailer, after all "we had a special relationship" so I spent the night with him. It was just me. Mother and Heather slept somewhere else. The next morning an unidentified (to me) woman found me alone in the women's bathhouse, crying and bleeding into the toilet. I was apparently taken to a local hospital, likely in either Petoskey or Charlevoix. Mother told the hospital staff I was suffering from a kidney infection. Later, when I was taken for a follow-up visit with my home pediatrician, Dr. H, he contrived to interview me without Mother in the room and subsequently reported suspicions of sexual abuse.

Two things prevented confirmation of sexual abuse.

> First: I couldn't talk about it. It wasn't just that I didn't understand or remember. I was so traumatized by the event that I literally couldn't hear the words when Dr H, and subsequently Ex Mrs. Supervisor interviewed me.
>
> Second: the only person in the region who investigated such claims was my father.

Because of these reasons the only consequences for my family were to stop the in-process adoption of five abandoned Native American children.

Of course, the allegations had a devastating impact on my father's career along with his relationships with his colleagues. I would be why he was demoted from case worker back to auditor.

My memories are still sketchy, but I remember Mr. Special Relationship. I remember the rain. I have a faint memory of hiding in the last stall of the women's bathhouse and trying not to cry so no one would hear me. The interviews with Dr. H and ex-Mrs. Supervisor have always been clear, though confusing, memories; the words that dissolved into unintelligible mutterings as well as the buzzing pain in my head when I tried to understand them. I clearly remember overhearing Mothers phone conversation and insistence that despite the opinion of multiple Drs. my bleeding was caused by a kidney infection.

The other things I remember are the pain, my parent's anger, and the accusations that I was touching myself and that touching myself was bad, and that people were saying bad things about us, and recognizing that for some reason I was the cause of Mother and Father's anger, knowing it was all my fault. I remember the buzzing and pain in my head and blurring at the edges of my vision when I tried to understand it all…

There is one more thing I remember with unabashed, self-righteous glee. I remember that Mr. Special Relationship was absolutely terrified when asked to babysit my cardboard shoebox with a large pine snake inside!

Reflection

From my current vantage point decades later, I can better trace the interaction of family dynamics and the life altering decisions that were made in the midst of crises.

My pediatrician found a way to question me without a parent present then he reported evidence of rape to local social services. This is why I was never allowed to visit him again; why Mother physically dragged me away the one time we ran into him by accident and I just wanted to say "Hi."

The outing to the state fair with ex-Mrs. Supervisor was a follow-up attempt to question me about the rape. For any other child this would have been my father's job, but he couldn't be tasked with investigating his own family. Unfortunately, I was unable to tell my story. I was a bright, articulate child who had been so traumatized that the questions and even the individual words became meaningless gibberish to my ears.

Then there was the overheard phone call between my parents, the questions she answered, the number of times she answered them, and her growing agitation as she pushed her version of events again and again becoming increasingly frantic with each volley.

Father knew that my trauma and injuries were caused by something more than an infection. He knew Dr. H had reported suspicion of rape. He had to make a choice between supporting his wife's fabricated version of events or putting his family through the trauma of a rape investigation. He could choose to admit that his emotionally unstable wife had put their children at risk, or he could pretend nothing had happened. He knew denying the accusation would cut me off from physical and emotional care, but he probably convinced himself that this had been a one-time, freak event. He probably allowed himself to believe that the trauma and family fallout of a formal investigation would outweigh any benefit of medical or social services intervention.

At least I hope he thought these things. I hope he at least considered my well-being before choosing to cut me off from any hope of medical care and emotional support.

I also hope he remembered that this was not the first time. Did he consider that the last time I attended a Church function with Mr. Special Relationship I was left unable to eat peanut butter from that day forward. Did he remember that my last interaction with Mr. Special Relationship left me so traumatized that they had to move out of town rather than take me back into the church?

He made the wrong choice. He took the cowards' way out. He chose to believe my injuries were minor and the accusation of rape was an exaggeration. He didn't examine me. He didn't question me. He didn't pay attention to my needs at all. He simply denied the abuse. He turned his back on his own child despite evidence of rape so clear it was independently reported to Social Services (his office) by medical personnel. He denied my rape knowing that his decision would also cut off my access to medical care and trauma support.

He must have rationalized his choice. He must have thought that surely this was a one-time event (except, of course, that this was actually the second time). He must have believed that we didn't need outsider involvement in a family matter; that children are resilient; that I would heal, and that the trauma would eventually blow over and everything would work out in the end.

He didn't know that the man who raped me had also sexually abused my mother when she was a child. He didn't look for, and therefore didn't see, how the dysfunctional patterns that started with her abuse subsequently led to my abuse and would continue to place our family at risk for tragedies yet to come. He couldn't see, or didn't want to see, how covering up one criminal act of child abuse would put him on a path of covering future acts, again and again.

In one of our last conversations before his death he told me he regretted "the times he chose to support Mother over his children." He explained that while he knew this was hard on us he felt bound by the dictates of his faith, that marriage was a sacrament; that he had to honor the sacramental relationship; that his faith left him no choice but to support his wife even when doing so harmed his children.

I was stunned by these words. I was struck dumb.

Was he trying to tell me that it was his faith that justified turning his back on his children in the face of criminal sexual abuse? Did he believe that by denying care and support to my sister and me he was honoring God?! Did he continue to believe this even in the face of event after event after event?

I couldn't find words, any words, to respond. I wish I could have answered him, but the opportunity passed, and we never finished the conversation in this life. I doubt it would have mattered. I believe this conversation is more than humans can handle on this mortal plane.

The truth is I talk to him more, now, after his death, than I ever did when he was alive. I wonder if he hears me. What would the great preacher, teacher and theologian say in response to my accusation. "You were nothing but a coward! You turned your back on your children. You profaned your own religion by twisting the name of God and your religious beliefs to support the person who exposed your children to pedophiles. You twisted your religious values into an excuse to deny care and support to your own children despite multiple rapes! You used the name of God and your religious values to blame the victims, your own children, for being raped! You chose to deny that rape occurred and instead accused a five-year-old child of masturbation. You nurtured your resentment for years, even decades. When you decided it was finally time to clear the air between us you accused me of 'fornicating' against you. You claimed I owed you 'atonement!'

Somehow in your mind I became the offender (for being raped) and you the victim!

How did this work out for you? What was that moment like when you finally met your maker and explained how righteous you were, how you twisted the message of God's love for all his children to support your cowardice and your fear, how you sacrificed the needs and safety of your own children in order to remain faithful to your God?"

My father gave in to the sin of pride. He allowed desire for a fictional perfect family to outweigh the most basic needs of his children. One cowardly response led to another and another... replicating itself throughout our lives and sadly even into the next generation.

He was the only social services case worker in the region. He was Child Protective Services, and his inability to protect his own children destroyed his career as well as his family.

He had hopes for a career with Michigan Social Services. He didn't plan on remaining a case worker for long. He was ambitious. He believed he deserved to be on the fast track to bigger and better things.

Then there was a family of five abandoned children. How could anyone deny the devotion and compassion of a man who adopted five needy children? Was he really motivated by compassion or was this a just a shrewd move to support his ambition?

All his potential dried up when he denied my rape. He went from enjoying his job to complaining bitterly that his supervisors "had it out for him," that they would actively block him from ever being promoted. Of course, they would! How could anyone promote a social worker who stonewalled the investigation of the rape of his own child?

All joy went out of his job at that point. There wasn't enough evidence to fire him or remove Heather and me from his home and place us in foster care. Was that a possibility? Was he threatened with the loss of his own children?

I was threatened with it. I was told again and again that my behavior could result in the loss of Fathers job and/or removal from our home and to a foster facility. I was treated to all kinds of horror stories about what happened to children in foster care.

How close did we come? How much evidence did they document? Obviously not enough for a criminal investigation, or to fire him. Seemingly enough to discipline and demote him.

Did he try to quit? I don't think he could. I believe he still owed a service obligation in return for his education. If he did look for other work, what kind of reference would he receive from his current employer? He was stuck. He couldn't quit, not for another year or two. So he brought home the State Car and worked a year or more on the road as an auditor building up more and more resentment with each passing week.

As soon as my father completed his service obligation to the State of Michigan, he started a long-range job search. Anywhere but Michigan. At one point we thought we were moving to Australia. In the end he found work in northern Maine, a thousand miles away. Sometimes the course of life turns on a single choice, for our family August 1968 was one of those times.

Daily Life in Northern Michigan

Maine was in my future but for now it was still just a distant and unlikely possibility.

My world in Northern Michigan was that of a child. Children are resilient. We do heal. We also live in the moment. And we fail to understand how much our lives are shaped by the adults in our lives.

We lived in a modern home in a trendy neighborhood. Our neighbors were primarily young professionals with growing families. Mother was excited, thrilled, even just to be there. She once said Father started his Marquette job with a salary over $10,000. She felt like they had really made it!

The house was a three-bedroom ranch with a bath and a half. We were at the bottom of a hill. Each lot has been cut out of the hillside like terraces. The resulting grade connecting us to the next house up the hill was taller than the house itself and quite steep, a perfect sledding hill. On the far side of hill was a gentler slope, almost like a ramp. In winter we used the ramp to climb to the top of the hill with our toboggans, sleds, and flying saucers…

Deep winter snow in outside our home in February of 1968.

At the low end of the ramp, where the different elevations came together, sandy soil from the untamed woods met the grassy lawn. The previous owners had built a low rock wall to contain the sand. The result was an elevated sand box; perfect height for a five- or six-year-old sitting up on her knees. It was even better than the sand table in my kindergarten classroom. I was getting bigger. I could wander further. And in this new neighborhood there were fewer restrictions. My focus was on me, my friends, my life at school, my free time to wander and explore…

The school bus stop was the triangle of land across the street from our house which we creatively named, “The Triangle.”

On an average day as many as three dozen children gathered at the Triangle each morning and packed into the bus. One bus served the entire neighborhood. We were packed in like sardines, literally sitting six to a seat. The bigger kids sat three across on the bench seat and the smaller ones sat on their laps. The bus filled from back to front. There was no complaining and no choosing where to sit. Each child took the next spot available. If you wanted to sit with a friend, you needed to make sure you were together in line before boarding the bus. The upside to riding that overcrowded bus was getting to know every child in the neighborhood.

Another oddity of my elementary school was that we were bussed home for lunch and back to school afterwards. By the end of the day each child had ridden two complete circuits of the bus route. It wasn't long before I knew every child in the neighborhood, their friends, their brothers and sisters, what grade and classroom they were in at school, and what bus stop they used.

When I wasn't in school, I roamed free throughout the entire neighborhood. We lived in a relatively new subdivision that had been designed for a "park like" experience with each home backed to woods. We children wore a network of pathways through those woods. These were our secret routes to each other's houses and to the hiding places and sun dappled glens where we played. I knew my way through backyards and woodland paths better than the streets.

By the end of first grade many of my classmates had graduated from shoe leather transportation through the woods, to bicycles on the streets. Groups of children I played with the summer before were now speeding by on brightly colored banana bikes. I was left behind. I had to get my hands on a bicycle!

My birthday is in August, so I started a summer campaign for a bicycle. It ended up being a long process. Mother's first answer was a cheap scooter. This was not one of the smooth wheeling, power assisted scooters available today in the year 2023. This scooter was a clunky thing with small wheels that always stuck. As long as I kicked it along the wheels would turn but it never coasted on its own, not even down steep hills. Uphill and even on level surfaces it was no better than walking or running. Most significantly, it wasn't a bicycle!

Mother's second attempt to satisfy my insistent requests for a bicycle was to offer up her old Schwinn. This was the bike with the child's seat on the back that she and I had ridden to all her pregnancy checkups before my sister was born. It was a fine bicycle, but it was waaaay too big for me. Even in its lowest position the seat was so high it was practically level with my shoulder. The girls bike cross bar was high enough that straddling it, even while standing up, I couldn't reach the pedals. And it was heavy; it weighed at least as much as I did.

Taking Mothers too big bike away from home, joining the flocks of children racing their bikes around the neighborhood, was out of the question. I did find a fun trick though. Our driveway was several car lengths long and steeply sloped from the house down to the street. I would stand the bike up in the carport, then balance with my right foot on the left pedal and shove off. On a good run the bike would fly all the way down the drive and across the road before I lost balance. Once or twice, I managed to make a turn at the bottom of the drive and steer it out into the intersection. This wasn't a very safe game, but no one paid attention or told me to stop, so I found it to be great fun.

Eventually, I think it was for my seventh birthday, my persistence won out and I became the proud owner of a blue banana bike with high handlebars and white streamers. Oh, what fun I had on that bike!

There was a community park(ish) at the far end of the neighborhood. The developers had never completed the project. We were left with a set of monkey bars, a piece of pavement for playing foursquare, and various holes and mounds, the result of unfinished excavations and unused piles of fill dirt. It was the perfect environment for banana bike motocross. We wore trails into the ground and added planks for bridges and ramps. I was as much of a daredevil as any of the older boys.

A year later I broke both my front teeth on that bike. I took the long route to a friend's house so I could start down her street from the very top of the hill, then I raced down it as fast as I possibly could only letting up at the very last minute (okay, obviously a little after the last possible minute). I skidded around the 90 degree turn into her driveway and laid both the bike and myself down flat, somehow presenting my face, front teeth first, into the pavement. I was a teenager before I finally got my teeth fixed, but a couple of broken teeth did not stop me from continuing to challenge the laws of physics and gravity on my banana bike.

Life in Marquette also introduced me to Girl Scouts, and to the mothers who volunteered their time and effort to lead our scouting troops. I loved the structured activities and the opportunity to make even more friends.

My elementary school was a mix of social classes. The children from my suburb were from white-collar, middle-class families. The children who lived closer to the school were from blue-collar, working-class households. What I didn't notice until many years later was that the caring, hard-working mothers who took time to be scout leaders all came from the working-class families.

A Battered Sister

One hot summer day, in June or July of 1970, I came bursting into the house, panting from whatever breakneck adventure I had been engaged in. The moment I stepped through the door I knew something was wrong. Mother and Father were both sitting at the kitchen table, except sitting is not the right word. They were limp, sagging, and ashen faced. They looked like their world had come to an end.

Mother looked up at me and said, "Your sister was hurt."

I answered "Oh." and "What happened?"

Mother said, "She was running through the woods, and she fell."

I asked, "is she okay?"

Mother tried to explain that Heather had tripped on some tree roots and hit her head.

I was confused because I knew every square foot of woods in the neighborhood. The tripping hazards included brambles, fallen branches, and occasional rotten logs from trees downed long ago. My sister had just turned four. She didn't wander like I did. She had never been past our yard or the woods just behind our house. There weren't any trees with trippable roots in our little patch of woods.

I asked what tree had tripped her and Mother responded that it was a big tree. I asked Mother about a specific tree in our patch of woods, or if it was the rotten log that we sometimes played on.

Mother said "No. No, it wasn't the woods behind our house. She was in the woods over on the other side of the Triangle."

Again, Mother's explanations only added to my confusion. Getting to the woods past the Triangle required crossing two busy streets. My four-year-old sister didn't cross streets by herself yet.

I asked how/why she was over there and was told she ran because a group of children were chasing her.

The story made less and less sense. Children came into our yard and chased my four-year-old sister across two streets causing her to fall and hit her head? I did not know any children who would do that.

I asked who the children were. Mother told me they were older children. I wouldn't know them.

Now I knew for sure that she was lying. I had ridden a single school bus packed with all the other children in our neighborhood, every day from kindergarten through second grade. I knew every child who was in my school now, or who had been in my school for the past three years. If Mother had said a single child, one I did not know, had chased my sister and caused her to hurt herself I might have believed her for a while, at least, until I combed the neighborhood and failed to turn up such a child, but a whole group of unknown children? This was a bald-faced lie!

Mother went on. She insisted it was a sizeable group, five or six children. But still, no one that I would know. These mythical children chased my sister out of our yard, across a wide street, across the Triangle, across another street, and into a patch of woods that was a low-lying poplar thicket. There, apparently, these fictional children caused my sister to trip on the roots of a big tree and to hit her head so hard she was knocked out.

There were no big trees in that grove of young poplar. It was a unique patch of woods, flat and sandy like a riverbed, with a shallow stream flowing through it. The poplar trees, related to aspen, grew close together and straight up. None of the trunks were more than two or three inches in diameter but they were so close together that even a small child had to push them aside, like walking through tall woody grass, to get through. Nothing to trip on, but plenty of reason to go slowly enough that a fall would be unlikely to cause major damage.

Mother answered every question I asked with more details; obviously fabricated details, that made her story less and less plausible. My sister was running when she tripped and fell. If she was running, she should have fallen forward, but somehow, she hit the back of her head, not her forehead, against a hard tree root.

She tripped on a tree root and hit her head on a tree root? How many exposed roots did this tree have?

The gang of unknown children were callous enough to chase my sister across two streets and through the woods until she tripped, fell, and did not get back up. But these same children (who Mother was still quite sure I would never have met) were then caring and responsible enough to come back to the house (of a child they didn't know) and find a parent to report their misbehavior to. How did they figure out what house we lived in? If these mythical children actually came to find Mother and lead her back across two streets and into the woods how come Mother had no idea who they were?

Throughout the conversation Mother was the only one who spoke; Father just sat there. He was ashen faced, slack mouthed, and shaken to his core. I am not sure he even followed what we were saying. He just stared blankly into space, looking like his world had come to an end.

The only part of the story that seemed to be true was that my sister had somehow been hit on the back of the head hard enough that she was unconscious for at least ten minutes, probably more, but she eventually woke up and my parents insisted she would be okay.

If she fell while running how could she hit the back of her head?

I finally gave up. Talking to Mother was hopeless. She was never going to give me a story that made sense. Heather had fallen and hit her head hard enough to be knocked out but she woke up and was going to be okay. Got it.

I casually wondered what being knocked out would feel like. This was a thing I had only ever seen on TV, in shows like Bonanza, or in Tom and Jerry cartoons.

Aside from that casual curiosity I didn't give it too much thought. I was sorry she got hurt but Mother assured me that my sister woke up and would be alright. Father still looked stunned. He did not move or speak.

I stood in the kitchen for a few moments longer wondering why grown-ups were so weird and if it was okay for me to go back outside. Then I realized that no one was paying any attention to me, so I left.

I am sad to say that it was a long time before I recognized the significance of that day. It only stood out in my memory because of my parents' odd behavior. By the next day everyone in the family was behaving normally and no one ever brought it up again.

In 2016 I traveled to Michigan to visit my sister. Family tensions were high. Heather claimed to have photographs of Mother with John, her birth father. (These pictures are included in chapter 5, "A Visitor.") Mother's denial of an affair remained vehement and brutal. According to her, Heather, now an adult and mother of four, didn't have even a basic understanding of how babies were made

Heather had met her birth father a few years earlier, near the end of his life. She visited with him on several occasions before he passed away about six months later. He acknowledged his paternity and expressed joy in the opportunity to get to know her. The two of them did what they could to make up the lost time. Heather remained in contact with her half siblings after their father passed. They gave her several photographs of Mother and John together.

Heather and Mother were engaged in a long, drawn out, heated battle. Neither one was willing to budge from their version of the truth and both parties were campaigning for my support. I was receiving phone calls at all hours of the day, venting frustration, and anger. I was also receiving long drawn-out letters packed with a lifetime of bitter accusations and dripping with vitriol towards the other side. Each one expected me to take their side, step in, and force the other side to back down.

I get tired of always being stuck in the middle of family drama. I wanted everyone to go away and leave me alone, but it was clear that this was not an issue that would ever blow over. I had never questioned Heathers paternity but now I was truly stuck between the unmovable rock and the impenetrable hard place and had no idea which way to turn. At least one party was choosing to fuel the fire with hatred and lies and using me in the process, but I had no way to know who. I did not want to be used to push falsehoods and cause needless trauma. I needed to see the photographs and judge the evidence for myself.

My husband, Wesley, was deployed overseas so I had a summer all to myself. I took a couple of days off and drove from Maryland to mid-Michigan.

Heather's photographs are compelling. One is of John and Mother side by side as a young couple. Another is the same pose about a decade or so later which would have been about the time of my sister's conception. The body language speaks volumes. My mother looks so happy, physically cuddled up to John. She exudes joy and a level of intimacy I never witnessed between her and father. And then there is John's face. He and Heather have the same gap between their front teeth and the same vertical folds on each side of their smile. From the instant I saw the photographs there has been no doubt in my mind that this man is Heather's father. What's more, I immediately recognized him as the "friend from church" who had visited Mother on my third birthday.

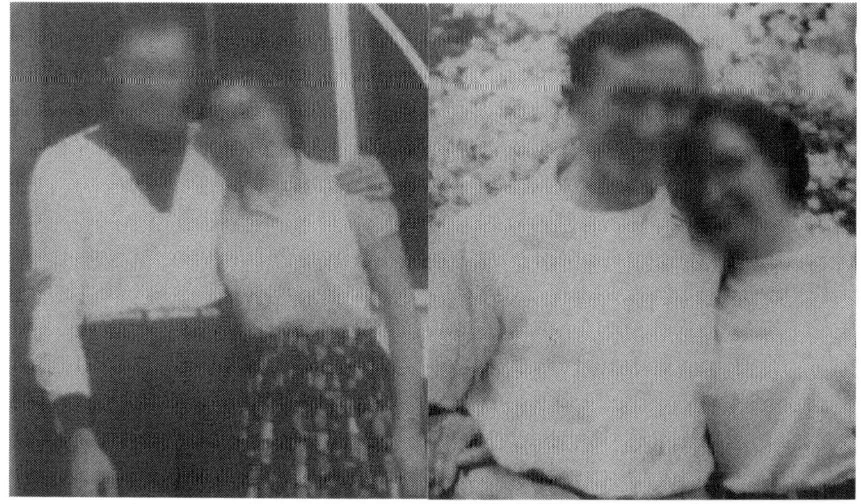

Left: Mother, age 18, with her fiance John.

Right: Mother, age 28, with John at about the time my sister was conceived. (The photo was given to my sister by members of John's family. We have no idea who took it.)

It had been many years since I had seen my sister. We talked almost non-stop for two days.

At one point she told her story of mother hitting her in the back of the head with a brick when she was a small child. She said her doctors had identified a long healed traumatic brain injury which she believed dated back to the day Mother chased her into the woods and hit her on the back of the head with a brick, causing her to lose consciousness.

I paused for a moment to let the comment sink in, then I asked her to tell me again. After Heather repeated her statement, I asked if she knew any more of the story. Heather said she had spilled a glass of milk which launched mother into one of her "blow-ups," (violent temper tantrums that could last hours). Heather wanted to get away. She ran out the kitchen door, across the back yard, and several yards into the woods before she felt something hard hit her in the back of the head and everything went black.

I took another moment to let this sink in then asked her to repeat the story one more time. After the second re-telling I asked if she remembered how old she was. She responded that she was four. I asked if she remembered which way she ran; if she knew what time of year this occurred; and if there were any other details she could add. She said that she ran across the backyard toward the woods, and that it was warm and sunny outside.

I realized I was hearing her side of the story; the story of the day "unknown children" chased my sister into the woods and caused her to fall and hit her head.

We had never talked about this event. I always assumed she had no memory of it. But she did remember. She had a clear memory of the events leading up to Mother's blow-up, she remembered running across the back yard, and feeling the blow of a hard object hitting the back of her head before she passed out.

I saw myself as a seven-year-old, standing in our family kitchen trying to understand why my parents were so shaken and why they were lying to me as I listened to my mother trying again and again to spin a plausible tale of how and why my sister had been hurt. I visualized our house, the backyard, and the patch of woods behind it. I realized I now knew what had occurred that day. And I knew that Heather had lived all these years not knowing what had happened to her. I took a deep breath and told her.

I said, "It wasn't a brick. It was a rock." I reminded her of how the back yard was laid out. At the far edge of the grass was a row of un-mortared, stacked, flat rocks forming a small retaining wall, the wall that formed my beloved sand-table. The wall was no more than 12 or 15 inches high on the left end and sloped to only a few inches on the right as the ground level rose to meet it. The ground behind it was sandy for a few feet before the edge of the woods.

By the age of four Heather could have scrambled up and over that that little wall like it was nothing but Mother, who enjoyed wearing nice pants and cute shoes, wouldn't have wanted to chase her child past the sandy edge of the yard and uphill into the woods. In her frustration she must have grabbed one (or more) of the rocks and thrown them at her child.

I have no trouble believing this. Her blow-ups were violent and irrational, like hurricanes or tornados. They eclipsed everyone and everything else.

Then I remembered that the wall had changed. It was nicer when we first lived there. I remembered a day, a couple of summers later, wondering what had happened. I wanted to play in my nostalgic happy place, but it wasn't the same. Part of the wall was missing. It didn't have a nice edge, like a sand-table, anymore. The sand just kind of sloped into the yard. At least the little bit of sand that was left. At first, I thought I was just seeing it differently because I was bigger but even when I got down on my knees I couldn't place where the edge of the wall had been. I tried to reposition the remaining rocks but there weren't nearly enough to rebuild the wall. I remembered wondering where they had all gone.

Mother was the one who hit Heather in the back of the head! There never were any strange children. There we as only Mother.

Mother threw the rock that almost killed her own child!

This was why Mother and Father were so shattered. This is why they desperately tried to come up with an alternate story and location. This is why they were so shaken they couldn't even fabricate a lie plausible enough to convince a seven-year-old.

Mother had thrown rocks at her child. Multiple rocks. So many rocks were missing that I couldn't rebuild the wall!

Mother kept throwing rocks until one hit her four-year-old in the back of the head causing her child to fall unconscious to the ground. She must have thought she had killed her.

Mother admitted Heather had been unconscious for as long as ten minutes. How long was it really?

What does it feel like to pick up the limp body of your child, knowing that you were the one who harmed her and not knowing if she will live?

I tried to remember if Father was supposed to be home that day. I was home because it was summer. But it didn't feel like a weekend. I feel like I was surprised to see him in the house. Shouldn't he have been at work?

How does it feel to call your husband home from the office because you think you have killed your child?

This event occurred less than two years after I was raped, in August of 1968. It occurred less than two years after my pediatrician reported suspicions of sexual assault to the social services office where my father worked. It occurred less than two years after my father refused to acknowledge my rape; less than two years after he had put his job on the line by obstructing his own organization's investigation into the sexual assault of his own child. Now my sister, the only other child in our home, was hit by a rock in the back of the head, knocked out cold, and likely concussed. It was another act of criminal child abuse in the same household.

My father still worked with the only Social Services facility in the region. He knew exactly what would happen if anyone reported Heather's injuries.

It was the same drill all over again. Create a cover story. Keep the child away from medical personnel who could identify the cause of the injury. No doctors, no palliative care, no evaluation of possible damage to mental or motor skills.

Because they had lied about my rape, they had to lie about Heather's injury. If anyone learned that Mother had hit her child with a rock, knocked her out, likely concussed her, and potentially caused long term damage, they would certainly take another look at the earlier allegations. There would be criminal charges, everyone would talk, Father would lose his job this time…

I am sad to say that there is another piece of this story that I missed. After returning from my visit to Heather in Michigan I shared these revelations with my therapist and she asked a simple question. She asked, on the day when you were confronted with both of your parents, sitting in the kitchen, looking as if their world had ended, "Where was your sister? Who was with her?"

I was stunned by this question. Yes, I was only seven when the incident occurred, but I was in my 50's when Heather and I pieced together our separate memories of the event. It had never occurred to me that my parents tucked Heather into her bunk and simply left her there, alone. When I found them, sitting stunned at the kitchen table, no one was with Heather. My parents were sitting together in the kitchen. They could not have known if Heather would live or die. Was she merely concussed? What if she was suffering a brain bleed?

I was only seven, but I knew that someone with a head injury should be kept awake for the first 24 hours, and I knew that someone should stay with them to assist or call for help in case of vomiting or seizure.

The reason I knew this was because it had been a recent plot in a sit-com I watched. I thought it was a funny rule. Mother explained the why of it to me, how a person could get sicker and if they were not awake, how it would look like they were just sleeping but they could be bleeding inside their skull, they could be dying. *Mother had explained that if you let someone go to sleep after they got hit in the head, they might die instead of waking up!*

There were only the four of us in our household. There were no close friends or family to take a turn at watching an ill child. Three of us were in the kitchen. No one was with my sister. She had been knocked out cold and then just put in her bunk to sleep it off; or not.

I want to take a moment here to string these events together. In August 1968, when my father made the decision not to report (or even acknowledge) my rape, he probably thought it was a onetime fluke event. He probably believed they were good parents, and we (his children) were in a safe home. I am sure he convinced himself that this wasn't a pattern. There wasn't any risk of future abuse. Children were resilient. This would pass. It was okay to lie to his co-workers and Social Services authorities just this once, because it would all turn out alright in the end.

Of course, even that wasn't true. He was conveniently forgetting my first encounter with Mr. Special Relationship and our abrupt move away from Mothers hometown and the farm they owned.

By hiding my rape, he chose to believe he was protecting us. He did not choose to see how he and Mother were weaving a web of deception that would trap all of us.

Both of my parents became wary of medical personnel. If anything happened to a child in our community or extended family, one or both of my parents would tell me how awful it was that the parents told people what had happened to their child; how awful it was that they even took the child to a doctor because if people knew that something bad had happened authorities would come and "take their children away."

Mother was frantic after one of my cousins broke an arm while wrestling with his brothers and father. The boy was taken to the hospital and when asked how he broke his arm he responded, "My Daddy did it." Mother was convinced her brother would be charged with child abuse. He would be sent to jail and the boys would all end up in foster care. She refused to believe that police and social services personnel could tell the difference between isolated accidents while roughhousing and patterns of abuse.

Foster care was the specter that hung-over Heather and me throughout our childhood. We were never, ever, to say anything bad about our parents. If we ever told any of the bad things that happened in our house, people would come and take us away. If we were taken away, we would end up in foster care and horrible things happened to children in foster care. Mother told us again and again, and in great detail, about all of the horrible things that went on in foster care.

So we lied.

My parents lied because if they ever told the truth about any single incident, they would be found out for all of the other incidents and then Heather and I would be placed in foster care.

Heather and I lied because we were conditioned to believe that none of the bad things were real. The bad things were just events we made up in our heads and if people knew we made up all these bad things they would know we were evil children. If people knew we were evil children, they would figure out the lies about our being a perfect family and then the really bad things would happen. Our family reputation would be ruined, our church reputation would be ruined, and Fathers work reputation would be ruined. Father would lose his job. People wouldn't believe in our church. We would lose our house. Heather and I would be taken away and made to live with bad people who only took care of foster children so they could hurt them and steal their money…

This is a simple form of bullying. Today we would call it gaslighting. Make the subject more afraid of the consequences of asking for help than they are afraid of you. It only works if the person being bullied has very little power and no one else in their lives to offer support. But we were children, and they were the adults who ruled our world.

My parents were terrified of being found out, so they passed that fear on to us. They bullied us with their fear. They told us stories again and again of children who were innocently injured but when they went to a doctor or hospital the police came and questioned or arrested the parents. They told us that the police and other authorities were always looking for reasons to place children in foster care, and they told us about all the awful things that happened to children once they were in the system.

It didn't matter that I never saw any examples of families torn apart because their parents took them to a doctor. The police talked to my uncle about my cousin's broken arm, but they didn't arrest him or threaten to take his sons away.

It didn't matter that I never knew a child who was in foster care. Of course, the five children my family intended to adopt all went to foster care, but I only ever met one of them, one time. And after the adoption plan failed no one ever talked about them again.

My parent's fear was real and so the fear they passed on to my sister and me was real too. Because of that fear, seeking help from anyone, doctors, teachers, parents of friends… was out of the question. With no one to turn to for help we would suffer even more abuse in the years to come.

I didn't understand that we were an isolated nuclear family. It took a therapist to point this out, many years later. She questioned me extensively about other adults in my life. She asked about aunts and uncles, close friends of my parents, the parents of other children I was close to. Eventually she looked at me in frustration and said, "Are you trying to tell me there were no other adults helping to raise you?"

She wasn't my favorite therapist. The question came across as if to say, "You must be lying!" and yet for me it was the first time I had reason to consider how isolated our family was. I recognized social isolation as an indicator of abusive relationships, I had just never looked at my upbringing in that light. I had never considered the lack of extended family or trusted friendships was itself a form of control and abuse. We had always lived far from family, friends, and even other church members. I didn't realize there was anything unusual about this. I never experienced anything else.

A few weeks later Mother and Father announced that Heather had been enrolled in full-day preschool. When school restarted in the fall we would both have a place to go.

I was livid! As a three and four-year-old I had begged and begged to go to school but I was told I was too young, that no one could go to school until they were at least five. But now, when my sister was only four, there was a special kind of school just for her!

Mother and Fathers explained that preschool cost money and when I was a child there hadn't been enough. This did not help at all. All I understood was that they could find money to do something special for Heather even when they hadn't had any for me!

I didn't have any idea that Father made the decision to send Heather to preschool, no matter the cost, because he was afraid of what would happen if he left her alone all day with Mother. Father couldn't leave Mother home alone with Heather for another whole year. He was afraid of what would happen next. The fact that Heather survived this time was simply a matter of luck. He was afraid they wouldn't be so lucky next time. Preschool was the best way to keep Heather out of the house, and hopefully, safe.

Baptism and Communion

In Community of Christ tradition Baptism is a choice made individually and freely. In keeping with this belief, we do not offer Baptism to children until they are old enough to understand the commitment and make the decision for themselves. Of course, the ability to understand and make commitments is personal, can be influenced by any number of outside forces, and varies with each individual. In practice we do not baptize children until they are at least eight years old.

For me Baptism could not come fast enough. My desire to be baptized had little to do with a mature understanding of Christian beliefs or a desire to serve. I desperately wanted to be treated as someone of significance. I wanted to belong. I wanted to find a way to purge the evil part of me that always made the adults in my life do bad things.

I also wanted to be included in the monthly ritual of communion. Except for the years in Detroit, I had only known small worship communities, often as few as two families who met in someone's home. My sister and I were frequently the only children. Communion was served on the first Sunday of each month but only to members who had completed the steps of baptism and confirmation. No one ever bothered to consider my child's perspective of a ritual that required everyone, including me, to kneel for sacrament prayers before sitting and watching patiently while everyone else is the room is reverently served a child sized portion of bread and yummy, syrupy, candy-sweet grape juice. (In recent years my home congregation has found ways to honor our children while still keeping the communion tradition, such as passing a small piece of candy to children too young to formally participate.)

I was also a child who suffered significant abuse and was expected to keep my sinful secrets to myself. Is it any wonder I saw Baptism as a magical portal that would transport me into the adult world, a world where I would be seen and valued?

No one ever asked about my understanding of a ritual that claimed to wash away the sins of the participant, returning them to a pure and holy state at the beginning of each month. I knew that I was sinful. Wasn't I told again and again that it was me who made Mother lose her temper and spend hour after hour taking out her anger on all of us? Wasn't it me who ruined "Special Relationships" with good and honorable men by making them do unspeakable things? Wouldn't everybody's lives be better if I could have my sins cleansed too? These were the reasons I begged to be Baptized as early as possible.

As it turned out, my eighth birthday fell on the last Saturday of Reunion and it didn't take much effort to convince my family to allow me to participate in the Baptism service that was traditionally held on that day. I am pretty sure they felt proud of their child as I put on my new white dress and walked into the lake at literally the earliest possible moment I could be baptized.

They explained that Baptism is only half of the ritual, that (at that time) becoming a full member of our church required rebirth of both water and the spirit. There was a second service the next day at home. This would be a "laying on of hands" where I would be welcomed and blessed as a new member. Father Baptized me with his friend Jared, the only other Elder in our tiny church group, assisting. The next day Jared Confirmed me while Father assisted.

That was it! It was done. I was in! Surely this was what I needed. This was what it took to make me a real person. This was what I needed to stop being evil. Everything would be better now!

Wouldn't it?

Left: Heather and me on the day of my Baptism

Right: Being Baptized by my Father, Aug 15th 1970
(My eighth birthday.)

Tithing

Shortly after my baptism (possibly at the beginning of September but I am not sure) Mother said she had a surprise for me. A package had arrived in the mail containing a blue, paper-bound book, about the size of a school notebook. It was a children's version of "Stewardship and Accounting."

Mother explained that now, since I was a full member of the Church, I needed to practice stewardship and pay tithing. The book contained instructions on completing a first tithing statement and ledgers for tracking subsequent income and spending.

I do not believe I had ever heard the word tithing before that day.

Mother and I sat on the floor of the bedroom I shared with my sister and made a list of all my assets. There was my bed, my clothing, my toys, my crappy blue scooter, and my beloved banana bike. Then we shook out my piggy bank and counted my cash.

Once everything was inventoried Mother added up all the estimated values. She talked about the law of tithing and how the word tithing meant one tenth, and the tenth was the amount I was expected to give to God for all of the things he Had given me. When she finished her first calculation, she said that I owed an initial tithing amount of just over $70.00!

The year was 1970. I was eight. My income was a weekly allowance of 35 cents and the total of my piggy bank was about $2.50. Mother said she couldn't help me pay the $70.00 because tithing was between me and God. No one else could pay God for what I owed.

As I sat on the floor wondering how in the world I was going to come up with $70.00, Mother said maybe she could reconsider some of her value estimates. Maybe, since none of my stuff was new, we should estimate rummage sale value rather than replacement cost. She wrote down some new numbers and did some more math, cutting the overall total by about 50%. Great now I was only in debt by an amount equal to 100 weeks of my allowance!

Mother adjusted some more numbers, and then adjusted them again. Finally, she came up with a tithing owed of just over $2.00. As congregational treasurer she took the $2.00, leaving me with about one week's allowance in my piggy bank.

The next step was to show me how to record all of my income and expenses in the blue book. There was a two-page section for each month. It was set up as a grid and looked a lot like a modern-day spreadsheet with columns for income and various expenses.

The expenses were divided into two categories, "Necessary" and "Unnecessary." Unnecessary was also referred to as "Increase." Across the columns was a row for every day of the month. When I received any money, I was supposed to enter it in the Income column. When I spent money, I had to decide what column it fit into best and record it there. At the end of each month I was supposed to add up all the totals, calculate how much of my income had been spent on necessities and how much had been spent on increase, then I was supposed to calculate a tenth of my increase and give that much to the church as tithing.

One of the first things I noticed was that the columns for moneys I gave as church offering or tithing were on the "Increase" page. This bothered me. As I saw it there was no way to ever catch up. It looked like a trap. Every time I paid tithing, because I was spending from my 'increase' I created another debt, and when I paid that debt I still owed more, and on and on.

Mother had explained that the "Law of Tithing" was very important. A sure way to tell the sinners from the righteous was to check if they were up to date on their Stewardship and Accounting. This just made it feel more like a trap to me. If paying tithing meant I just owed more tithing, then the whole thing was simply a set-up. I knew all about set-ups. Mother and Father were constantly complaining that this thing, or that, was a "set-up." They also liked to use phrases like, "This is how they get you!" Now she was telling me that paying tithing was necessary for a person to be seen as 'good' by God, but since you could never be caught up by paying all of your tithing, than no matter how hard you tried, you could never be good enough.

I should point out that the real reason I was bothered by the supposed half-life of tithing had little to do with tithing itself. My anxiety was the result of being raised by a parent who was capricious, frequently irrational, often violent, and always willing to make up new rules as needed so that she could blame her loss of control on the actions of others, especially her children. Here she was explaining a process where there was no possible way to be fully compliant. I felt like I was the one being set up!

I also couldn't help but notice that the law of tithing was less about the rules in the book and more about the rules as Mother decided to enforce them. I could tell this by the way she didn't bother to try and answer my questions about the half-life of tithing debt, and by the way the amount I owed had varied from $70.00 to just over $2.00 depending on her interpretation and calculation. She had the power to decide if my debt was $70.00 or only $2.00. How could there be any consistent rules in this system?

What neither of us saw at the time was that the columns for tithing and church offerings were separate from other "Increase" expenses. They actually made up a third category. There was no half-life and no trap. My anxiety was unfounded, but Mother didn't know the answer so she didn't bother to consider the question. Instead of assuring me that God was a loving being who cared for me; that God's law was about valuing everyone, not about trying to trap them into being unworthy, she resorted to being irritated and dismissive of my concern. Obviously, I continued to be a difficult child who was always looking for ways to 'push' her.

After we got past the first stewardship and accounting process, I was careful to keep track of all my monies and spending. This wasn't very difficult as my 35-cent weekly allowance didn't support many financial transactions. I usually put about 5 cents in the weekly offering plate and liked to buy a 10-cent candy bar on our weekly trips to the grocery store. This gave me about 20 cents left that I saved so I could buy birthday and Christmas presents for friends and family.

Mother had promised to help me balance the book at the end of the month, but when that time came she insisted she was too busy and suggested we could wait until next time then we could balance the two months at one time.

A month later she was still too busy.

Finally, after three months and many requests, she agreed to help me balance my books.

I brought out my book and proudly showed all the records I had kept. Every ten-cent candy bar and 5-cent offering contribution was properly recorded. Mother added and balanced all the columns and then we went to my bedroom and shook out my penny bank to validate the cash total against the ledger.

I was nine cents short.

We counted it again.

I was still short by nine cents.

Mother asked me what I had done with the missing money. She told me I needed to give it back. She said that God would know if I was hiding the money and that doing so was worse than stealing, because it was stealing from God!

I tried to tell her that I didn't know why there was money missing, that I had been really careful to record everything, and that the only place I ever kept money was right there in my piggy bank. I was very afraid, but I couldn't tell her where the money was because I didn't know. I didn't know why the numbers were off. Was she sure she had added everything up right? By now Mother was dangerously angry. She said if I didn't give back the nine cents then I was a horribly sinful child. I was stealing from God!

I was scared and crying. I screamed through my tears that I didn't know what she wanted me to do. I didn't take the money. I didn't hide it. I couldn't give back money that didn't exist. Please! Please! Please believe me! Please help me! Maybe we could look at the numbers again. Maybe the mistake was there. Maybe we made a mistake the first time we counted. Maybe the nine cents was gone because it never existed to begin with!

Please try not to get so angry. Please don't lose control and become the evil screaming monster!

It was too late.

Mother had passed her point of no return. She began to scream at me and slap me. I screamed back. I tried to tell her that there was nothing I could do, but it didn't matter. The screaming, slapping, and then kicking, continued. We were both standing in the bedroom I shared with my sister. My back was to the open closet door. As she repeatedly slapped and kicked me I backed further into the closet until I pushed through the hanging clothes and my back was pressed against the closet wall. She kept on coming. I edged to the side until I was trapped in the corner of the shallow closet. Then I sank down to the floor, brought my knees to my chin and did my best to protect myself from the ongoing assault of screaming, slapping, and kicking. This is how we stayed for the rest of the afternoon. My best guess is that I sat huddled on the closet floor for two or three hours. She just kept screaming, and slapping, and kicking, as if nothing was ever going to stop her.

And then she did stop. She gave one last volley, stepped back and said that my father would be home soon. She told me that she was going to be late making dinner and I had better hope he didn't ask why because she would have to tell him about the horrible thing I had done. She told me I had better wash my face and clean up or he might ask why I had been crying, and again she would have to tell him about the horrible thing I had done. Then she walked out to the kitchen and left me still crying and huddled on the floor of the closet.

A few weeks later I overheard her talking about me to some of her friends from our small congregation. She puffed up with pride telling them that she had taught me about tithing and I how had kept such wonderful records that after three whole months I was only off by nine cents!

I feel a need to explain to the reader how significant this event was for me. By now the reader understands that children in my parents' home were never safe but I, as a child, had not realized this yet.

I was the child of a woman who had gifted me with a kitten only to take it back to the pound a few weeks later, and then carefully explain how it would be "put it to sleep."

I had been molested as a toddler and raped as a five-year-old, but my memories of those experiences were fuzzy at best. What little bits I remembered did nothing to help me understand. I had no knowledge of sex and no understanding of the significance of those acts.

My sister had been seriously wounded and knocked unconscious for at least several minutes when mother threw a rock and hit her in the back of the head, but I was not present when this occurred. All I knew was that my sister had been hurt and that my parents lied about how this happened.

I had never been safe in my parents' home, but I didn't know that. Acts of violence against my sister and me were routine, as was the expectation that we cover up the evidence of that violence, that we prioritize the wellbeing of our parents and abusers, that we protect them and their public image while we, the innocent children trapped in a violent home, suffered in silence, without access to safety, medical care, or emotional support.

This day, the day of the tithing and the nine cents, was the day that I began to understand. This was the day I got my first glimpse of the Pandora's box that was our home and family. This was the moment in time when I knew I had done nothing wrong, in fact, as evidenced by her bragging to her friends, I had done an impressive job of accepting the new concept of tithing and tracking my income and expenses. But as good as it looked to the outside world and as happy as Mother was to brag about me to her friends. I could still become the target of her rage at any time, for any reason, or for no reason at all.

Nothing I could ever do would ever be enough to please her. No matter how hard I tried, I would never be enough. And when she was done, when she realized she had wasted her whole afternoon screaming at and battering her child, I was expected to clean up, hide the evidence of her behavior, and hope Father didn't ask any questions.

This day was also the moment I understood that she was the primary threat. Until now I believed the bad things were always caused by outside forces. There was always a circumstance that presented a plausible excuse for her actions.

I could forgive her taking Butterscotch away because, even though I never saw him lash out at me, it was plausible that Mother had seen him do something that I missed; it was plausible that she was trying to protect me.

I could forgive her for the sexual abuse because I didn't understand what had happened to me or what it meant and (to my knowledge) she didn't know that anything had happened.

It was the same with my sister and the rock. I didn't know what had happened or how. I could allow myself to believe that my mother was not the kind of person who would throw rocks at her own child until she hit her child, knocking her unconscious, or the kind of person who after knocking her child unconscious would focus solely on protecting herself. I didn't know she was the kind of person who would tuck her battered child in bed and walk away, not bothering to offer medical care or even knowing if her child would live or die.

In all of the above situations I could imagine myself in her position and I could, with not too many mental gymnastics, contrive a narrative that allowed me to feel empathy towards her. The event of the tithing and the nine cents was, for me, the first time she absolutely crossed the line.

Yes, I knew she could be explosive and violent. Yes, I knew she could become so angry she stomped around the house muttering hateful things for hours, and sometimes days, at a time. Yes, I had experienced physical violence from her before. But this day was different, it wasn't a momentary loss of control; it wasn't a relatively harmless period of frustration or anger that led her to stomp around the house muttering angry thoughts while banging pots and pans, slamming kitchen cabinet doors, or kicking laundry baskets as she went about her day. On this day when I knew I had done a good job of the task she requested (done such a good job, in fact, that she later bragged about me) she pushed a terrified child onto the floor in the back of her closet, and she stayed there, for hours, yelling, screaming, kicking, slapping, calling me vile things, telling me how my mere existence was an unwanted burden that had ruined her life.

There was nothing I could do to justify her behavior that day; no barely plausible way to convince myself that she didn't mean what she said, hadn't seen, or didn't understand.

This was the day I finally understood that nothing I did, or ever could do, would make me good enough to please her. Nothing I could ever do would keep me safe from her anger and hatred.

But I was still a child. I still lived in a world controlled by the adults around me. My understanding that there was no way for me to be good enough to please her didn't do me any good. I still had to find a way to make my life better and the only things I could change were my own behaviors. I didn't want to believe that Mother was the problem because if I did, then I had to accept that nothing was in my control; nothing I ever did could ever change anything in my life. I had to continue to believe that I was the problem, I was responsible.

Identifying Mother as the problem didn't make my life any better and it didn't make any sense in my understanding of the world around me. I knew that all mothers loved their children, it was God's Law and the natural way of things, but clearly my mother did not love me.

If my mother could not love me, it had to be because there was something terribly wrong with me. I tried so hard to follow all the rules. I really did try to be a very good little girl, just like God and Jesus wanted me to be. Obviously, I still wasn't good enough. I had to try harder. If I only understood what the problem was, I was sure I could fix it. I wished I could understand why there was such evil in me, what it was and how I could overcome it. It had to be a powerful evil because it hid so deep inside me that I couldn't find it or root it out. I wanted to make it go away, but I just couldn't figure out how.

A thing I did not yet recognize was that she was hiding her blow-ups from my father. I was still a trusting and gullible child. When she told me to wash up and clean my face so that Father would not see that I had been crying; when she gave me a chance to avoid telling him what had happened, I accepted the pretense that she was looking out for me. I believed she was giving me a chance to protect myself. I did not understand that she was using me to protect her.

I also did not know who my father was in the bigger, wider, adult world. I did not understand his professional role in our community. I had no knowledge of how it was his job to evaluate the impact of unsafe homes on the children who lived in them. I did not know that every time my sister or I survived a violent event it had to be covered up because it was he and his bosses that investigated reports of battered and abused children. It was he and the people he worked with that were supposed to keep all of us safe. If he couldn't keep his own children safe, how could he be trusted to keep all the other unfortunate children in our community safe? If he couldn't keep his own children safe, maybe he wasn't any good at his job, maybe he shouldn't have his job at all anymore.

Of course, the people my father worked with already knew that my sister and I were not safe. They had known this since Dr. H reported evidence of rape when I was barely six. They had sent "ex-Mrs. Supervisor" to interview me because they knew something was terribly wrong and because they couldn't allow my father or his supervisor to conduct the interview. The fact that I was so traumatized I couldn't answer, or even understand her questions, prevented further inquiry but it didn't make his employers any less suspicious. Cleary something traumatic had occurred. Maybe they didn't have enough evidence to accuse my parents of child neglect and abuse, but they found sufficient cause to stop the pending adoption of five abandoned children. They even went so far as to demote my father back to auditor. They knew they could not trust him.

My father's office must have been a horribly unpleasant, hostile environment. Only the three of them, my father, whose hopes for an emotionally and spiritually satisfying career with potential for upward mobility had been ground to dust; his supervisor, responsible for the protection of children across the community with only one case worker and him the father of an abused child; and a single clerk who was trapped between the two of them, day after day.

I did not understand that my parents were afraid. They were always afraid. They were afraid that if anyone ever learned the truth, then my father and our family would lose everything!

If anyone ever learned that Heather and I were abused then my father would lose his job and his income, and we would lose our home.

If anyone ever learned the truth of my family, there would be public scandal. If the children of the one local Social Worker were abused how could people trust anyone in Social Services?

If my father couldn't do his job who would protect all the children who really needed him? Children who were really at risk; children who needed help from the state to support them, to keep them clean and keep them safe and keep them fed, would lose their only protector.

Then there was the church. My father was an ordained member of the priesthood and pastor of our local (miniature) congregation. Most people had never heard of our church. For those people the only thing they knew about our church was what they knew about us. If people learned that my sister and I were abused, our church, our whole church, including all of the people that lived far away and attended distant congregations and Reunions, would be shamed and discredited.

What about the people who didn't know about our church yet? What about the people who needed to hear our message of salvation? If the world learned that Heather and I were abused and the whole church was discredited, who would be there to bring the message of God and Jesus to these people.

What if the Church took away my father's priesthood? He used his priesthood to help people. He spent Saturdays visiting men in the local state prison, he even baptized a couple of them; he visited with them and prayed with them, he took the Communion Sacrament to them. Who would take care of them if my father wasn't priesthood anymore?

It was my responsibility to protect everyone. I had to protect our family, and my father's job. I had to protect all the people he helped in his job. I had to protect the church and all the people, all over the world, that were part of, or helped by, the church. I had to protect people who could someday be helped by Jesus and our church even if they didn't know about any of it yet.

I was still a child, and these were just some of my burdens. These were the things that I had to protect every day with my secrets and lies. I hadn't learned the whole list yet, but I was starting to. Every time I thought about my responsibility to protect our family, my father's job, our church, and all the distant people in all the distant places that we could impact, I felt myself become smaller and smaller and the weight of my responsibilities grew heavier and heavier.

I was the one responsible for covering up all the bad things that happened around us. If I ever told anyone about the things that happened in our house, then all kinds of bad things would happen. All the various people; my family, my father's co-workers, his clients, members of our congregation and our denomination, at risk children and men in prison, hundreds, maybe thousands of people, people I did not know and might never meet, all of them would be horribly hurt. If I ever told anyone about the things that happened to my sister and me, all of these bad things would happen. And it would all be my fault!

Eight & Nine

That fall Heather went to preschool and I went to third grade. My friends Lisa and Cindy moved away, and a new classmate named Nancy moved into their house. Nancy was a nice enough girl, but I missed Lisa and Cindy a lot.

When school started and I resumed riding the bus that allowed me to interact with all the other children in our neighborhood I met a new friend named Bethany. Bethany was only in second grade. She lived all the way at the far end of our subdivision and got on the bus from a different stop. She was an only child and was heartbroken and lonely because when her family moved into our town she had to leave all her friends behind. Her parents were older than mine. She had her own room. It was pretty and sunny and had all the best toys.

Bethany's new house had two tree houses in the back yard. One was old and partly broken down, but the other had a beautiful, up in the tree, gazebo with an actual staircase leading up to it. It was a glorious, gracious staircase; the steps were at least four feet wide. A little girl could feel like a princess walking up or down those beautiful, wide steps.

Bethany's mother liked it when I came over to visit. She never bothered to ask if I wanted to stay for lunch or dinner, she just included me. She taught me to like grilled cheese and other child friendly foods that I had never eaten before. Being around her made me feel warm, cozy, safe and (for reasons I never understood) a little sad.

That winter Bethany's father, whom I rarely saw, built a sledding trail that started just behind the house and wound its way down the hill and through the woods, for 100 yards or so. Zooming down it in our flying saucers was a fabulously joyful experience.

I tried to imagine building a sled run with my father. He was born and raised in Montana, so it was easy to picture him outdoors in snowy weather, but he was always grave and focused on more important, grown-up things. I couldn't imagine him taking the time to build something so fun and special for his children. I couldn't begin to imagine him engaging in such a lighthearted task.

I graduated from Brownies to real girl scouts. A classmate spilled the beans about Santa Claus. I attempted the high-speed turn on my beloved banana bike and managed to smash myself, face first, into a friend's driveway, breaking both my, not quite grown in yet, front teeth on the pavement.

It was a good year, a healthy year. It was an island of peace and calm in my life.

Me, left, at a Girl Scout activity with my friend Nancy, being photobombed by my sister Heather in the foreground

Shots

One challenge for my eight-year-old-self occurred at a vaccination clinic.

In my generation vaccinations were an unquestioned requirement. The devastation of diseases like polio, tetanus, smallpox, rubella, scarlet fever and so on, was barely behind us. Every family had its own stories of a loved one who had barely survived, or not survived, or been left blind or crippled. I've known polio survivors who are not many years older than me.

Children were vaccinated in mass and no child could register for school without an up-to-date shot record. Sometimes vaccines were brought to school where we all lined up to receive them. Other vaccines were distributed through pop-up clinics at churches or community centers.

One day, when I was eight, Mother took Heather and me to a large church that was hosting a vaccine clinic. It was the biggest, busiest clinic I ever attended. Chairs had been set up in one large room where we sat waiting for well over an hour before we were finally called to the next room and took our place at the end of a long line. This second room was at least as large as a gymnasium. There were several vaccination stations, but the line barely moved. It felt like we stood there forever.

By the time we reached the head of the line we had been waiting for over two hours. (I knew this because Mother was watching the clock and kept updating me on how much of her time was being wasted on getting us our shots.) I was tired of waiting, tired of standing and tired of listening to Mother complain about how we were wasting her time.

The room was large, the acoustics were harsh, and I had been subject to the cries and screams of unhappy children for too long. The sounds were bouncing off the hard surfaces, echoing, magnifying, and filling my head so that I couldn't see, hear, or feel anything else. I tried to stay calm; I really did. I probably tried too hard, clamping down on my anxiety rather than relaxing and breathing it out. (In adulthood I have learned more about the Vegas nerve and how fighting for calm, rather than relaxing into it, can cause panic, fainting, and (in one case for me) seizures.) By the time we finally got to a vaccine station I was used up. I didn't have any self-control left. An aid approached me with an uncapped needle, and I reacted in terror. I said "No!" and tried to pull away. Mother gripped my wrist and pushed me forward. I said "No!" again. An attendant grabbed me by one arm. I screamed "No!" and struggled to get away. Another attendant grabbed me by the other arm, but I only struggled harder. There was no rational thought left in me. I was fighting for my life, kicking and screaming. In the end it took four adults to pin me, spread eagle, on the floor while a fifth administered the shot.

This experience left me with a fear of needles that continued to be a problem for much of my life. For years I fought to overcome my anxiety. I was a rational, competent person. Why was I always reduced to a quivering mess every time I required a little shot? Nothing I tried made it better.

My fear of needles grew. It became a real problem. It was a bigger problem than my aversion to peanut butter. I didn't need peanut butter. I was perfectly free to live my life without it. Shots, needles, medical care; these are things we all need from time to time. Knowing that I was going to have to fight my anxiety just created more anxiety. Even the thought of a shot triggered physiological reactions such as nausea and headaches. This wasn't pleasant but I could live with it.

Blood draws were an even bigger challenge. I suffered from vasovagal syncope, a condition that frequently caused me to pass out during a blood draw. If the tech was good enough to get the vein on the first stick, I was usually able to walk out on my own power. But even for the best tech it was challenging to get my veins. My emotional attempts to clamp down on, to push away my anxiety also caused me to constrict my veins, making them harder to find and stick. With each additional stick, second, third, sometimes fifth, my chances of ending up on the floor increased exponentially.

I was in my mid 50's when I suffered a seizure during a routine, blood draw. I am told my eyes rolled back into my head and I thrashed uncontrollably for at least 30 seconds. I had no idea. I had felt the unconsciousness coming on. I had asked for a place to lie down, but the clinic didn't have a reclining chair or cot. The tech called my husband in from the waiting room. He ended up sitting next to me, holding my hand, for the whole thing.

I thought I had passed out for a minute or two. I didn't understand why it was so much harder to wake up than normal or why the medical staff was so agitated. Someone offered me a drink of orange juice. It tasted soooo good for about two seconds, before my body said no and sprayed it back out at the people around me. I didn't even notice the other messes I had made until after they transferred me to a wheelchair.

My poor husband described it as the most frightening moment of his life. He says he pushed his hand into my mouth to keep me from biting myself. The hospital nurse told him he was lucky he didn't lose any fingers.

Follow-on activities included an ambulance ride, a cat scan, half a day in the local hospital, bone chilling cold that I just couldn't shake until my electrolytes rebalanced … and best of all, additional blood draws!

Eventually, I began to ask 'Why?' What is it about needles that triggers such a traumatic response? Are there any conscious thoughts or images behind my anxiety? I had to ask these questions many times. I needed clues. I had to search my emotions. I had to try to focus, to remain rational despite my fear and anxiety, so I could analyze my irrational reactions of fear and panic. I had to learn to open my psyche instead of pushing against it. I needed to be able to explain what happened to me before I could look for a way to get past it.

For many people this would seem impossible. My secret weapon in this quest is that I am a nerd. Once I was able to frame my fear as in intellectual puzzle, I could shift my focus from the fear to the puzzle. The quest itself was part of the solution I was searching for.

First, I discovered that at the base of my shot anxiety was sound. When the anxiety spikes there is a roaring sound inside my head. The sound blocks out my ability to focus on the present, to communicate and to cope. I tried to re-live the sound when I was not facing a needle. I needed to analyze it and understand it, but the mere memory of the sound didn't provide enough information. I needed the stimulation of an actual needle to provoke my anxiety so that I could try to analyze the root cause.

Just knowing that I needed to focus on the sound helped. It gave me a focus point. I understood that I couldn't try to block the sound, if I did, if I clamped down on what I was feeling and tried to block it or push it away, I was likely to end up on the floor again. I had to let myself enter and experience the sound.

This is not an easy task. Imagine trying to explain this mindset to the medical tech. Imagine saying, "Hello stranger. Nice to meet you. Please feel free to root around in my sensitive flesh while I attempt some weird form of self-hypnoses to see what hidden secrets I can uncover about why I am so likely to be that horrible patient that passes out on you."

The next time I had to face a needle I was ready. Choosing to focus on your own terror isn't at all easy but it is way better than being overwhelmed by that terror. I allowed my psyche to enter that black pit of sound and fear. I metaphorically walked inside, stood in the darkness and let myself feel and listen. I was able to identify the sound! It was a cacophony of children crying and screaming. It was the sounds of that long-ago day at the shot clinic. It was as if someone had recorded the sounds of that large room with its many vaccination stations and even more sounds of children crying from anxiety, fear, and pain. It was as if there were a dozen recordings of that event, playing all at once, poorly synchronized, and at max volume. There was also the smell. The tang of rubbing alcohol and disinfectant. It is the same smell, whenever or wherever we walk into a room full of needles. The smell is the first trigger followed by the cacophony or terrified, screaming children. Then I realized another thing. That day at the vaccine clinic wasn't the source, it wasn't the root of my anxiety. It was only a bad experience that triggered another, older, trauma. I realized that there was a link between the fear, and the screaming and crying, from that day at the vaccine clinic when I was eight, and the many pediatrician visits, years earlier with my mother and new baby sister. That day, when I was eight, I wasn't just hearing healthy babies scream and cry because of a single needle. I was also hearing my baby sister howl in pain and fear as her pediatrician held her upside down and slowly squeezed from thigh to ankle trying to force a single drop of blood out of the prick in her heel. I was hearing a baby, suffering from the injustice of jaundice and too many trips to the doctor's office. I was hearing my sister; another child struggling to grow and thrive in the hostile environment of our home. I was hearing a little baby who had been sick all of her life, screaming in fear and rage at being poked, prodded, and treated roughly. With that realization I finally understood my fear, my anxiety, and my reaction. I knew what it was that I was fighting. I was back in charge, I was able to understand my anxiety, and to honor it and work with it rather than clamping down, shutting myself down physically and emotionally, and waking up on the floor. I haven't passed out since.

Where to Next?

My father's service commitment to the State of Michigan was over. He was still the only social services case worker in the region. He was also the uncooperative parent who had stonewalled his own supervisory chain when my pediatrician reported the rape of his child. A couple of years later he was the man who covered up a traumatic head injury to his youngest child caused by Mother when she threw a large rock at her four-year-old child, hitting her in the back of the head and knocking her out for several minutes.

My father was the man who covered up our injuries and denied us access to medical care in order to prevent additional reports from physicians of the injuries his own children suffered. He was the man whose application to adopt a family of abandoned children had been denied by his own colleagues because of allegations of mistreatment of his own children in his own home.

Professionally, my father was still the man who evaluated the safety of at-risk children throughout the region. He was the man who made recommendations to remove children from abusive families and place them in foster care. He did this while hiding the risks, and very real trauma, his own children faced every day in his own home.

His career prospects as a State of Michigan Social Services employee had ended the day Dr. H reported suspicions of my rape. He would never see a promotion or even an opportunity for increased responsibility. In fact, if anyone learned the truth of our family both he and Mother could face criminal charges. After my rape he had been reassigned as an auditor but that couldn't last forever. The role did not match his education or experience, so he was offered an administrative position in the state capital of Lansing 400 miles away. It was a bit of a promotion, but it was also a dead end and if he accepted he would never work as a clinician again. It was time to get out of Michigan.

It was 1970. There was no internet, no LinkedIn, no computers, or word processers. Employment ads were listed in local papers or in the back of professional journals. Mother acted as secretary, producing stacks of multi-page, resumes on her manual typewriter, and sending them off in fat manila envelopes.

He interviewed for a position in Australia. The interviewer, a woman, came to the house for dinner and answered questions about life in that faraway place.

He interviewed in multiple locations across the country. I thought he must be very important every time he packed his suitcase and got on an airplane to travel to a faraway place and talk to people about hiring him for a new job. I didn't know of anyone else who had a father who was so important people bought him tickets just to fly in just for a job interview.

Other than that, I did not pay much attention to the job search. I knew not to bother Mother when she locked herself in the study. I knew the resume packets were important, that they required special paper and had to look 'professional.' I knew I shouldn't interrupt her and risk being the cause of a misfired keystroke that could ruin a full page of precious text.

Mother used the study for other tasks as well, including preparation of church bulletins, congregational treasury tasks, and household Stewardship and Accounting. Adding one more task to the 'grown-up' work didn't mean much to me.

I wasn't anxious about moving. In one sense I am sure this was because there was no timeline. Moving was a thing that was going to happen 'someday.' But who knew when 'someday' was, or if there really would be a 'someday?' Why should I fret about things that were so far in the future I didn't know for sure if they were really going to happen?

I also didn't worry about the challenge of finding a new home, new friends, or a new school. I had done all these things before. Moving from Trenary to Marquette had been a good thing. Kindergarten in Marquette had been soooo much better than in Trenary. I liked being a person who had experienced different places and different people.

My friend Bethany didn't see it that way. She couldn't understand how I was okay with the thought of packing up and leaving everything and everyone behind. She told me that when her family moved away from their old house, she had grabbed hold of the screen door and refused to let go. She said her father had to pry her off the door and carry her to the car.

I could not imagine doing such a thing. Temper tantrums were not tolerated in our home. (Well, except for Mother's blow ups, they were not tolerated.) We children knew better than to ever lose our tempers. Any tantrum Heather or I could create would be matched and magnified by Mothers screaming rage. We didn't, ever, dare behave in such a way. We didn't ever, dare draw that much attention towards ourselves. If we ever did, we knew that there would be a price to pay and we knew that it would be absolutely, unquestionably, too high.

Of course, the other thing Bethany was trying to tell me was that she didn't want me to move away because she would miss me. Bethany was still the new kid in town. I think I may have been her only friend. Sadly, I didn't understand her message. I didn't see myself as special enough or important enough that anyone would miss me if I wasn't around. I am sorry Bethany. If you ever read this, please accept my apology.

We did not go to Reunion that summer. I am not sure why. My guess is that Father had used too much vacation time on out-of-state interviews and didn't have enough left for a week of Reunion. I can also guess that he didn't want the three of us to go without him. My rape, three years before had occurred at Reunion when Mother, Heather and I were there without him. It was the only time he had not been with us and he may not have wanted to risk sending us alone again.

I missed Reunion. I missed the campgrounds. I missed the lakeshore, the playgrounds, the big dining hall full of loud happy voices of hundreds of people dining with friends and family. I missed the endless array of scheduled activities for children.

It was a wonderful surprise when Mother announced that she and I could still go there together, just the two of us. She explained that there was a whole weeklong camp just for grade school children, that I could go as a camper and that she would go along to help in the kitchen. Why had I never known about this before?

The campgrounds were not quite as full and busy for Jr. Camp as they were for Reunion. There were no tents on the lower terrace, and only a couple of trailers (for staff) on the upper level. One of the chapels was set up with rows and rows of cots for girl campers. I have no idea where the boys slept, for that matter I don't even remember if there were any boys. (There must have been boys. I have never known my church to segregate boys and girls. I just didn't pay any attention to them.)

Mother seemed concerned that I would be anxious about sleeping in the big chapel without her. She showed me the dorm where she was staying and let me know that I could come find her if I needed to. It was as if she forgot about all the times I had happily slept away from home, visiting relatives, attending sleepovers with my friends, and even Reunions. She may have had some concern that sleeping without her in this place might trigger memories of rape, but the rape had happened years ago, for me it was almost half my life ago. I had not seen Mr. Special Relationship since, and the dissociative fugue that had blocked all my memories for days on either side of the incident still held and protected me from such thoughts.

I am sure the camp staff included plenty of adults teaching classes, chaperoning activities, and so on, but my experience was all about lots and lots of girlfriend time. From the moment I assured her I would be okay sleeping alone with all the other girls, and practically pushed her out of the chapel, until the ride home at the end of the week, I didn't give her any thought.

It was a wonderful week.

The rest of the summer came and went. I turned nine and started fourth grade. Heather moved up to kindergarten, and Father continued to look for a new job.

At some point Father applied for a position in northern Maine. The job was for someone to manage a 12-bed psychiatric inpatient ward in a state funded Mental Health Clinic in Aroostook County Maine. The prospective employer paid the cost of a plane ticket, and Father spent a long travel day flying from Northern Michigan to Detroit, to Bangor, to Presque Isle in Aroostook County Maine. When he called from the hotel to tell us he was safely arrived we asked, "How was it?" and he responded, "They did everything but meet me at the airport in a dogsled."

As he told the story, the journey as far as Bangor was uneventful, but then things got interesting. The aircraft out of Bangor was a 12-seat plane, booked to capacity with one pilot and eleven passengers. Because all the seats were filled the luggage had to be left behind. My father was assigned the co-pilot seat, up front, next to the pilot. They got everyone strapped in and took off. About the time they hit altitude the passenger door, next to my father, popped open. My father grabbed for the door handle and pulled it as far closed as possible, considering speed, altitude, pressure, really cold air and such. (It must have been an absolutely terrifying experience!) The pilot circled back to the airport, landed, and attempted to secure the door before taking off again. As soon as the plane reached altitude the second time, the door popped right back open. They landed again, latched the door, and the pilot asked my father to keep a grip on it in hopes of preventing it from opening again. With my father holding the plane door for the third takeoff the latch still popped but the door didn't swing wide. They continued the flight, 250 miles north from Bangor, in freezing cold weather, with my father holding the door closed the whole way.

He was picked up at the airport by prospective co-workers and settled into a hotel room. He didn't have his luggage because with a full load of passengers there hadn't been room for baggage.

The next morning, he interviewed for his new job, in a rumpled, twice worn, shirt, unshaven, and without even brushing his teeth.

A week or so later they offered him the position. We were moving to Maine.

Moving

In early January of 1972 my father flew away to begin his new job as inpatient director of a small, county funded, Mental Health facility in northern Maine. Mother, Heather, and I stayed behind to prep the house for sale and pack up for a cross country move, while Father spent his evenings and weekends looking for a new home.

One of the first things Mother did was separate the bunk beds Heather and I shared and move my, previously top, bunk into the bedroom that had been Father's study. With all the work of moving looming in front of her I do not know why she took the time to do this.

Having my own room for the first time was simultaneously wonderful and awful. I felt so grown up and special. There was a full-length mirror (a holdover from the previous owners) behind the door. At night I would get ready for bed and close the door so I could see the mirror, and see myself, as I got into bed. Then, with the door closed, I could leave my nightstand light on for as long as I wanted.

I was preparing to write my very first book report. I was reading a biography of Father Jacques Marquette, the French missionary for whom our small city was named. If I looked off to my right, I could see myself, in my own room, in my own bed, with my book and my nightlight, I thought I was very grownup and scholarly!

Sadly, I learned that Father Jacques Marquette, him of the big bronze statue on a hill overlooking downtown, did most of his missionary work in Illinois and likely never set foot in the little city that would be named for him.

Also, sadly, being in that room was a constant reminder that things were changing, that we would only be living in that house a little while longer and that I wouldn't see my father again until after we moved away from everything else in my life.

One night I tucked myself in bed and opened up my scholarly book, but when I tried to read, I couldn't make out the words because my eyes were full of tears. After a few minutes of quiet crying Mother came in to ask what was wrong. I looked at her, feeling confused and embarrassed and explained that I didn't know. I had no idea why I was crying. Life and stress often work that way for me. I seem to have all the drive I need to push through the hard times. It is in the quiet, safe moments that I feel the strain.

I am sure it took a lot of work to prep the house and coordinate a move all by herself. I have moved enough times in my life to know it is no easy thing. I have heard Mother tell frustrated stories of how the pack-up date was scheduled and re-scheduled. How the day after being told it would be another two weeks before the movers arrived, she came home with a full load of groceries to a ringing phone and the news that the packing crew would arrive early the next morning.

For Heather and me the move was a breeze. One afternoon we were sent off to a friend's house (a friend of Mother's, not of my sister or me). I wasn't sure I wanted to spend the afternoon at a stranger's house so Mother tried to sweeten the offer by promising that her friend would serve us cheesecake to which my response was "Eww! Why would anyone make a cake with cheese?" Mother tried to explain that cheesecake was a wonderful dessert made from sweet, creamy, soft, moist cheese. I eventually fixed an image in my head of cottage cheese with pineapple, a combination I was not fond of.

The next afternoon I learned that cheesecake is indeed, very yummy. Mother's friend kept Heather and me well entertained and when Mother came to take us home that night the house was fully packed. Why hadn't we known about this person and this wonderful food sooner?

The next morning the three of us drove away in our family Jeep Wagoneer. We headed east across the Upper Peninsula of Michigan and crossed into Canada at Sioux St Marie, Ontario where we continued along the northern shore of Lake Huron, on through Ontario, Quebec, and New Brunswick, and finally into Northern Maine. The total distance was almost 1200 miles. I think it took us four days to complete the trip. We spent one night in Quebec where we struggled with a dinner menu written in French and a wait staff who spoke little English. I had no idea we were moving so far away that that we would pass through places where people spoke foreign languages!

We arrived in Maine on the day after Valentine's Day. We met up with Father and he showed us the yellow Volkswagen he had bought to be our second car. When Heather and I climbed into the back seat there was a chocolate filled, red, heart-shaped, candy box on each of our seats. I had never been given chocolate on Valentine's Day before.

I wondered what it was that made this Valentine's Day so special. Then I thought about it and realized that February 15th is exactly six months after August 15th, which is my birthday. February 15th was my half-birthday! That must be the reason for the chocolate!

Of course, this explanation did nothing to explain why Heather and Mother also received boxes of chocolate. (Mother's box was much bigger.) My theory also failed to explain why we never celebrated half-birthdays at any other time or for anybody else, but it made me feel special in that moment, so I was happy to declare it as the reason for celebration. I was, however, disappointed a year later when I happily declared my half-birthday, and no one else seemed to think it was a thing.

We arrived in northern Maine in mid-February. Aroostook county includes all of northern Maine from east to west as well as a panhandle extending south along the Maine, New Brunswick border. Locals just call it "The County." Its land mass is 25% of the state but it has only 10% of the population of an otherwise sparsely populated state. Most of the land is a region known as the Allagash wilderness while the rest is rural, agricultural, and poor. It is wild, beautiful country with brutal winters that are long, harsh, and very cold, and we had arrived at the very coldest time of the year. In February temperatures in the County routinely dropped below -20 degrees Fahrenheit. Most years have a handful of nights when the overnight low drops to -40 or lower.

County schools closed every February for a week termed "Mid-Winter" break. I believe the entire point of mid-winter break is to keep people inside during the coldest week of the year. No one wants to leave the house so why not let them stay home and save on the cost of attempting to heat school buildings?

A year later I was excited to learn that the local ski hill offered free lift tickets during mid-winter break. I requested a ride to the ski hill a couple of times but in the end the experience of skiing in below zero (sometimes double-digit below zero) temperatures was too extreme for me.

Despite being 1200 miles apart, Maine and most of Michigan (excluding a few counties in the western end of the UP) share the same time zone. This put Marquette at the very western edge of the eastern standard time zone and our home in Maine a mere two miles from the eastern end. (New Brunswick and its maritime Canadian neighbors are on Atlantic time.)

We had traveled from a region with later than average winter sunsets to one with very early sunsets. On the shortest days of the year in northern Maine the sun comes up at about 4:00 am and sets by 2:30 in the afternoon.

Father had rented a small house about 12 miles away from his

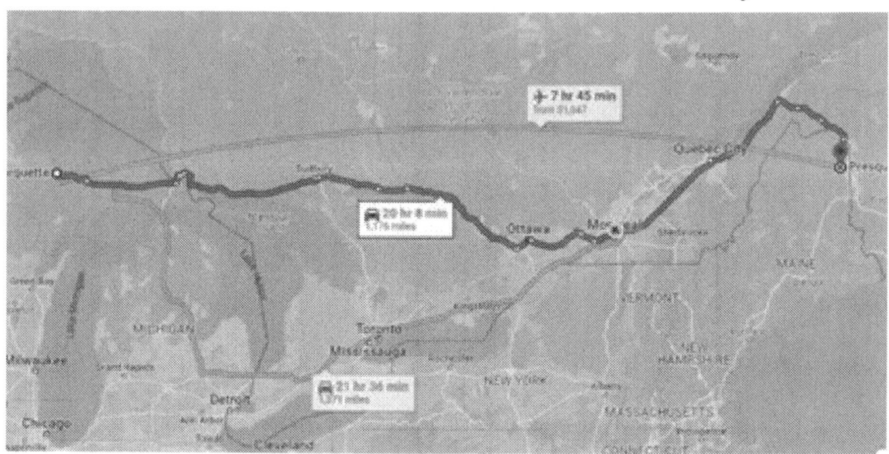

The route from Marquette MI to Presque Isle ME and from end-to-end of the Eastern Standard time zone.

job. The house had only two bedrooms and one bath. It had a detached garage, separated from the house by a three-foot breezeway, an actual dining room, and possibly the smallest kitchen I have ever seen. The drive and yard were hidden under several feet of snow.

And then there was the water. The regional cash crop was potatoes, most of which ended up as frozen fries or dehydrated products. The small city of Presque Isle had built a potato processing plant a few years earlier and the plant dumped untreated wastewater directly into the Aroostook River; the same river that provided the water supply for multiple towns in the region.

Presque Isle was awful. In the dead cold of mid-winter particles of air pollution that would otherwise evaporate and/or dissipate, freeze and become trapped at ground level, as a result the whole town smelled like rotten potatoes. It was a deep pervasive odor that seemed to cling to your clothes and the back of your throat.

There was a McDonalds restaurant in Presque Isle, an exciting and new cultural experience we had not had access to in the UP. Our first visit to Presque Isle was specifically to show Mother some housing possibilities and to buy her first ever McDonald's milkshake. (Mother was particularly fond of ice cream, floats and milkshakes.)

Drive-throughs hadn't become a thing yet, so we parked and walked across the rutted frozen parking lot and through the miasma of sulfurous smelling air, in the pitch dark of late afternoon. By the time we came out with our precious milk shakes, we were running to get to the car and drive away from the horrible smell as quickly as possible. We all felt at risk of throwing up!

And that water... The plant was downstream of the Presque Isle municipal water source so it didn't taint their drinking water, but it was upstream of the town where we rented our little house. The water out of the tap had a sulfurous odor and a brownish yellow color. Toilets always looked like they needed flushed. It only took a skim of water in the white porcelain tub to show the discolored, sulfur stained, hue. Hot water coming out of the shower head could smell up the whole house. No one had any desire to taste it.

On top of all this there was the snow. I like snow. My family liked snow. My mother had been born and raised in Michigan's upper peninsula. My father was from Montana. We expected snow. We were used to long, cold winters buried under thick white blankets of fluffy snow, but even those places hadn't prepared us for the volume of snow we encountered in Aroostook County.

Snowplows roamed the roads seven days a week. It didn't matter if there was snow falling or not, there was so much snow on the ground that it was always blowing and forming drifts across the roads.

Because we arrived in mid-winter the snowbanks were already at full height, which is to say that every road was bordered by a five-foot vertical wall of snow on either side. Our family vehicle was a Jeep Wagoneer, but five-foot snowbanks were still high enough to block everything we could see from inside it. Driving the roads in winter in northern Maine was a lot like being a rat trapped in a maze.

Years later my Driver's Education instructor would provide specific instruction on how much to accelerate when approaching a drift and exactly what part of the drift to aim for to prevent getting stuck, or worse, hung up on it. I was in the car when one of my fellow students misjudged and high centered us on a particularly large drift with none of our wheels touching the pavement. A nearby farmer tried, and failed, to pull us free. In the end it was a massive snowplow that 'rescued' us after explaining that he was going to push us out of his way whether we wanted him to, or not.

In addition to plows the County maintained snow movers, kind of like super industrial snow blowers. The snow movers traveled in small groups, a single snow mover followed by a line of dump trucks. The snow mover, at the front of the pack, would groom the bank down to the five-foot level, throwing the excess snow into the truck behind it. When the truck was full it would head off to the municipal snow dump and the next truck in line would take its place. Local snow dumps were piled so high that they generally retained blackened piles of melting road snow until well into June.

Despite all the plowing, and snowbank grooming there was no bare pavement visible on the roads. Salt does not melt snow or ice when the temperatures fall below zero, so the plows and snow movers were supplemented by trucks that spread a mix of sand and gravel. The roadbeds were icy trails buried under several inches of compressed snow, ice, and gravel from late November until early May.

Grooming the snowbanks ensured they never got so high they risked collapsing onto the road, but it also converted every road into an open topped snow tunnel with five-foot walls on either side. We learned our routes from one community to another much like that rat in the maze. There were no landmarks and not very many street signs. Luckily, there also weren't too many roads. Traveling from one town to another was simple; get on the right road before you leave the first town and stay on it until you reach the next.

All of these things, the cold, the dark, the small, tired house, the sulfurous unpalatable water, and the outside world of seemingly endless tunnels through snow and ice, along with the fact that she had both of us children home and underfoot while unloading a moving truck and watching cold, rough strangers mishandle her precious things, combined to make life hard for Mother, and when she was stressed she was also irritable and likely to lose control and blow-up at any moment. We were off to a bad start.

Tension in our little house was high. Mother was volatile, the smallest thing, a dropped object, a single crossword between Heather and me, or just being in the wrong place at the wrong time would set her off. My physiological response was to clench my muscles. I walked around with stiff shoulders and tightly clenched fists. I also clenched the muscles in my abdomen and core.

This is an unconscious response and like any prolonged muscle strain it can lead to secondary effects. That winter my persistent muscle tension resulted in a painful and prolonged case of colitis. All of my abdominal muscles were rigid with stress and anxiety and absolutely nothing was able to pass through. As days passed into weeks my discomfort grew, but I didn't understand the problem or have the knowledge to seek a solution. Eventually I reached the point where I couldn't hide my discomfort. I began to complain of stomach aches, my appetite decreased, and the stomach aches grew into horrific, gut-wrenching cramps, the kind that take your breath away and cause you to double up in pain.

One night, after little food and hours of lying on the floor complaining of cramps and stomach pain, I was getting ready for bed when I overheard an argument between my parents. My father insisted it was time to find me a doctor. Mother pushed back. She said I was always whining about something. She didn't want to risk talking to a Dr. She reminded Father of all the trouble we had to deal with after taking me to see Dr. H, years before.

The argument bounced back and forth for a while growing more heated with every volley. Eventually, Father raised the stakes. He told Mother he thought I had an ulcer. He told her she had gotten out of control. He said there had been too many blow-ups and too much tension. He insisted it was all her, that being around her was making us children sick. He said that if she didn't curb her behavior, I was likely to end up in the hospital with bleeding ulcers. He reminded her that we had just moved all this way to make a fresh start. He reminded her how important it was for his colleagues and peers to see us as a happy, functional family. He pointed out that none of his co-workers had even met us yet, and that he didn't want the first thing they knew about us as a family to be that his children lived with so much stress that his nine-year-old developed bleeding ulcers. Then he upped the ante further and told her that if her behavior continued, he might have no choice but to leave their marriage. To my knowledge it was the first time he threw out the threat of divorce.

It was a small house. I was tucked into my bunk with the bedroom door closed but I heard every word. I heard my father tell my mother that she had made me sick. I heard him say that he might have to take me to a doctor, and that if he did the doctor would know the reason I was sick was because of how my mother behaved and how she was angry all the time. I heard my father threaten to divorce her, to divorce us! I heard him blame all of it on me because I was the one in pain and because I kept complaining about it.

I pulled the covers up over my head and curled into a tight ball. My stomach hurt so bad, but I knew I couldn't complain about it ever again. I knew that if Father went through with his threat of taking me to a doctor, the doctor would start asking me questions and then all kinds of bad things would happen. It wouldn't even matter how I answered the Dr's questions or if I didn't say anything at all.

I hadn't answered any of the questions Dr. H asked but he still caused all sorts of trouble for our family. Of course, the only reason I hadn't answered his questions was because I couldn't. I tried to listen to him and answer him like a good little girl but every time he spoke his words got all funny and I couldn't answer him because no matter how hard I tried I couldn't understand the words, they all somehow fell out of my brain sounding like nothing but gibberish. I was older now. I was pretty sure I could talk to a grown-up without all of the words dissolving into nonsense syllables. If a new doctor asked me questions, I knew I would have to answer him. Doctors were grown-ups, and men. When grown-ups, especially grown-up men, asked you questions or told you to do something you had to answer them or do what they told you to. It didn't matter how bad or gross it was. It didn't matter if talking to them really, really scared you. You always had to do what grown-ups told you to.

Had Father really threatened to divorce Mother? Had he threatened to divorce us! Surely, he didn't mean it. Divorce was a sin; a big one. Marriage was a sacrament. If he divorced us, he would be breaking one of the sacraments, he would lose his priesthood. Would he leave my sister and me alone with Mother? What would happen then? I couldn't live alone with

Mother, ever! I was terribly afraid of what would happen to Heather and me if my father wasn't around to keep us safe.

There was only one way out of this. I could never, ever, tell my parents that I had a stomachache, ever again! No matter how bad my muscles cramped or how bad it hurt I had to make sure they never knew I had pains, because if they did Father would take me to a doctor, and the doctor would ask me questions, and I would have to answer them because he was a doctor, and then the doctor would tell people about us, and then all the bad things would happen. Father would lose his job, and we would lose our house, and he would divorce mother...

Did that mean we would have no house, no place to live, and no job to make money to take care of us, and no safe person in the house to see if we were even fed, and alive? And all the other bad things would still happen too. All the people would think bad things about the place my father worked, and all the people would think bad things about the church we went to, and those places (the hospital where my father worked (now) and our church) would all be broken, and all the people who needed them would have to do without and it would, all of it, would be my fault!

I never complained about my stomach again. I tried to stay away from Mother and Father as much as I could, which was probably the best medicine of all. Eventually the issue resolved, and no doctors were involved.

Although Mother disliked the house intensely to me it was just fine. The bunk beds had been re-stacked, and I was on the top again. In this house they were against an exterior wall with a window right at the level of my bed. As the days lengthened the sun came up earlier and earlier. I remember one early morning waking at about 3:30 am and watching my first sunrise, all orange and rosy and promising, from the warm safety of my very own bed.

The house had a small dark basement tightly packed with all of the boxes we didn't have room to unpack. It was so crowded it was like a rat's maze with blind corners and dead ends so tight I could barely turn around in them. It was kind of scary, but scary in that good way that makes it fun to challenge yourself to brave it.

When school reopened after mid-winter break, I enrolled in fourth grade. My teacher, Mrs. D. was a woman of about 50. She was one of those stylish, energetic, always composed, women that truly make 50 fabulous. She genuinely loved her students and was always in control of her classroom.

One day Mrs. D. asked for volunteers to tell a story to the class. I was new but still an outgoing child. I raised my hand, walked to the front of the room and told a funny story that I had learned at camp the summer before. When I proudly delivered the punch line (the focus of which was poop) I expected to hear a room full of happy laughter, but the class was dead silent. Mrs. D. looked sternly at me and explained that my story was inappropriate.

I felt humiliated.

Obviously, there were rules about this sort of thing. Obviously, all the other children in the room knew the rules. I had no idea. I was nine. Almost all the jokes and funny stories I knew involved poop. No one had ever told me there was anything wrong with that, in fact I had learned most of my poop stories from adults and camp counselors who, from my perspective, were also adults. I loved Mrs. D. and now she was upset with me. She was so upset that she asked to talk to Mother! It was the first time I ever had to take such a note home from school. I still loved Mrs. D. She was still a kind lady who loved her students, but I never told any more stories in her class.

Despite my embarrassment in front of Mrs. D. I was still a child who made friends easily. I made friends at school; I made friends roaming around the community and I joined a local Girl Scout troop and made friends there.

February moved into March, another long, cold, dark, hard month. By April the sun was coming back. The bright sunlight sparkled on all the white snow, even though the temperature remained below freezing, direct sunlight kissed the tops of the snowbanks and the roofs of the houses melting the snow in the places that it touched.

As soon as the days grew long enough for me to walk home from school before sunset, I stopped riding the bus in favor of walking, making stops along the way, and meeting people that interested me.

Paula was a year older than me and lived in a big house on my route home from school. Once I realized we walked the same route the two of started walking together and we became fast friends.

Paula was the youngest child of a local physician and the only child still living at home. Her house was huge. It was one of those big old New England houses that were built to allow access to all parts of the property without ever having to set foot outside in cold weather. It was a long building with a porch and living room in front, a kitchen in back, and a family room that had once been servants' quarters behind that. Some large, long New England houses were practically a block long from front to back, including woodsheds, chicken coops, machine sheds, and barns; all built as one extended property. Mother used to call them "a house, attached to a house, attached to a shed, attached to a barn."

Paula was like Bethany in the sense that she had a lovely house and all the best toys but didn't seem to have any other friends to enjoy them with. Paula was also older than me, more worldly, and as the youngest child of a well-off family, she was used to being spoiled.

The first time Paula suggested we go to the store for junk food I happily dug out ten cents for a candy bar and joined her. The next day she wanted to go to the store again, and the day after too. When I explained to her that I couldn't go to the store every day because I didn't have that much money, she said we would have to figure out a way for us to make some.

Paula's first money making idea was to find something we could sell. After some consideration she settled on potholders. A common toy of the era was a square plastic loom, about 8" across, with raised pegs around the perimeter. The loom came with soft, slightly stretchy, loops of fabric that were the right size to stretch from one side to the other. The activity was to fill all the pegs across the loom then weave the cross loops in by hand. Once all the loops were woven the edges could be finished with a simple crochet stitch and the final loop was left free to be used as a hanger. The finished product was about 6" square, looked like it had been made from old T-shirt rags, and had the problematic disadvantage that when used as a potholder it was possible for a finger to push through the weave and be burned by the hot pan.

The looms were also an inexpensive and popular toy that allowed children to make something 'useful,' but they could only produce one product. This meant that every household with children had a lifetime supply of ratty, handwoven, not so useful, potholders.

Nonetheless, Paula had the thought that there must be households that did not have children and therefore did not have wonderful handmade potholders. She was sure we could find someone willing to buy them from us. We spent a day or two in her basement game room using up her supply of fabric loops and then headed outside to begin a door-to-door canvas of the community.

Let me remind the reader that this was spring of 1972. Girl scouts still sold cookies door-to-door and children with paper routes canvassed their neighborhoods once or twice a month collecting subscription fees and tips. Paula and I were ten and nine but no one was surprised or bothered when we walked up their drives without a parent in sight. No one asked to call our parents or questioned our behavior when we knocked on their doors. They generally just smiled indulgently and sent us on our way. After about two days of door-to-door canvassing we had made only one sale and were finally convinced we needed a new business plan.

Idea number two was simpler and more profitable. In the course of walking door-to-door we had noticed a number of discarded beverage bottles along the side of the roads. Maine had a bottle recycling law. Single serving glass bottles were worth two cents. Larger bottles were worth a nickel. It was also spring in a region of long snowy winters. The snowbanks were melting and each one yielded several months' worth of litter that had built up over the long winter. For two children seeking candy cash they were a treasure trove!

There was still slush and ice in some places but most of the pavement was finally clear. We pulled our bicycles out of winter storage and started grooming the community one block at a time, gathering all the empty bottles we could find.

We found a windfall at the community snow dump. All the snow that had been gathered by the snow movers, blown into dump trucks and dumped in a low-lying field; a whole winter's worth, was melting and revealing its hidden treasures of trash. Many bottles did not survive the grinding blades of the snow movers, but a surprising number did. There were literal piles of them, heaped here and there across the soggy field of snow melt. Every time we filled the baskets on the front of our bikes, we made a trip to the store to trade them in for all kinds of yummy treats.

For the first several days the cash came fast and easy. I didn't have to limit myself to a single 10 cent candy bar. We supplemented candy bars with bags of chips, or popcorn. I bought my first whole bottle of soda; I think it was Mountain Dew. (Mother wouldn't let me drink Coke. She said it was full of caffeine and just as bad as coffee. She probably didn't know that other flavors, like Mountain Dew, contained even more caffeine.) We took our goodies out to the stoop in front of the store and sat in the bright spring sunshine enjoying our feast.

We bought some other treasures as well. A local treat was an ice cream cone filled with homemade maple sugar which sold for 15 or 20 cents. Yes, we simply ate the whole thing, about half a cup of straight sugar. I bought a rabbit's foot key chain and kept it in my pocket for good luck. The only pets I'd had since Butterscotch were a couple of guinea pigs that we gave away before leaving Michigan. The act of stroking the soft fur was comforting to me.

In a small city of about 10,000 people, it didn't take long for two motivated children on banana bikes to cover the whole territory. We canvassed our own streets first, and others nearby. The snow dump was on the edge of our neighborhood, so we cleared it out early. Then we focused on main street and the few other commercial blocks. When we had finished all this territory, we re-canvassed all the same places but the week or two between passes could not compare to the first canvass after snow melt. We scouted the local warehouse district but were disappointed in the results, so we crossed the river and began our search in the lower rent district. Again, it didn't take long for two enterprising children to clear out all the intact, returnable bottles.

Eventually we admitted that there just weren't enough bottles left to keep us in the style of filling our bellies with junk food that we had become accustomed to. I was ready to call it quits but

Paula had another idea. She thought there must be lots of people who had tons of empty bottles inside their houses. She said we should just ask people to give them to us.

I was dubious. Picking up trash people had thrown away was one thing, asking them to give you valuable property was another. Paula said we would be performing a service. If people had bottles stacked up that they had not had time to return, we were willing to do it for them. If the people still wanted to get the deposit money for themselves, they could just say, “No thank you.”

Since we were already across the river, in the low rent side of town, we decided to try her new idea then and there. The first few homes we tried were family dwellings. After multiple disappointments we worked out that families with children didn’t want to give up their bottles because they could let their own children return them.

Next, we started looking at the even grubbier houses. Again, the first few answers we received were “No.” The people who lived there didn’t have much to spare and were not willing to give up a stash of returnable bottles that could be the last-ditch source of cash at the end of a lean month.

We had worked our way almost to the end of a tired, grubby street. The days were still short and the shadows were getting long. There was only one house left and Paula was heading resolutely towards it when I asked her to wait. I didn’t like the look of this last house. The yard had piles of trash and the screen door was hanging askew on a broken frame. I wasn’t even sure that anyone lived there; but Paula was on a mission and wouldn’t be stopped. I argued with her as she climbed the front step and banged on the door. I didn’t expect anyone to answer, but a moment later a very large, unkempt man, in a dirty white t-shirt, appeared on the other side of the door.

“Yeah? Wha da ya want?”

I was ready to bolt and run. I could feel myself shaking with fear, but Paula was standing firm. She was on the top step and I was still on the sidewalk. I couldn't reach her to pull her back and I couldn't leave her. She stepped up to the threshold and explained our mission. The man scratched his head, then scratched the wedge of bare belly pushing out from beneath the dirty t-shirt. "Yeah. Okay. Knock, yourself out kid." He pointed to a group of boxes just inside the door. Each one was filled with quart sized empty beer bottles. I stood there, stunned as he loaded our arms with the boxes, full of oversized, five cent bottles. It was a windfall! We filled our bicycle baskets, propped boxes on top of the handlebars and somehow managed to get all of it to the store (easily a mile away) without dropping and breaking anything.

I wondered if the store would accept beer bottles from us. We were nine and ten, way too young to buy beer. Would we be able to return the empties? But the store clerk didn't bat an eye over our windfall, and we enjoyed yet another feast, sitting on the curb looking out at the parking lot, feeling proud of ourselves.

To this day I cannot shake my sense of irony toward that experience. To me it was the scariest moment in a childhood full of wild risk taking. There were so many times when I was unsupervised, far from home, alone or with a single friend. I took so many risks. I never told anyone where I was going or when I would be home. No one ever asked. As long as I was home in time for dinner no one ever cared.

The irony is that nothing bad ever happened, not when I was out in the world alone, or with whatever other children I encountered while roaming the streets, playing daredevil on my banana bike, swimming in rain swollen ditches, catching snakes with my bare hands, climbing so high in the tops of tall trees that I could feel them swaying with my weight, knocking on the doors of indigent alcoholics…

I suffered many horrible experiences. I survived physical, emotional, and sexual abuse, but all the bad things occurred at home or with trusted caretakers. On my own, no matter how risky my behavior or how dicey the situation, I was always safe.

Spring warmed its way toward summer. One day I found myself sitting on the grass of the broad lawn between the Elementary and Jr. High schools; I was eating a hotdog provided by the Budweiser wagon that had come to our Girl Scout event. The wagon was pulled by two glorious, perfectly matched Clydesdales that were bred on a nearby farm. I was quietly pulling at the verdant young grass beside me and feeling the warm sun on my back when I realized how exquisitely beautiful the setting around me was.

Maine is wild and beautiful. Each of the four seasons compete to display the best they have to offer.

Yes, there are also a couple of extra seasons. There is the season of hibernation from the brutal cold and darkness. I suppose it could be called Deep Winter. It is so much colder and darker than the beautiful Norman Rockwell scenes of snow blanketed churches and pines that it deserves a name of its own. If asked, locals might have guided us towards a more hospitable arrival date.

There is also a season of slush and flooding, followed closely by a season of mud. Some call it Spring Breakup. Trickles of melt water work their way below the solid ice of frozen rivers. As these trickles grow into channels of flowing water, they exert tremendous pressure on the tons of ice above, pushing harder and harder until the ice fractures into chunky burgs that attempt to flow away only to run into other burgs and pile up like a dam. The pressure behind the dam continues to build until it forces its way through again, flooding the lowlands on either side of the riverbank and carrying massive ice boulders along with it. On good years the flood waters would recede quickly leaving house sized blocks of ice stranded in fallow fields a mile or more from the river. In harder years the river swelled above its prior boundaries submerging Main Street, 50 plus feet above the train tracks that ran alongside the river.

Spring Breakup might sound awful, but it is also an enthralling display of the power and majesty of nature followed by anticipation of the glory of blossom and growth that is spring in the north.

Spring! People might groan and say, “Don’t blink or you’ll miss it.” Better advice would be, “Don’t miss it!”

Don’t let yourself miss that magical handful of days when all the plants and all the trees compete to put on the best show. Don’t miss the sight of a hardwood forest sprouting forth in amazing, soft, fragile, spring green; forcing itself into the world so rapidly you could swear you were watching time lapse photography. Don’t miss the fragrance of that growth. Don’t miss that undefinable aroma that feels like it charges your soul with boundless joy and renewal. Don’t miss it!

Next there is a season of biting insects. Mosquito’s and black flies who take advantage of the standing water from snow melt. Stay inside for a few days. It’s just another step in the cycle of life.

And then there is summer. The morning sun arrives early and stays late. The days are surprisingly warm. Inland temperatures can hit triple digits in July and August but cool off beautifully at night. The rapid cooling creates the phenomenon of heat lightning, exquisitely beautiful broad fans of multi-pronged lightning bolts that light up the sky in total silence.

Vintage homes were built with screened porches on the second floor where people sleep in the summer, enjoying the cool night air and the sounds of crickets and loons.

School let out. I was excited by the promise of summer. I captured a million insects, quivering with excitement every time I found something new and different. I climbed to the top of a huge poplar tree, bigger than any I had seen before in my life. I climbed so high the trunk was only two or three inches across, the size of a sapling. I held tight to the topmost branches, feeling them sway in the breeze as I looked out over the roofs of our little house and nearby neighbors.

Paula told me she would be leaving soon for summer camp. She said it was a beautiful place. It wasn't like Reunion where we went as a family and came home after a week. Paula got to stay at a children's camp all summer. There were canoes, and swimming and all kinds of fun things. She wished I would come along with her. I asked Mother about this. She told me that Paula's camp wasn't nice at all. She explained that Paula was just being sent away. She said Paula went to the kind of camp that rich people sent their kids to so they wouldn't be bothered by having them around all summer. She explained that we were better than that. We were people who valued children and didn't send them off for someone else to raise. I wondered where she got this information. How did she know so much about the specific camp Paula went to? But I knew better than to ask.

Another New House

With the school year complete and the lease on our little house running out, the search for a new home intensified. I was particularly drawn to the wonderful, big old farmhouses. We toured one that had a servant's wing with several small bedrooms off a long hall. I fantasized about claiming the whole row of them as my "room." I could have a room just to sleep in, a room for my closet, a room for reading…

My parents settled on a smaller house in town. It was about half a mile from Father's work at the local hospital. The ability to walk to work was high on his list of priorities.

The house had other positive attributes as well, including separate living and family rooms, plus four bedrooms. A fourth bedroom meant that even after Father claimed one for his study there were still two rooms left for Heather and me. We could each have a room of our own!

The house was across the street from the municipal park and community pool. It was also within walking distance of all the other schools, the local Armory, and community center. As a final bonus it was less than half a block to the local Carnegie Library.

Moving in was a scramble. We settled on the new house in early July but still owed rent on our temporary house and had not yet sold the house in Marquette, so it was a month of three house payments plus the cost of a moving van. This was hard on my parents but, again, not so hard on my sister and me.

A handful of my father's co-workers showed up to help load and off-load. One of the first things off the truck was my beloved banana bike. I immediately rolled down the drive and set off to survey the streets and blocks of my new town, building a map in my head as I went.

Heather ended up in conversation with the elderly couple across the street. I do not know how this started. She was six and left to herself while the adults unloaded the rented moving truck. At the end of the day, she explained to Mother that she had discovered a Grandmother and Grandfather living right across the street, that this Grandmother and Grandfather did not have any grandchildren of their own, and that they had asked if Heather and I would be grandchildren for them. Mother thought this was wonderful. She declared it a blessing from God and a sure sign that we had made all the right choices. She said that this lonely couple were the reason this was the right house for us and that spending time with them was an opportunity for Heather and me to form new 'special relationships' and provide special ministry.

The next day I crossed the street with Mother and Heather to meet this grandchild-less pair of grandparents. Their names were Edith and Vance. They were both in their 70's and seemed genuinely excited at the prospect of regular visits from a six and almost ten-year-old.

With Edith and Vance welcoming our company and Mother convinced their proximity was divine intervention, visits across the street became a daily event. Edith and Vance taught us the card game Forty-five. It was suitable for four, with or without partners. There was a kitty, bids, and a trump suit, basically just enough complication to engage the minds of a couple of bright children. After an hour or two of Forty-five, we would take a snack break and enjoy a couple of Edith's peanut butter cookies (which I liked very much despite my peanut butter aversion) or a piece of the cinnamon rugalach she made from excess pie crust. After our snack we would turn on the television and watch a game show before heading back to our house just before Father arrived home from work.

Our favorite game show was Match Game, a 70's gathering of over-the-hill celebrities swapping innuendo laced questions, answers, and sometimes drawings, that pushed the censorship boundaries. Watching with Vance was great fun as he unabashedly explained the double entendre. It felt good to be treated like an 'adult.' I felt smart and special at being included in the grown-up jokes and expressions.

Once the house was unpacked and set up, Mother invited Edith and Vance to dinner. She cooked a nice meal and we used our new dining room furniture for the first time.

Near the end of the meal, while the adults were talking, I reached out to Vance and took hold of his hand. I was used to holding hands with Vance. I liked to feel the super fine, smooth skin on the back of his old hands. He usually reached for my hand during the breaks while waiting for Heather and Edith to complete their moves in the game. (Heather and Edith always paired up against Vance and me when we played Forty-Five.) But on this day, in our house, he snatched his hand away like I had hurt him. I was confused, so I tried again, careful this time not to startle or scratch him, but he pulled away even faster the second time and threw an angry look my direction, hissing angry words under his breath that sounded like, "What are you trying to do to me?" I felt hurt and confused but this was obviously not the time to ask questions.

Despite spending all of my afternoons with Edith and Vance I still had plenty of time to explore my new community in the mornings and the long after-dinner daylight hours of northern summer. It didn't take me long to identify all of the other girls my age who lived in town.

There was an elementary school at the far end of our block. On summer evenings local children would gather in the playground. I decided we should give ourselves a name so declared us to be the Hacker Street Gang. The fact that Hacker was the name of the school, not the street, didn't bother me at all.

By the time my birthday arrived, in mid-August, I had a good group of eight or ten girlfriends to invite to an overnight slumber party.

School started the next week.

In Michigan, the first day of school was always after Labor Day, but I would learn that in Aroostook County children started school in August. This allowed time for a three-week hiatus in the fall for everyone to work the potato harvest.

I was excited for the first day of school. I always had new school clothes at the start of the year. I would get to show off the first wearing of my new outfits and meet all the other children my age.

My grade, the class of 1980, was the largest the town had ever seen. Most classes averaged about 80 students and were easily divided into four separate classrooms, but our class had over 130. We didn't fit. The Grammar school, grades four and five, had exactly eight classrooms. Starting with sixth grade the school administration would pack us into only four classes but for fifth grade they designated a fifth, overflow class and co-opted a classroom from the adjacent elementary school to accommodate everyone. I was placed in this class.

Our teacher, Miss M was a small thin woman. She was close to retirement and the strain of keeping up with an overfull class of fifth graders was starting to show. On the first day of school Miss M took role by reading the list of assigned students. As she identified each one, she would pause and connect the student with other family members she had known or taught. She would say, "I had your brother Tom in class last year." Or "I taught your mother and your aunt Sally." When she got to my name, I thought she might ask when I had moved in or where we had moved from, but she didn't say anything at all. She read my name, I raised my hand to indicate that I was present, and she immediately moved on to the next student and a happy conversation about a long list of siblings and other family members.

Grandchildren

The school year did nothing to interrupt our daily visits with Edith and Vance. When I came home from school at the end of the day Mother would tell me that Heather was already across the street and I should join her. We would play Forty-Five for an hour or so then watch Match Game before going back home for dinner. This was the routine, every day.

I was surprised a couple of weeks later when Mother told us not to visit Edith and Vance that day. She said Edith had called to tell her that they were being visited by their grandchildren and to ask that Heather and I stay home.

Grandchildren? But they didn't have any grandchildren. Wasn't that part of the story? Wasn't that why Mother thought it so important for Heather and me to visit them every single day?

I had already learned that the story wasn't exactly true. I had learned that Edith and Vance had five grown children and that at least some these children had their own children, so there were technically some grandchildren but apparently, they all lived far away and never came to visit. Except that now these grandchildren, that never visited, were visiting.

If Edith and Vance's distant grandchildren were there for a visit, why would they ask Heather and me to stay home? Wouldn't they want Heather and me to meet the actual grandchildren? If we were so important to them that they called us family, wouldn't they want to introduce us?

Heather was feeling lost and hurt. She was younger than me. She wasn't as good at spending time alone or at wandering the community until she found her place in it. She had literally visited Edith and Vance every day since the very first day we moved into our house. Now she was being told she was not welcome.

I looked at Heather and said, "This can't be right. It doesn't make sense. They must have told Mother they were having a visit and that their grandchildren were coming over, but they wouldn't have asked us to stay at home. They would want us to meet their grandchildren. They would want us all to be friends."

I suggested we go outside and walk to the end of the driveway. I was sure that once Edith or Vance saw us there, they would smile, wave us over, and introduce us to the other grandchildren.

We walked out to the foot of the driveway and stood waiting. Directly across a road that was only about a lane and a half wide Edith and Vance were sitting on their porch swing. A group of four or five adults were standing in front of them on the porch and on the front steps. Several children were playing a game of tag in the front yard. We smiled and waved but no one seemed to see us.

I took Heather's hand and said, "We'll just wait a minute. They will call us over. You'll see." We waited, but no one even looked our way.

We weren't quite at the end of the driveway, so I inched us forward a foot or two. We smiled and we waited.

I looked at the children and recognized one of them as a classmate. My grammar school was just far enough away that I had a choice of riding the bus, when I did, we rode by this girl's house to pick her up, along with her younger brother and sister. All three of them were there now. They had the same last name as Edith and Vance. They must be real grandchildren.

I pointed out my classmate and siblings to Heather. Heather indicated a couple of other children that went to school with her, she told me that one of them lived just a couple of blocks away.

Apparently, Edith and Vance had a whole bunch of grandchildren and at least half of them lived in town and went to school with Heather and me.

Why wasn't anyone inviting us to come join the fun? I waved at my classmate and called her by name. We were only 15 or 20 feet away, standing with our toes just across the line from the driveway to the narrow street but no one would even look at us.

We were six and ten. We didn't understand. There were a lot of clues that day that we didn't know to consider. The positions of different parties didn't mean anything to us. Edith and Vance were sitting on the swing at the far end of the porch, a group of adults stood at the foot of the steps. Another couple were on the porch, between the steps and the swing. The remaining adults were on the front walk leading up to the steps and at least one was standing in the grass between the paved walk and the group of playing children.

The children were all in the yard. Not one of them came near the steps, if they had they would not have gotten within reach of Grandma or Grandpa because there were at least four adults standing as a barrier between Edith and Vance and any of the children. Edith and Vance were fenced in. They were blocked from any physical contact with their grandchildren. None of the children came near the walkway or steps to the porch. No one went inside the house. No one acknowledged the two confused little girls standing just across the street. Everything was carefully designed to ensure Grandma and Grandpa could look but not touch. Edith and Vance couldn't even speak directly to any of their grandchildren.

My grammar school did not have its own cafeteria, instead we were bussed from the school at the far end of town (not quite a mile away) to the cafeteria in the elementary school where I had formed my summer "gang" of friends. We lined up by classroom for our meal trays, ate our lunches in the basement cafeteria, then trickled back on to the waiting bus and rode back to school for afternoon classes.

A few days after the confusing grandchildren's visit, I contrived to sit next to the grandchild I had recognized as a classmate. She was sitting alone in a window seat when I slid in next to her. She nodded as I sat down but then turned her face to the window. I was undaunted and said what I had come to say. I said, "You know, my sister and I visit your grandparents sometimes too."

I was still absolutely sure the only problem was a simple misunderstanding. I was sure she would be happy to know that another child was there to keep her Grandma and Grandpa from being lonely when she could not be around. I was sure that she would like to visit them with us from time to time, that she and I could be friends who had the same grandparents in common. I knew these things had to be true. I couldn't understand why they wouldn't be; but my classmate kept her eyes firmly pointed out the window. The only sign that she even heard me was a visible stiffening of her back and shoulders.

I didn't have any idea what I had done wrong, but I could tell that for some reason I was hurting her. Just by being there and speaking to her, by wanting to be her friend, I was hurting her. By now the bus was moving so I had to stay seated where I was. We rode the rest of the way in silence. In all the years that followed I never interacted with her again.

I feel that I need to pause here and talk about the things that didn't happen, the opportunities that were missed, opportunities to protect us from the path we were headed down, simple things that could have made all the difference.

The first opportunity was Mother's. She could have asked. She could have noticed. She could have wondered why Edith and

Vance would lie about their family. Why would the patriarchs of a large local clan insist that they were alone and neglected? She could have paid attention to what Heather and I did on that day when she told us not to visit them. She might have overheard me telling Heather that there must be a mistake. She could have asked the same questions I did. "If you do have grandchildren here in town, why wouldn't you encourage them to get to know the two new children across the street that you claim to be so fond of?" She could have come outside with us or asked us what had happened when we came back into the house feeling sad and rejected.

In my adult life I have asked her again and again, "Why didn't you pay attention? Why didn't you help us and protect us?" She always pushes the blame back on me. She says there was no way she could have known that anything was wrong. She says that if I suspected something I should have told her. She says that the fault is all mine, that it was my job (not hers) to protect my sister. That I wanted to visit them, that I was the one who let the bad things happen. Of course, she only says these things when she is willing to acknowledge that anything happened at all. The rest of the time she just accuses me of making up terrible stories so that I can turn everyone against her.

There was also the opportunity for Edith and Vance's adult children to intervene. They knew! They knew not to let their own children within arm's reach of their grandparents, ever! They saw us standing there. They knew who their parents were and what their history was. They could have, should have, spoken up! They should have protected us.

In over six years this was the only time we ever witnessed a family visit. It was carefully staged. The adult children acted together to form a shield between their parents and their own children. They saw us standing there. They could have offered warning. They could have suggested we not spend time alone in that house. They could have walked across the street and spoken to our parents. They could have found some way to offer some protection.

This is the great challenge of sexual abuse. Social taboos run deep. The unwritten rule is that no one ever talks. This rule has such power that those of us who suffer the most are the least likely to share our stories, the least likely to call for help, and the least likely to protect others. These adult children were quietly protecting their own, but they would not admit it, and they certainly wouldn't explain their actions to a stranger, not even to protect two innocent children.

There is another part of the story that I cannot explain at all. We moved out of Michigan. We moved away from the setting of past abuse. We traveled over a thousand miles to a new state and a new community where no one knew us, and we knew nothing about them. We bought a new house based on availability and suitability. What unfortunate twist of fate, what malignant act of karma placed us in a new house directly across the street from the local pedophile? As long as I live, I will never know the answer to this question.

Sometime later (I feel like it was only a couple of months, but I do not have a good way to measure timing in this case) I was told that a woman who lived a few blocks away committed suicide. She stuffed a rag into the tailpipe of the family car, turned it on and sat in her own driveway waiting for the exhaust fumes to end her life. She was the mother of my sister's classmate. The mother of the little girl Heather had pointed to on that day when we stood at the very end of our drive, with our toes edging into the street, wondering why Edith and Vance wouldn't invite us over to meet their grandchildren.

I learned of this suicide from Mother, who was particularly affected by the event. Mother was highly agitated and remained so for several weeks. She would bring it up at random moments, obsessively relating the details over and over to herself. It didn't seem to matter to her if I or anyone else, was in the room. She would talk about how awful it must be for Edith and Vance to live with this death. She sometimes worried about the family and the children, but her main focus was on Edith and Vance as though she believed they were more affected by the suicide than anyone else.

Heather tried to remain friends with the child. I remember her coming to our house for a play date, a very quiet, sad child whose presence left Mother even more agitated for the next several days.

Despite Mother's anxiety, the suicide didn't seem to have any effect at all on Edith or Vance. Heather and I still made our afternoon visits. We played cards, ate cookies, and watched grown-up game shows, just like we always had before, as if the visit with the real grandchildren and the subsequent suicide had never even happened.

At ten I was too naive to string these events together. Heather's classmate, who was a grandchild to Edith and Vance, had a different last name. Did this mean that the woman who killed herself was Edith and Vance's daughter? This connection could explain Mothers agitation but not Edith and Vance's lack of interest. How could they lose a child to suicide and not vary their routine or show any signs of grief? Was there a funeral or memorial service? I never heard mention of one.

Even if the woman wasn't their daughter, even if the family connection was more complicated, their grandchildren, grandchildren who lived just a couple of blocks away, lost their mother in a horrible public suicide. How could they possibly have continued on, as if absolutely nothing had happened?

There is obviously a lot more to this story, but I will never know the answers to my questions and if I did it would not be my story to tell. As it is I know almost nothing. It took me too long to fit the pieces together. By the time I knew to ask the questions I was an adult living far away without any active ties to that small town in Maine. I don't even know what happened to the child. Heather moved on to other friends. I never saw her again and our focus shifted to other things.

Picking Potatoes

Three weeks into the school year classes stopped and everyone went off to support the potato harvest. I do mean everyone. By the mid 70's most communities in Aroostook County were only closing High School for the harvest, other towns recessed for both Jr and Sr High. Our town was the last holdout, closing all grades, K through 12. Any child old enough to attend school was old enough to pick potatoes. Housewives worked the potato harvest. Teachers and other school staff worked the harvest. I have seen whole families work the harvest, including children as young as two.

It is probably helpful here if I take a minute to explain the process. Potatoes are planted in mounds. The planting machinery tills the soil, plants the seed potato (a portion of a potato with one or more sprouting eyes) and covers it with about 10" of mounded earth. The result is a field of long raised rows that looks a bit like giant sized, corrugated cardboard.

In the fall, once the tubers are grown, the fields are dusted with defoliant (sadly in the 70's, the chemical of choice was agent orange). Once the tops are dead and dry it is easier to dig the potatoes without fighting to keep tangled greenery out of the equipment.

A simple potato digger is pulled behind a tractor. The digger has a wide blade that spans two rows. As the tractor drags the blade under the raised rows, dirt and potatoes are pushed onto a conveyor belt of open steel links. The soil and dried plant remnants drop through the chain links and when the potatoes get to the end of the conveyor, they are dropped on top of the dirt to be harvested by a waiting picker.

Each picker was assigned a section of the row, usually about 15 to 20 paces long. Once the digger passed, we gathered the potatoes into our baskets and dumped them into a waiting barrel. Full barrels were marked with a tag displaying the picker's number. A good-sized basket was enough to fill a quarter of a barrel. One barrel held 125 pounds of potatoes.

Local farmers would drive through town in the pre-dawn hours picking up the children who were working their crop. We packed into the back of a covered pick-up truck, sitting on makeshift wooden bench seats for our ride to the fields. The workweek was Monday through Saturday from 7am to 4pm plus an hour or so of transportation at the beginning and end of each day.

There had been some contention in our home about whether or not Heather and I should be allowed to participate in the harvest. Mother didn't like the idea of sending her children, ten and six, off to the fields. Father felt that if we wanted to become a part of this community, we should not sit out an activity that held such local significance. Then there was the question of finding a farmer to hire us. Father had an answer for that too. He had a colleague whose husband farmed. While his co-workers farm no longer relied on hand pickers, her sister's farm did. So, it was decided. Heather and I would work the S farm. A truck would come by at about 5:30 am to pick us up and take us to the fields.

The rate for a barrel of potatoes that first year was 35 cents. This amount increased slowly over the next few years. It was pushed a bit as other communities enforced limits on who could work the harvest. With fewer workers available a picker could choose to work on a farm that paid a nickel more. Sometimes a picker would change farms mid-season to earn a higher wage, or because a farm with a higher yield per acre made for more lucrative picking. At other times young people would change farms just to hang out with the 'cool' kids. As it got harder to attract pickers, farmers started offering a 5 cent per barrel bonus to anyone who stayed on their farm until the end of the season.

The most I ever made for filling a 125 pound barrel of potatoes was 55 cents (including the 5 cent bonus.) The most barrels I ever picked in a day was 54 or 55. Fifty to fifty five barrels a day was a good average for a fit young person. There were of course rockstars who rarely dipped under 60 as well as competitions and local champions that claimed to double that. 120 barrels might be impressive in a single day competition but across six-day work weeks I never knew anyone who claimed much above 60.

As children in the fields we always found time for play, roughhousing, and a death defying game. The potato rows that had been planted by tractors, were spaced just far enough apart to provide a sung wheel grove for the tractor pulling the digger. This meant that steering wasn't necessary. The digging blade and linked conveyor were vulnerable to rocks or even an excess of plant material that could get caught in the machinery and cause a breakdown, so the driver constantly watched backwards, never forward. The tractor also sported a radio, always on, turned up to max volume as that was the only way to hear it over the cacophony of the equipment. If a person wanted to communicate with the driver they had to get very close, yell as loudly as possible, and usually jump and wave their arms in the air in order to be seen.

Our daredevil game was to stand directly in front of the moving tractor, each foot atop a potato row. As the tractor approached we would lean forward, arms stretched out as far as possible, palm splayed and vertical. The goal was to palm the front of the tractor before jumping out of the way. It was a death defying act. Had anyone of us slipped we would have been crushed by oversized tractor wheels practically as high as we were tall. The tractor moved slowly but not slowly enough for a fallen child to scramble out of the way in time.

Most children challenged the tractor at least once. Many challenged it once or twice in a season. I challenged the tractor every day, several times on most days. I never cheated; never chickened out. Palming the tractor wasn't about proving my bravado to other children it was about proving my value to myself.

Palming the tractor was another ironic act. My wild, daredevil behavior made me feel special, empowered, and somehow it never brought me harm. The bad things only happened in settings that were supposed to be safe; when I was following the rules, doing the things I was told to do.

Mrs. S

I met someone that first year, picking potatoes at the S farm, that deserves her own chapter. I want to take a moment here to pay homage to her, yet another angel, a woman who, just by being who she was, made my world better.

Her name was Mrs. S. It was her farm that I was working. Her husband and sons were in the fields, driving the tractors and the trucks that gathered up the barrels and hauled them off to the warehouses. Mrs. S was home feeding her flock and keeping the books.

At some point there was a message that needed to get from the field to her in the farmhouse. In the era before cell phones this meant sending a runner to the house. I happened to be available and was given the task. It was midday. I was, of course, caked in dust and mud. When I ran to the house and banged on the door to the screened porch a voice called for me to come in. I was cautious. I was dirty and grubby and entering the house of someone I didn't know. I announced myself and was told again to come in, so I entered the screened porch and stepped up to the kitchen door. It was a big farmhouse kitchen; the full width of the house. It was also a very clean kitchen. I opened the door just a little and explained my errand. At the far side of the kitchen a small woman was standing at the stove with her back to me, stirring a pot of heavenly smelling soup. There was nothing between us except a large expanse of sparkling, fresh mopped, white linoleum.

She said again, "Come on in. Come over here and try my soup." I told her I couldn't. I was wearing boots from the field. They were muddy. My knees were caked with mud. My jacket was dirty and dusty and there was a pair of muddy, dusty, field gloves flapping from my back pocket. I was not going to walk across her sparkling white, freshly mopped, kitchen floor.

She asked me if I liked pea soup. I did. I told her so. (To those readers who do not like pea soup, my apologies. Please substitute something warm and satisfying that will make you feel welcomed and cared for.) She pointed to a table and told me to come in, sit down, and try her soup. I do not think she had even turned to look my way yet. She didn't know who was at her door and it didn't matter, anyone who came to her kitchen was going to get a bowl of warm soup.

I was still caked in field dust and mud. When I got home that night I would be expected to strip down to my underwear, carefully tucking all of my dirty clothes into a paper grocery bag, before stepping from our not enclosed back porch, into Mother's kitchen. Then I was to go directly to the bathroom, shower, and change into clean clothes before touching anything else in the house. In my current state I was not worthy to sit at my own kitchen table, let alone hers.

Mrs. S turned and looked at me. She gave me an appraising stare, pursed her lips and nodded her head slightly. She said, "Okay. Will you sit on that stool?" and tilted her head towards a step stool just inside the door.

I looked at the stool. It was right there. I could reach out and touch it but I would still have to put at least one muddy boot on her beautiful floor before I could climb up onto it. I took another look at my host and realized that this was the best compromise I was going to get from this fiesty woman. I nodded, took one gingerly step, and climbed up onto the stool, trying to keep myself as small and still as possible in order to minimize the amount of dirt I would leave behind. Mrs S came over and placed a warm bowl of soup in my hands.

Her soup was wonderful!

This was not my mother's, stand a fork in it, full of chunky carrots and potatoes pea soup. Mrs. S's soup was silky smooth, perfectly seasoned, and infused with richly smoked bacon. It was warmth, and welcome and generosity. It was a smell and a flavor I have remembered all my life.

Later, a few more years down the road, Mrs. S would become an important person to me. The kind of mentor that stands off at a respectful distance and lets us find our own path. The kind of support that makes its impact not because you use it, but because you know it is always there, always ready, always capable of catching you if you fall, but even happier to step back and rejoice as you fly away without ever needing the assist.

I have wondered. If for me heaven will look like Mrs. S's kitchen; a warm, beautiful and inviting place that I am afraid to enter because I feel unworthy. I wonder if I will be welcomed by someone who urges me across the threshold and then comes forward to greet me and meet me where I am, and to make it clear that despite all my soil and my grubbiness I am welcome in that space.

Will I find myself stepping out of the woods and into the yard of the Hippie House? After warming my hands by the fire in the oil drum and playing with the spinning wheel will I step over the threshold and find myself in Mrs. S's kitchen? I believe I could appreciate that version of heaven.

A Hard Year

The harvest ended and school resumed. All my classmates came back to school showing off the new clothes they had bought for themselves with their potato picking money. They were surprised that I didn't have anything new. I told them that my mother always took me shopping for new clothes before the first day of school and I had already worn my new school clothes at the start of the year. My classmates thought this was weird. They couldn't understand why anyone would let their mother buy new school clothes for them when they had the opportunity to make their own money and buy their own things.

Back to school also meant back to spending afternoons with Edith and Vance. It was the same routine. We played cards, had a snack, and then watched innuendo laced game shows with Vance while Edith went off to the kitchen to prep dinner. We never stayed and ate with them. As soon as the game shows ended, we headed across the street to have dinner at home. I asked Mother about this. Why were we never offered dinner with Edith and Vance? Mother claimed that they were too poor. Vance was a retired laborer and the only income they had was from Social Security.

I enjoyed the quirky card game and very much liked talking to adults who seemed to enjoy listening to me. Vance and I still held hands. We never talked about why he had gotten upset the one time I reached for his hand while my parents were present. I let myself believe it was just a silly one-time concern.

One day Vance showed me an incense burner. It was a little tableau with a tiny log cabin and a pine tree sitting on a flat base. You put the cone of incense inside the little cabin and when it burned the smoke curled out of the chimney like a real cabin with a real fire in the fireplace. He had a few other incense burners too, but the log cabin was his favorite. Lighting a cone of incense every day became a new part of our routine.

Another day Vance asked me to sit on his lap.

I was ten. I didn't know of any reason I should not sit on his lap, so I climbed on up. He was sitting on his recliner with the footrest up and his legs stretched out. When I sat down on his lap, I felt something large and hard. It wasn't at all the soft cushy lap I had anticipated, in fact it was awkward, uneven, bumpy and uncomfortable. I didn't have any idea what that hard lump was, and I was genuinely concerned that I had hurt him. I said I was sorry and tried to get up and leave but he pulled me back and told me to stay.

A day or so later he asked me to sit on his lap again, and I encountered the mysterious lump again.

The next time he asked me to sit on his lap I told him no. I was still afraid that I was hurting him. I could tell it caused him pain. He squirmed and groaned whenever I sat on him, but when I said I didn't want to hurt him he still insisted I sit on his lap and held me firmly in place. I couldn't understand why he would ask me to do something that hurt him so badly. I tried to move to the side so I would not be directly on the lump, but he shifted me back so I was directly on top of it. It felt like I was sitting on a rock. It was not comfortable for me and seemed like it was awful for him. I could not understand what this was about and certainly didn't know what to do.

I ask the reader to remember that I was a girl with no brothers and no knowledge of male anatomy. I was also an oldest child. I had no older siblings to show off their guilty early knowledge of carnal activities. Because we moved frequently, I had no long-term friends with older siblings and no interaction with older cousins. I had never even changed diapers on a male baby.

I knew that I had a 'private' place. To my understanding that private place was the same as the place I urinated from. I understood that boys were different, but I thought their privates were basically in the same region. I had already experienced sexual abuse, but my only memories were of pain, confusion, and adults who's carefully asked questions mysteriously morphed into unintelligible words and phrases.

Vance had a hard lump several inches above the crotch of his pants. It was closer to the round, soft tummy region just below the belt than it was to the 'private place' which I believed to be in the protective nook of his crotch. There should not be anything hard in the region of the tummy. I certainly didn't have anything private or hard in my tummy.

Something was very wrong.

I thought about this. I tried to reason out an explanation. I didn't ask questions. I couldn't ask Mother. if I did, she would only tell me I was being disobedient. I couldn't ask Vance because he clearly wasn't willing to explain. He acted like he was sharing a special secret every time he asked me to sit on his lap, like I was supposed to know something, it was just that I didn't know. I didn't have any idea, and I didn't have anyone to help me understand.

I remembered that Mother had been talking a lot about cancer lately. She said we were living in a region where too many people had cancer. She also said that members of Edith and Vance's family had a lot of cancer, that someone specific in their family had cancer now, that it was bad, and that the person was likely going to die. I didn't understand cancer either, so I tried to ask questions about it. I learned that cancer happened when something went wrong in the body and caused it to grow tumors. Tumors were described to me as hard masses, or lumps, that grew inside people. If the tumor kept growing it could damage all of the important parts around it, until it killed the person.

Vance had a hard lump on his stomach. He had a big, hard lump in a place where there shouldn't be anything but soft tummy! He wanted me to know about this lump, but he didn't want to talk about it. That must be why he was acting so strangely. He had cancer! He was going to die! He wanted me to know that he had cancer and that he was dying but he couldn't bring himself to say it!

Armed with this misinformation I resolved two things. First, I would never sit on his lap again. It didn't matter how much he begged me to do so, I would not do anything that would hurt him. Second, I had to be as kind to him as possible. He was sick. He was probably dying, and I had to do everything I could to make him feel better.

The next day, after Vance lit his cone of incense, put his feet up on the recliner and asked me to sit on his lap I said "No." He said "Please." And I said no again. He said he had something he wanted to show me, but I still said no. He asked me to give him my hand. I thought that might be okay so I did, but then he pulled my hand and put it on top of his lump and told me I should feel it. He asked me what I thought about it, and if I liked it.

I thought this was a horrible question since I had worked out that his lump was a cancerous tumor, and it was very likely going to kill him! How could he possibly ask me if I liked it? I tried to pull my hand back, but he had a firm grip on my wrist so the best I could do was to make a fist and not let him force me to feel the evil lump that was making him sick! We stood there like that for a minute, him holding me by the wrist and pushing my clenched knuckles up against his lump, me pulling away. Finally, he let go and I walked into the kitchen and asked Edith if I could help her prep for dinner.

Things went on like that for a while. Heather and I still went to visit every day after school. We would still play cards and later we would turn on the TV to watch game shows. Vance still asked me to sit on his lap, but I never did. A couple of times he reached for my hand. At first I let him, but every time I gave him my hand he tried to make me feel his lump, so eventually I quit giving him the opportunity. I still enjoyed watching the game show with him and learning all the secret adult meanings to their answers, but I made sure to sit out of reach on the couch. It would be nice to be able to say that this is as far as things went but of course that was never going to be true.

Vance's next move was to ask me about toilet paper.

There was a special roll of grown-up paper in the little toilet closet under the steps. (This was an old, poor, house in Maine. The only plumbing was a cold water tap in the kitchen and a toilet in the closet under the steps.) Each square of the special toilet paper was decorated by a black and white cartoon of a very old couple with no clothes on. They had exaggerated knobby knees, oversized noses, chins and earlobes, saggy breasts and bottoms, and other parts the cartoonist must have made up because I had never seen anyone with such things.

The cartoon toilet paper was clearly not intended for children. I knew that some things were for adults only and I had never touched that role of paper, but Vance told me that I should use it. This was an odd request, but I didn't see how it could hurt anything, so the next time I used their toilet I made use of the kinda-scratchy, special paper.

When I came out of the bathroom Vance asked if I had used the special paper and I told him that I had, but only because he had asked me to. Then he asked me if I liked it and what I thought of it.

This was an odd question. It was cheap, scratchy toilet paper. What did he expect me to think about it?

Vance tried again. He asked if I had looked at the cartoons and if I liked them. I said I had not. They were clearly grown-up cartoons, and I didn't feel right looking at them. He told me that the next time I used the bathroom I should read the cartoons so I could tell him what I thought of them.

A day or so later I dutifully read the cartoons on the squares of paper. There were captions along with the drawings of a flabby breasted and boney kneed old couple in odd positions. Were they looking at each other's butts? The captions were obviously intended to be funny, but I didn't get the jokes and didn't feel like asking for explanations. When Vance tried again to ask what I thought about them I grunted a noncommittal answer that I guessed they were okay. This was not the answer he was looking for. He insisted I should look at all the different cartoons and be prepared to give him an opinion.

With every visit to the toilet, I tried to understand what he wanted. I counted the different drawings. There were twelve of them. I described the faces and features. She had a long chin with a mole and a hair growing out of it. Both of them had outrageously large noses and ears. Some of the pictures had a bit of background, like a chair or a bed.

None of my answers seemed to be the response he was looking for. On my part I didn't understand this game and I was getting tired of it. I quit using the scratchy paper. By now I had looked at and tried to answer questions about all twelve cartoons. What was the point of looking at them again and again?

One day I decided not to sit and watch the game shows with Vance. After I came out from the toilet closet and washed my hands in the warm sudsy dish pan Edith kept in the sink, I offered to help her finish the dishes.

I loved Edith's kitchen. I was fascinated by the way she made it all work. She cooked on a huge, antique, cast-iron stove. When the stove was new it had been wood burning but it had later been modified to use kerosine which was delivered to the house in five-gallon bottles, much like the bottles used in today's water coolers. The stove didn't have any buttons or controls. There might have been a way to adjust the flow of kerosine but from what I could tell it was just always on.

Edith kept a couple of oversized tea kettles on the back of the stove to provide hot water for washing. She simply filled her dishpan with a mixture of cold tap water and hot water from the kettle. I knew they took their "baths" in the same sink, presumably using the same dish pan and soapy washcloths.

Edith and Vance's house had other quaint, old-fashioned attributes. Heat was provided by a gas stove in the living room that had been converted to wood. (Don't ask me why, but the kitchen stove had indeed been converted from wood to kerosine while the heating stove had been converted from gas to wood.) She did her laundry in an old-fashioned wringer style washing machine that rolled up to the kitchen sink and connected to the faucet.

The house had electricity but during one, particularly long, power outage I was impressed by how well they could light it using just old kerosine lanterns from earlier times. Hanging with Edith in the kitchen was a lesson in domestic history. One of the ironies of my life is that she taught me so much. To this day I rely on recipes and skills I learned from Edith in her kitchen.

Spending time with Edith, helping her with her chores, seemed like the perfect way to avoid Vance and his odd behavior, but it didn't last long. After a couple of blissful afternoons in the kitchen Edith said I should leave her be. She said this was time for me to spend alone with Vance. She said he needed me and spending time with me was important to him. I wanted to say no. I wanted to ask why he was always so weird when we were alone, but I knew there wasn't any point. She stopped her task, turned around, stilled her body, looked me straight in the eyes and told me to go.

Of all the moments I have had to resolve this is the hardest. I cannot understand this warm, loving, comforting woman, raising her hand, pointing the way and knowingly sending me into the arms of her pedophile husband.

I have come to accept and understand that my mother was what she was because she lived her own life of abuse. I have never learned much of the who, where, how, or why of that abuse, but I know it happened and I know she was broken by it. I know that she did not love any of us because she wasn't capable of love. I wasted too much of my life trying to be the perfect daughter, trying to find the elusive key that would heal her and my relationship with her. That key doesn't exist, at least not on this earthly plane. I eventually made my peace with that and turned my focus towards a healthier life.

I have come to accept that my father was a coward. He never had the strength to stand up to his wife, so he warped the tenants of his religion to justify placing his ego above the safety of his children.

As for Vance, I don't get it. I cannot begin to understand the broken soul of a man who would choose such sin; who would commit his life to such sin; who would throw away love and family, joy and life... I cannot begin to understand it, but I don't need to. Somehow, he just doesn't matter to me. He is responsible for the condition of his own soul. In whatever afterlife he has or has not found, he is the one who can or cannot redeem himself. I honestly do not care. I have tried to search my soul for any feelings towards him, shouldn't there be something; hate, pity, revulsion, anger... anything? All I can find is an empty place in my heart, a void, a little well of nothingness.

But Edith. Why? How?

What were the justifications in your head? How did you find yourself in such a place and what was it that broke you? I honestly believe you loved us, maybe it was a warped, tortured love, but you needed us. Our presence was a comfort to you. Were you so broken you were willing to lead us into the arms of your pedophile husband just to have us around?

So, what else happened? The story above contains almost all of my firsthand evidence against Vance. I would like to tell you the rest of the tale, but I cannot.

My memory of our time together is like Swiss cheese. It is rich, and detailed, and full of holes. It is like a jigsaw puzzle with key pieces missing. Like the Mona Lisa without her smile. Is she smiling? Rumor has it that this piece of art stands out among all others because of a simple, subtle curve of her lips. Is it really there? Does the curve of her lips highlight what might be a gleam in her eyes? I will never know for sure. I have completed what I can of the puzzle. I have used all the pieces in the box and crawled around looking under the couch for lost ones, but they are not there to be found. The image is complete except for the two pieces where her mouth, her smile, should be. I can only guess at what it is doing.

What I do have are secondary clues. Some of the holes in my memory have sharp edges. There are places in and around the home where I know I spent time, but I cannot remember. The shed at the back of the house is one. The shed was accessed by a door at the back of the kitchen and a partial flight of unfinished wood steps, sturdy enough but gray with age. I remember Vance getting up and leading me across the kitchen asking me to come with him to get a 'stick' for the fire. In my mind I can see him, below the steps, walking across the dirt floor of the shed asking me to join him. I step through the threshold, right foot first, and there the memory ends.

Pain is another clue. It came back. It came back with a vengeance. That constant, nagging, burning, itch that made me feel like I had to go to the bathroom every minute of every day.

My obsession with stories of kidnapping returned. I gravitated to police shows with female victims and made-up horrible stories in my mind. I seemed to be pulled to them in ways I couldn't understand.

I also remember part of a conversation. I tried to say "No." I said I would tell. He looked right back at me and said, "Okay. Go ahead. Try. Who are you going to tell? No one will listen to you. No one will believe you. No one will help you. No one will even hear you."

He was absolutely, supremely confident that no one would lift a finger to help me, but then, why wouldn't he be. Everyone I could possibly turn to, already knew.

This was the beginning. There was much more to come but for now I want to shift focus to other threads in our lives.

A Hard Year at Home

Home was still a rocky road.

Mother was struggling to find a place for herself in our new community. In Marquette, after Heather started preschool, Mother had joined the League of Women Voters. It had been good for her, and good for the rest of us in return. Now, in Maine, she didn't have a niche. She attended a meeting of the local hospital auxiliary (Father was the new director of the mental health ward after all) but she didn't feel welcome. She told a story of being introduced to another 'newcomer.' This 'newcomer' was the mother of one of my best friends. She wasn't from Maine but had married into one of the towns oldest families more than 20 years before.

Mother took that statement to heart. If my friend's mother was still considered a newcomer after 20 years, there was no hope for Mother. She had been moved to a faraway place, one where she would never, ever, belong. She was irritable and unhappy and that made life hard on all of us.

Mother and Father were fighting a lot. Heather and I developed a routine in response to their battles. When the argument got loud, I would head to the kitchen and Heather would run upstairs to the bedrooms, then we would close and latch all the windows in our respective parts of the house. This didn't stop the fighting, but it prevented Heather and me from becoming secondary targets. It kept us from being accused of "broadcasting their arguments to everyone in the neighborhood," as if we were responsible for their behavior!

From time-to-time Heather and I talked about what we would do if they divorced. Heather was always wary of Father. She claims she always knew she didn't quite belong and felt that he treated her differently because on some level he knew she wasn't his child. She would not feel safe living with Father. Of course, she wouldn't be safe with Mother either but to her it seemed like the best option.

I couldn't imagine staying with Mother. I was her emotional punching bag. I was afraid of what my life would be if Father wasn't around to provide even a small amount of protection.

The primary concern, for both of us, was that we might not get a choice. What if our parents divorced and one or both of us was forced to live with the parent we feared most?

One day Father came home from his job with a pill bottle of valium. There hadn't been any medical visit or any prescription. He could have asked one of the staff psychiatrists to write a script but that would have meant telling someone outside the household about Mother's blow-ups. To the best of my knowledge, he simply took a bottle of valium out of the medical supplies at his workplace and brought it home to his wife.

Bootleg valium wasn't the only attempt at curbing her mood swings. Father, who considered it his irrefutable professional opinion that Mother's 'blow-ups' were related to her menstrual cycles, insisted it was time for her to stop taking oral birth-control, so he booked a hospital procedure to have her tubes tied.

These measures worked briefly. Mother proved highly sensitive to valium. The smallest dose left her limp and silly, but she quickly tired of being told to "take a pill" every time she was at all disagreeable.

I appreciated the few weeks of relative calm when instead of a screaming, yelling, monster my mother became a listless giggling child, but I understood her anger and frustration the day she refused the valium and stomped around the house for hours yelling, "Take a pill J! Take a pill! Nobody cares what the problem is. Nobody wants to hear your complaints. Nobody gives a damn about you. Just shut up and take a pill!"

A Hard Year at School

At the same time life in my new school and classroom was proving to be harder than any of my other school years had been.

I was no longer the little girl who became Queen of the Bus on my first day of school or the girl who could pick out a new best friend on my first day in a new kindergarten. In this place and this school things just weren't coming together the way they always had before.

I have told you that our class was an overflow group. We didn't fit in the Grammar School so were housed in an adjacent elementary school where we were both isolated from the other classes of our grade and deliberately segregated from the younger students in the building.

Then there was my teacher, Miss M. I have already told you she was small, worn, and ready to retire. I was used to getting along well with my teachers but for me and Miss M, this was not to be.

One of our first clashes occurred during a science lesson. Starting in sixth grade students rotated between teachers who specialized in reading, math, or other subjects, but in fifth grade we only split into different groups for reading. All of the teachers still had to manage teaching all the other subjects and science was not Miss M's best thing.

This particular lesson was about states of matter. Miss M explained that everything was made up of matter, that matter came in three states; solid, liquid and gas (plasma hadn't been identified yet) and that all matter could exist in each of the three states depending on environmental factors such as temperature and air pressure.

I was hooked. This was amazing and unexpected new knowledge. I began to wonder about the places this new knowledge could take me.

I thought about different kinds of matter I was aware of and how each one manifested in the three states. Water was easy. There is water, and ice, and steam. Most people have known for most of our lives that water, ice, and steam are the same matter; that water becomes ice when you freeze it and steam when you heat it. I tried to think of other kinds of matter and how they could manifest in different states. I remembered a craft I had made a few years ago. The goal was to make jewelry from a pill bottle and colored beads. You were supposed to place the beads in the pill bottle and put it in a hot oven until it melted down into a multicolored puddle, then you could poke a hole in it while it was still hot, put it on a string and wear it like a necklace once it cooled.

The craft hadn't worked very well. The bottle didn't melt all the way and it had smelled so bad I didn't even argue when Mother made me take it out of the oven before it was ready. But the bottle was melting. I could understand that if I had left it in the oven the bottle and beads would have eventually become liquid. And that smell, maybe that was an indication of the bottle becoming gas. Maybe what Miss M was teaching us was true! What about other things? Could I come up with other examples that supported her theory?

I rummaged around in my mind and stuck on butter. Now that was a conundrum. Butter was a solid if you put it in the refrigerator and it was definitely a liquid if you melted it in the bottom of a pan, but most of the time butter just sat around on the counter in a soft squishy state that wasn't quite a solid or a liquid. According to Miss M's rules, solid required a constant mass and a constant shape. Squishy, soft butter didn't really have a constant shape so it couldn't be called solid, but it wasn't a liquid either because it didn't need a container to keep it from flowing away. Oohhh, this is a hard one. I might need help with this one.

“Miss M! What about butter? Butter isn’t solid, not according to your rules, but it isn’t liquid either. How do you account for things that aren’t really liquid, or solid, or gas?”

I can’t tell you if I raised my hand. In my excitement I probably just blurted out the question. But I can promise you that it was a real question. It was a genuine attempt to apply my new knowledge to things in my everyday world. Unfortunately, Miss M heard it as a belligerent, “stump the teacher”, challenge and she was not going to tolerate insubordination in her classroom. She seemed to agree with Mother that my primary goal in life was to irritate the adults around me and she had some very firm things to say to me about my behavior.

Another science-related clash came directly out of the challenge of being the only child in the class with unique religious beliefs. When my parents got together with other adults of our faith, they seemed to enjoy what to me is a game of “My miracle can top your miracle.” I knew all the various stories. There was a relative with a tumorous growth on her face. The Elders were called for Administration (a prayer for healing the sick) and the next morning the woman woke up to find the tumor had fallen off and was lying next to her on the pillow. There was another relative who froze her fingers stiff. As the story goes, they were so frozen there was concern that they might break off, but again the Elders were called and she was miraculously healed.

What got me in trouble with Miss M was the story about Father’s tonsillectomy. According to this story, he went home after the procedure seemingly fine until he began to hemorrhage and vomit blood. He continued to vomit blood throughout the night. Someone grabbed a pan out of the kitchen for him to vomit into and he filled it again and again and again. This was a story I had known most of my life. It was absolute. It was gospel.

When Miss M told us as part of a biology lesson that the adult body contained only five quarts of blood, I had to tell her that this was not true. Father had vomited way more than that when he was just a little boy, and he was alive. This was incontrovertible evidence that we all had lots more than five quarts of blood in us!

What is a teacher supposed to do when a ten-year-old child stands up and refutes science with stories of family miracles?

These early conflicts were far from our last.

The next conflict was a simple matter of terminology. In Michigan there were two teacher parent events. The first was an open house. As students we did special art projects and lined the hallways with our efforts, then on a single evening all the parents, and other family if they wished, came to the school. Someone usually provided cookies and punch. We students walked our family through the halls and into our classrooms. We showed them our special art. We showed them where we sat. We introduced them to our teachers. Sometimes we introduced them to friends and parents of friends. It was a happy evening of celebration.

Parent/Teacher conferences were a separate event. Each set of parents received a specific appointment and had the opportunity to meet with the teacher and discuss any issues or concern. As a student who usually got along well with my teachers and peers I never paid much attention to this event.

When each student in my fifth-grade class was given an "Open House" invitation to take home I didn't think to look at the other students notes. If I had I might have noticed that each invitation listed a different time. But why would I, the event was clearly labeled "Open House?"

We arrived at the Open House as a family. We opened the door to a classroom empty of everyone but Miss M. She stepped up to the door, looked directly at me and exclaimed, "What in the world are doing here? You know better than to show up for a parent teacher conference!"

The saving grace for me was that my parents were so offended by her outburst they jumped to their own conclusion that I had been stuck with a bad teacher. That said, there were now three strikes between Miss M and me.

The rest of fifth grade was no better. The conflict between Miss M and me only got worse with time. I do not remember what set us off, but one day when she told me to take my desk and go sit out in the hall, I stood, picked up the square student desk, flipped it over my head, bench pressed it toward the ceiling, exclaimed that I didn't want to stay in the same room as her anyway, and stomped out holding my inverted desk above my head the whole way.

Please understand that this was very abnormal behavior for me. I was generally the child who tried too hard. I have never been someone to seek out conflict. When I do get angry it is usually a quick flash followed by regret. In fact, I cannot think of another incident when I have owned my anger in such a way. On this day I felt absolutely no remorse. I spent the rest of the afternoon sitting in the hall fruitlessly wearing out my pencil by trying to draw on the rough, red bricks.

My social skills with my peers weren't any better. I developed the habit of greeting my friends by slapping them on the bottom. I cannot explain what was behind this need, but the compulsion was strong. There was something about the physicality of the gesture that I needed, that I craved. The slap had to be hard. It had to be so hard it left my hand stinging for several minutes afterwards. Thankfully, this wasn't a need that stayed with me. I grew out of the habit quickly, but while it lasted it was so strong that it left what I can only describe as muscle memory. To this day I can rub the palm of my hand and feel the desire for that sting.

The miracle is that in that class, in this new town, where everyone had known everyone else for generations and I was a particularly strange outsider, I made two wonderful friends. As my closest friends they were primary targets for my slapping antics, but somehow the friendship remained. They were still my best friends six years later when my family left Maine to move back to Michigan.

People who stand by us and care for us even in our worst moments are one of the most precious gifts life has to offer.

As an outsider and a genuinely awkward child it's no surprise that I became a common target for insults and teasing. One boy particularly bothered me. He was a large child, quiet and soft spoken. He didn't join in with the teasing. He just hovered. He may have been trying to protect me, but I didn't understand his intent and he made me nervous.

One day, out in the frozen playground, I found a round, baseball sized, ball of rock-hard ice. I picked it up and tested its weight and solidity. It made me feel secure, so I tucked it inside my mitten. The next time the boy blocked my path I used the ball of ice to threaten him away. I gripped the mitten by the cuff and swung the enclosed ball of ice like it was a club. His response surprised me. He deftly stepped out of the way while reaching out to disarm me. He grabbed the mitten out of my hand then he looked inside, pulled out the ball of ice, gave me a look of hurt and betrayal that cut me to the soul and said, "That was a very bad thing to do."

I can still feel the shame of that moment. The realization that I had attempted to physically harm this quiet young man who had never actually threatened me created a knot in the bottom of my stomach. I realized that day that I didn't ever want to be the kind of person who hurt others.

The boy and I avoided each other after that. Aside from one afternoon, years later, riding tight circles around the park in his snowmobile, we rarely interacted. I think I lost a good friend that day.

My worst fifth grade moment had to do with baggy, soggy winter tights.

In the days before Lycra, hose and tights did not have any intrinsically elastic properties, the only thing holding them in place was the springiness of the knit and if they got at all wet, they became baggy and shapeless. My tights were generally a little large and worn to begin with. After 20 minutes of running around in slush and snow the act of pulling off tall winter boots could tug my tights down far enough to leave several inches of sodden sock flapping past the end of my toes. Squeezing such a floppy toe into dressy shoes was simply impossible.

Most of the students didn't bother to carry shoes to class in the winter. Since they simply wore their snow boots in class they were already back at their desks while I stood in the coat nook trying to figure how on earth I was going to pull my shoes over the long, soggy, tight flaps at the end of my feet. I felt harried and rushed. Since I was the only child still in the closet nook, I guess I also felt I was in a relatively private space.

I turned my back to the classroom, stepped into the back corner of the nook, and discretely tried to pull the soggy tights up as best as I could. Of course, I was still in full view of the rest of the class.

Someone yelled out, "What is she doing?" Someone else added, "Ohhh, is she pulling up her dress?" and "Miss M, make her stop!" I was totally caught out. There was no hope of recovery. Miss M's less than helpful response was to send me to the nurse's office and call Mother to come get me and take me home.

The incident of the baggy tights became the "worst thing I had ever done." I thought it was bad when I had been off by nine cents in my Stewardship and Accounting book but that episode had remained solely between Mother and me.

The incident of the baggy tights was broadcast to everyone. It had been publicly seen in the classroom. Then the school called Mother, who of course told Father. Father chose to chew me out at the dinner table in front of Heather. Heather, not surprisingly, took full advantage of not being the bad child who had to be brought home from school because she "took her clothes off in front of everybody" and taunted me more mercilessly than my classmates.

There was no quarter given, no excuse sufficient, and no viable alternatives offered. One would think that three competent adults could have come up with a safe plan to allow for necessary personal clothing adjustments when changing from boots to shoes.

Father insisted I should have gone to the bathroom and refused to believe me when I tried to explain that the bathroom in our building was off limits because it was for the elementary school children and the bathroom in the middle school wouldn't work because it was in a different building. To use the Grammar School bathroom, I would have had to change back into boots to cross the 20 or so yards of ice-covered pavement between buildings then when I got back to my classroom, I would still have to change my boots for shoes which was, of course, the same problem that caused all the trouble in the first place.

Obviously, I just had an excuse for everything.

No one helped me put together a plan to make things better next time. No one conferred with Miss M to see if we could identify a safe place for adjusting tights. No one even offered boots that were easier to pull on and off; or suggested it might be okay for me to give up wearing dresses in the winter months and just keep my boots on all day; like all the other children.

Mother bluntly accused me of lying. She insisted none of my excuses or challenges were true. Father somberly explained that making public scenes while pretending to be innocent is something bad children do, that it was an attempt to make themselves the center of attention. He said that was why I had undressed in front of all my classmates. He said telling bold faced lies to pretend I was innocent was just another part of the "behavior pattern" and he was too smart for that. No child of his would ever get away with such manipulative behavior.

Feeling Lost

The list of accusations grew. Eventually it fell back into the same old song. I was responsible for the reputation of everyone. My actions reflected onto the reputations of every other member of the family. We had moved all this way to give us a fresh start, but I was still a shameful, disobedient child. I brought shame on everybody. I brought shame on our family, on my father and his professional status, on his workplace, on our church…

It didn't matter that I believed I was doing the best I could. Mother and Father both continued to insist that I actually did these things deliberately. I was told that if I was really honest and thought about it hard enough, I would see that they were right, I would have to admit that deep down, I wanted to cause drama, that I sought out actions that I could pretend were innocent, when they really weren't. This was my pattern. It had always been my pattern. Social workers and professionals had a name for it. It was called "passive aggressive." It was the kind of thing a bad child would do to "get attention." Seeking attention; good, bad, or indifferent was the mark of a sinful, passive aggressive child.

I have never felt so utterly trapped and alone. I tried to do better. I tried to look deep inside myself and understand why I had such a need to make bad things happen. My parents were wise and Godly adults. If they said there was sin and/or evil in me that caused me to do bad things, then it must be true. If I could find the sin in me, hopefully I could make it go away, hopefully I could cleanse it. If I could do that then I wouldn't be bad anymore and all the bad things would stop happening and our family could be happy, and we could love each other, and life would be so much better. I really wanted to find the bad part of me so I could make it go away and make everybody's life better but if there was any sin in me it was buried so deep I couldn't find it.

Was I evil? Was there some dark mark on my soul that made everyone around me do bad things? What could I do? How could I find it and make it go away? How could I make the bad things stop?

I didn't want to be evil. I didn't like to see people hurt. I had realized that when the boy told me I could have hurt someone with the ball of ice in my mitten. In that moment I understood that I absolutely didn't want to hurt another person. I was not someone who could ever deliberately set out to hurt someone else. Yes, I felt ashamed of myself because he told me I had done a bad thing, but I felt even worse when I realized he was right, when I realized I could have really harmed someone, and that this boy who made me nervous and afraid was actually nice enough to explain my error and walk away without telling anyone. The thought of hurting another person created a heavy lump in the pit of my stomach.

How was it that even as a person who never wanted to see people hurt, even as someone who genuinely wanted to be a good person and interact well with others, I couldn't get rid of the evil blackness that lived in my soul?

I was ten. I was the weird kid, from the weird, far-away place, with the weird family and the weirder religion. I was being bullied at home, bullied at school, and molested in the afternoons. There didn't seem to be a safe space anywhere in my world.

I was also dauntless. I knew I could do better, wanted to do better, and kept trying to figure out how to do better. I was learning about other people and social pressure and how to interact, how to take turns, how to share, how to listen and, hopefully someday, how to be heard.

This was all the harder because I was an outsider in a small, insular community. Worse, I was from a dysfunctional family who didn't know how to support each other and were horribly self-righteous, always looking to point out the flaws of everyone else.

I knew that God loved my Father and that he was a holy person. I knew that God loved Mother and didn't want her to be angry all the time. I knew that God loved Miss M and didn't want me to be such a constant irritant to her. I knew that God loved Edith and Vance and had sent Heather and me to live near them so we could visit them and they wouldn't be lonely all the time.

I had been taught to ask God for help. I had been taught that if you were a pure and righteous person God would always be there and as long as you asked with pure intentions, humility, and sincerity, God would help. But no matter how I tried to be good and do what my elders taught me to do, I was still evil.

I knew I was evil because Mother was always angry at me and when she got angry, it was always my fault. She told me so, over and over again. If I didn't know what I had done to make her angry, or if I hadn't intended to make her angry when she said I did, I would try to say so. I would cry that I hadn't done anything wrong and I absolutely did not deliberately try to make her angry. But she still insisted her anger was my fault and that I always knew exactly what to do, and when, and how, to make her lose her temper. If she didn't have a specific act to refer to, she would just say that I 'pushed' her and that pushing her was how I used my 'passive aggressiveness.' She would scream at me and insist that no matter how hard I tried to pretend I was innocent, she knew better.

We lived more than a thousand miles away from the nearest relative. We were strangers in our community. There were no trusted aunts or family friends for me to turn to. Mother blamed me. Father supported Mother. My teacher was her own hostile entity and the 'kind old' couple across the street included a pedophile and his enabler.

All I could do was pray, but no matter how hard I tried to do better and how much I asked God to help me nothing ever changed. I knew I didn't want to be evil. I was sure of it. It seemed to me that I put much more effort into being good than other people did. How come God still loved everyone else, no matter how often they failed to be good and perfect, but God couldn't love me?

Why did God forgive everybody else, even when they were just awful, and never apologized about their behavior or even admitted they could do better. Why didn't God ever help me? Why was I so evil that God could never forgive me?

I would keep trying. I really would try to listen to all the grownups in my life. I believed that as long as a person wanted to be good and do good, and if they loved God and asked him to guide them, then God would help them. I wanted to be good. I really did. I prayed to God to make me a good person. I tried to make goodness the first thing I thought about every day and yet none of it helped. God still didn't love me.

Despite all my praying and all my trying, life just seemed to go from bad to worse.

One day, after stepping off the bus and watching it pull away, I found myself surrounded by all of my girlfriends from the Hacker School gang of the summer before. I tried to step aside but I was surrounded. One girl stepped up and asked why I had to be so weird all the time. She said no one liked me anymore and they all wanted me to know it. This was followed by several minutes of pushing, shoving, and name calling. My bag and schoolbooks were pulled away and scattered in the snowy street. My trumpet case was thrown across the road and the instrument dented. Most importantly, this group of friends; girls who had joyously shared the summer with me; who had filled the seats and sleeping bags at my birthday party only six weeks after moving into town; these girls, these one-time friends, wanted to make it very clear that they were not my friends anymore. They did not like me. They did not like anyone else who liked me. They wanted to make their message clear to me and everyone else. I was weird. I was an outsider. I did not belong.

I walked the one block home from the bus stop cold and heartsick. I tried to explain what had happened to Mother. Her only response was to sing the jingle, "Sticks and stones may break my bones, but words will never hurt me."

She didn't teach me this in a warm loving way. It wasn't a silly song accompanied with a hug designed to make me laugh and feel better. Mother seemed to think this was a talisman, as if throwing out the singsong phrase would magically stop the bullies in their tracks, cause them to hang their heads in shame and walk away. If it didn't work, if her silly phrase wasn't enough to call off a whole pack of mean girls, well, it was just one more example of how I never managed to do anything right.

There was one other significant experience that year. I developed mysterious, periodic, abdominal pain. This was not the pain of colitis from the previous year. These cramps were lower. They were not related to any activity or physical position I could identify. They would simply begin and end for no discernable reason, like an unbidden monster trying to claw its way out from behind my hip bones. I could not hide these pains. I couldn't grit my teeth and suck air while waiting for them to pass. They would catch me unaware and leave me literally writhing on the floor crying in anguish.

After several episodes my father bundled me into the car and took me off to a local doctor. He walked me into the hospital where he worked and into the office of one of the two medical doctors in town. It was after dinner on a cold dark winter night. I don't think any phone calls were made. My father just walked us into the hospital. I suspect he knew that Dr. P was on duty that night. As director of the Mental Health ward my father would have known the schedule.

In any case, we walked into Dr. P's office. We talked for a few minutes. Dr P poked at a couple of spots in and around my stomach and declared that I did not have appendicitis. As for the cause of these mysterious pains he postulated that I was entering the early stages of menarche. He thought maybe my ovaries were 'ripening.'

Determining that I did not have appendicitis did nothing to elevate or mitigate the pain, but it seemed to be enough to satisfy Father. He had taken minimal steps to ensure I wasn't going to die for lack of medical attention. His conscious was clear.

There were no other attempts to identify what was wrong. I continued to suffer regular episodes, but no one ever even seemed to notice. No one ever asked me to describe the pain. No one helped me figure out when it was likely to occur, or what might have triggered it. No one offered hot water bottles or Tylenol or aspirin. In fact, no one ever seemed to notice them again not even when I suffered attacks right in front of them.

To this day I don't have an explanation. The pain was intense. It started and stopped at seemingly random intervals. As I sit here describing it, I can feel an unbidden shadow of those long-ago wrenching spasms.

Lifelines

In the midst of all the other challenges I need to pause and shift focus to a couple of good things. These were positive experiences that helped me find the strength to stay sane and persevere.

First on this list is the librarian at our local public library.

The house in Maine was less than half a block from the local library. I only had to walk past the house next door, past one empty lot, and around the side of the building to be at the Carnegie Library in our small town.

When we left Michigan, I was about two years ahead of my reading level but, despite being in the highest grade in my Elementary school, I always found good reading options at the school library. Sadly, in my first Maine school the options were more limited and targeted to younger readers. For the second half of fourth grade I contented myself with Thornton W. Burgess books. If asked I would have told you they were 'Baby Books' better suited to second graders, but they kept me focused and out of Mothers way during the long cold evenings and weekends of that first Maine winter. I often read through a whole volume in a single evening and on the weekends made a game out of seeing how many I could finish.

We moved to our new home on the first of July so the school library was not an option but there was the town library, literally within shouting distance of the house. I don't think it took me 24 hours to make my first visit.

The librarian showed me to the children's room which was warm and sunny. There were a couple of child sized tables adjacent to a bank of encyclopedias and other reference books.

Father had purchased a set of Encyclopedia Britannica for graduate school with the expectation that they would continue to serve Heather and I through our school years. Advanced or not, the experience of wading through entries in Encyclopedia Britannica at the age of eight, or even ten, with the goal of writing your very first report, is impossibly daunting.

I tried to ask for more age-appropriate material. I suggested the Farmer's Almanac or the Lincoln Library, but the answer was always no. Mother insisted they had spent good money to provide us with the best encyclopedia, and I was absolutely going to use it. It didn't matter to her that each of the volumes weighed half as much as I did, that the oversized pages were filled with transparently thin paper, covered with print in the world's smallest font, and prose written by British academics. Once or twice, she had tried to read from one herself in order to help with the assignment by translating the entry, but after a few minutes she became frustrated, put the book down and told me I could handle it on my own.

What a miracle it was to find an inviting study area stocked with full sets of both World Book and Encyclopedia Americana as well as the Lincoln Library, and even a long row of Farmers Almanacs! I never bothered with Encyclopedia Britannica again. Since I didn't ask for other books, or even bother to tell Mother that I was going to the library to do my schoolwork, she didn't know and didn't care that I had found an alternative to her impossibly high-brow reference books.

On that first visit I looked hopefully at the children's fiction for books from the Boxcar series by Gertrude Chandler Warner. (This was the original Boxcar series suitable for children of 10 and up. It was later republished for a younger audience.) When the librarian asked if she could help, I told her that I had started reading the series before we left Michigan and was hoping to read the rest of them. She apologized but said she did not know about that author or the series. I believe I left that day with one or two Thornton W Burgess volumes I had not yet read, and my first Nancy Drew.

A week or two later when I visited again, my friendly librarian came out from behind the desk to greet me. She was excited and wanted to show me the new books in the display case by the door. There, behind the glass was the full series of Boxcar Children books. She wanted to know which ones I had been looking for. I told her I was happy she had found them, and I would be grateful to read them if they were ever available for circulation. I was thrilled to see the books but sad that they were locked inside a glass case, like a beautiful object in a museum that you were supposed to view and admire but never, ever, touch. I didn't understand that she had ordered them for me. She had looked up the series and purchased a full set. I cannot express my awe as she unlocked the glass case and handed me a brand new, crisp, clean smelling, volume of the Boxcar Children.

I am sad to say that I do not remember this woman's name. She was a surprise ally in a challenging world. She encouraged and guided my reading list for the next six years. I was a child and didn't understand the value of her support. By the time I realized how much I had to thank her for I was a young woman living a different life in a different part of the country and had no way to reach back. She is on my list for the afterlife. I look forward to finding her and telling her how much she meant to a troubled and lonely child.

Fifth grade finally ended, and the long, beautiful days of northern summers returned. Father decided that we should take a trip back to Michigan. He probably hoped it would do Mother some good. At some point in the planning Mother decided to also let me visit my paternal grandparents in Montana. She had worked out that if they dropped me off at O'Hare, in Chicago, I could fly direct to Great Falls. Since I wouldn't have to change planes, she was willing to let me fly as an unaccompanied ten-year-old minor.

Wow! What I cool surprise! I had no idea it was even possible to wish for such a trip. I didn't bother to consider how I would get home. There were certainly no direct flights from Montana to Presque Isle. The nearest full-service airport was Bangor. As if even a direct flight from Great Falls, MT to Bangor, ME would ever be a thing.

But Mother had worked this out too. I could fly direct from Great Falls to Detroit, and we had friends there. My friend Amy and her family wanted to come visit us in Maine, so Mother arranged to have me fly 'home' to Detroit and join Amy's family for the road trip to Maine. Wow again! I loved Amy and I always felt safe and cozy with her mom and dad.

It was a wonderful summer! I spent three weeks in Montana being spoiled by grandparents who hadn't seen me since grade school. It would be the only time I ever spent with just them. I am grateful for every minute of it. They spoiled me with restaurant food and creamsicles every night after dinner. I snuggled on the couch at night with Grandma, watching scary movies that I would never have been allowed to stay up for if I was at home. They drove me out to the ranches of Great-uncles and aunts where I rode horses and bottle-fed baby calves (who were bigger than me).

Horseback on my Great Aunt and Uncle's ranch in Montana.

I felt valued, safe, and loved.

When those three weeks were over, I moved on to another adventure. I flew from Montana to Detroit where Amy's family greeted me and brought me with them on their trip to visit my family in Maine.

Amy's mom & dad had a pull camper. They took their time on road trips driving for only five or six hours a day, then finding a "Kampground" of America (KOA) to spend the night. KOAs were wonderful. They provided trailer hookups, big bathhouses and laundry facilities, and always a swimming pool. We ate simple, child friendly foods like SpaghettiOs's and hot dogs, and at the end of the day I snuggled up with my life-long friend and slept in a cozy camper with sounds of the outdoors all around us.

Back at Home

Amy's mom and dad were good friends of my parents and Mother was especially excited to see them again. She wanted to show off our new house and all the beautiful and wild places around it.

Our last visit from Amy's family had ended badly. They had come to visit the last summer we were in Marquette. We took them camping in a wild and beautiful, undeveloped site along the south shore of Lake Superior.

Part way through the week Amy's family, including Amy, her Mom and Dad, and a boy of about 13 (he was the son of friends and was enjoying this trip with them) headed out as a group to hike a trail we recommended.

This is not really my story to tell, so I will stick to the abbreviated version. At one point the rough trail crossed a stream by way of a beaver dam. This is where Amy's father lost his footing, one leg went through the dam, pitching him sideways and shattering his hip as he fell. The rest of the story is as harrowing as any wilderness rescue tale you have ever heard. His leg was hopelessly wedged, and he had landed with his head below the water line. Amy, at eight was too young to send for help. Her Mom was crouched in the water to hold her husbands' head up out of the water. If she left him, he would drown. Any hope of rescue was in the hands of a thirteen-year-old, a city boy in an unfamiliar environment. Sadly, I don't even remember his name.

It was about two miles from the bever dam to the trailhead and the trailhead was another nine miles from our campsite. I think he ran the whole way.

I have always been amazed that he found his way back to camp at all. I remember seeing him jogging down the road towards our tent. I remember listening as he explained to my father what had happened. There was a hurried conversation between Mother and Father. Then Father and the boy drove away leaving Mother, Heather, and me alone, at our wilderness campsite, with nothing to do but sit and worry.

All in all, it took over twelve hours to rescue our friend. There was no helicopter, just a stretcher carried by firemen and my father's Jeep driven down a too steep embankment with the help of a firetruck and a winch. And, of course, a friendship stressed by fear, trauma, and lots of rehabilitation.

Then there are the parts of the story I have never known. They replaced his hip with a metal pin, advanced surgery for 1972. I think the procedure took place in Detroit. Amy's mother didn't drive. How did they get home? How did she get back and forth to the hospital to visit him? Every bit of the experience would have been a major challenge.

We, Amy's family, and mine, needed a happier visit this time.

Two events conspired to make this follow-on visit to Maine almost as much of a train wreck as the earlier one in Michigan.

The first was, supposedly, caused by me. It was Sunday morning. In Maine we held church services in our house. This would be the day we introduced our Detroit friends to the handful of church members we had found in our new home.

Mother was upstairs working on her hair and makeup, and I needed a moment from her. I needed an answer. I do not remember the exact question, just that it had something to do with the preparations I was making for the Sunday dinner that would be served after church. (Yes. BTW. I was ten, and in the kitchen, prepping our Sunday dinner while Mother was upstairs primping.) I was at an impasse and needed an answer from her in order to continue my task.

She was, of course, agitated. She told me to leave her alone. I persisted. I just needed a simple answer. I was trying to complete the task she had given me, but I was still ten and I didn't know how to handle this part. I also knew that if I didn't get it right, I would hear about how I ruined an important Sunday dinner with special company for at least the next year.

We circled.

"Please, I just have one question."

"No! I don't have time right now."

"But I don't know how you want me to do this." We circled again.

I knew that if I didn't get an answer and didn't make the 'right' choice I would pay for it later. I just needed one answer.

She will tell you that I "pushed" her. She will say that I always knew just when and how to push her buttons. Apparently, I did, even if I had no desire to do so. We circled again, but this time she spun out of control. This wasn't a standard blow up. She lost all control of sense, reason, and civility. It was like the Stewardship and Accounting book except this time it was in front of witnesses.

She showed the very worst of herself in front of the best friends she had.

I doubt the screaming lasted more than 30 minutes or so, but it was enough to put everyone on eggshells for the rest of the visit.

The second event occurred a day or two later and came from Amy's father.

The house in Maine had a two car, detached garage with beautifully detailed, multipaneled carriage doors. Specifically, it was a two-car garage with a set of two carriage doors for each car; four doors in all, each with multiple panels, like fancy barn doors with a red background and shiny white cross bars forming an 'X on the bottom half of each door, plus multiple layers of additional trim on each panel. Mother had made it a project to paint those doors to match the sage green she had chosen for the house. She carefully highlighted all of the trim detail in bright white. It looked beautiful. It took a lot of work.

We had been out on a multi-family outing, all of us in our Jeep. (Four adults and three children in a six-passenger vehicle didn't raise any eyebrows in 1973.) For some reason Amy's father was behind the wheel. I suspect he may have just wanted to test four-wheel drive. Whatever the reason, he was the one driving. We arrived home and stopped three or four feet shy of the garage, as needed to swing open a set of carriage doors.

There was a pause as people started to shift in their seats and reach for door handles, etc. and then the car jumped forward! It lurched just far enough to ram right through those doors and at just the right angle to take out the center pole as well as the second set of doors before stopping just barely inside the garage, with shattered pieces of prettily painted doors scattered all around.

What happened? How did it happen? We never got a good answer. Something was said about the hip, the one with the pin in it, from the previous vacation catastrophe. Maybe it had twinged or caused him to jerk. But we had just come to a full stop. Shouldn't his foot have been on the brake rather than the gas?

In any case the relationship between Amy's family and mine would never be the same again and it had all started with me, pushing mother's buttons… She never forgave me. I mean this literally. She would bring that visit up again and again, decade after decade. I was the one who made her lose control. I destroyed her relationship with her best friends…

I remember visiting my parents as a thirty-year-old. I was recently divorced and heartbroken. I was working as a waitress, scrimping to pay my own rent along with graduate school tuition. The flights alone had cost almost a full month's rent, and the visit meant a week with no work and thus no income. I chose to spend the time and money to visit because that is what people do. People do what it takes, they sacrifice as needed to remain in each other's lives. And now here I was, trapped in the backseat of my parent's car listening to Mother detail her way through every imagined deliberate and malicious act, including how I ruined the only friendship she ever had.

Twenty years later and I was still the one who ruined everything.

Sixth Grade: Hairy Arms, Time to Grow up

There was one more item of note that summer. I grew body hair. I was ten and slightly small for my age. Puberty was a couple of years away but something within me decided it was time to grow hair. It was horribly embarrassing. My arms and legs went from smooth and childlike to softly furred. The hair on my arms was denser than on my father's. It's my theory that by ten I had developed all the body hair follicles I would ever have. As I aged and grew those follicles would spread out over my larger body but as a child they were densely packed on my smaller frame.

I begged to be allowed to shave my legs, but Mother insisted I wait until I was thirteen. Everything was supposed to wait until I was thirteen. At thirteen I would magically transform into a young woman. I would be able to shave, wear make-up, and bras. This was the natural order of things.

Grandma, back in Montana had been kinder but not any more helpful. She once tried to comfort me by reaching across the kitchen table, stroking my hairy forearm, and telling me my hair was beautiful and soft like fur!

Heather and I hadn't seen much of Edith and Vance over the summer. The whole family had traveled to Michigan. During my trip to Montana, Mother, Father and Heather took a leisurely road trip back to Maine. They took the southern route this time, driving along the southern shores of the smaller Great Lakes; Huron, Erie and Ontario. They visited the White Mountains of New Hampshire and subsequently spent a couple of weeks in a friend's summer cabin on the Maine coast. Once everyone made it home, we were occupied hosting Amy and her family.

When we finally managed a trip across the street Vance put his legs up in his recliner and lit the cone of incense just like he always had but he didn't ask me to sit on his lap or feel the horrible lump in his pants. Instead, he said we needed to talk. I listened politely to his little speech. He told me that I was growing up and that my life was going to be full of new and different things and that this would change the relationship between us. I had no idea what message he was trying to get across. Wasn't I always growing? What made this day, this week, this season, or this year any different than any other time?

My birthday passed and the new school year started. I was in 6th grade, Junior High in our school district. The school was an imposing gray brick building less than half a mile from home. I wanted to be excited about going to a big kid's school, but I was transitioning from the oldest class at the Grammar School to the youngest, and physically smallest, class in Jr. High. I had heard too many horror stories about how the eighth graders treated the wet-behind-the-ears sixth graders. However, like most stories these were overly exaggerated. In the end I never once witnessed an eight-grader shaking down a sixth grader for lunch money, forcing a younger child to carry his or her books, or any other form of hazing, but leading up to the first day of school all I had to go on were terrible rumors.

At the end of my first day of sixth grade I walked home, dropped off my schoolbooks, and told Mother I was going across the street to visit Edith and Vance, just as I had done every day the year before. I walked across the street but didn't even get inside the house. Edith met me at the door and explained that Heather, who now got out of school earlier in the afternoon than I did, was already there. She and Vance had decided to do something different and gone away somewhere else. They hadn't bothered to wait for me.

This was different and unexpected. I had never known Vance to go anyplace other than the golf course. Edith didn't drive so she relied on female friends to take her to the hair salon and grocery store. Vance didn't even leave the house to help her with shopping. In over six years the only place he ever went was to the local golf club.

I asked where they had gone. Should I meet them there? Should I wait for them to come back? Would Edith rather I stay and help her in the kitchen? The answers were no, no, and no. Before I could work out what was happening the door had closed and I was standing alone on the front porch.

I was more confused than hurt. I walked back across the narrow street and into my house. Mother asked why I had come back and I relayed Edith's message. Mother's only response was simply a disinterested "hmm."

Things continued like this for the next week or two. I would go across the street every day after school. Edith would explain that I had "missed them" as if things would somehow be different if I could only get out of school ten minutes earlier, and Mother would shrug disinterestedly when I came back home.

The amount of time Heather spent with Vance began to increase. One day there was a phone call asking if Heather could stay through dinner. Within another week or so Heather was staying through dinner with Edith and Vance almost every night. This bothered me. There had never been a single dinner invitation when I was visiting. Why was Heather getting so much special attention?

Heather took advantage of my hurt feelings and twisted the knife at every possible opportunity. Vance had showed her places in the house and in the multi vehicle shed (a holdover from his working days) that I had never visited. However, her attitude did not do much to upset me. We were not a family that ever supported or expressed concern for each other. Yes, I felt like she was being a snot, but I was also enjoying the unexpected opportunity to do whatever I chose in the after-school hours.

The milk shed which was off to the side of E & Vs house, was an old sagging building of tired gray wood that did not retain any indication of having ever been painted. It was literally condemned, a status confirmed by the remnants of a tattered notice that had been nailed to the exterior years before. Mother, despite having no concern for her children's welfare when it came to spending copious unsupervised time with questionable adults, was very tuned-in to the hazards of a tired structurally unsound building and had made us promise to never, ever, go inside.

For reasons I never thought about and would not have understood if I did, I respected her wishes but only with respect to this particular building. Our rural community was dotted with all kinds of vacant buildings, particularly tired old, abandoned barns and vacant, neglected houses that had once housed farm help before becoming unneeded or simply falling into disrepair. As children, alone or in groups, exploring these buildings was a favorite pastime. We didn't just wander in to look around. We played in them. We chased each other in and out through the vacant doors and windows. We climbed way up into the rafters. I remember looking down once, from high in the rafters of a friend's barn. I was higher than I realized. I was at least three stories up, looking down on tractors and farm equipment parked on a cement floor. I realized that a fall could likely kill me. I paused for a minute, but my friend was getting away, so I stopped looking down and continued our game of tag in the rafters.

Mother had only ever denied me this one building and although I could never have told you why, I took her warning very seriously.

Vance never seemed to worry about his condemned building. On nice summer days he liked to open one of the vehicle bays and practice his putting. He had a rug of fake green grass that he rolled out into the drive. He would stand in the shade just inside the door and putt golf balls towards a tin can near the end of the "green."

On any nice day you could count on finding him there. He would ask if I wanted to play too. But I never said "Yes." I didn't want to step across the threshold into that building. I never ever wanted to go in there and I didn't think I ever had.

One day, sometime after I grew hair all over my body, and moved up to Jr. High, after Vance and Heather started doing special, secret things without me... One day I came home from school and Mother told me we needed to make a trip to the next town over. She wanted both Heather and I to come with her. She asked me to go across the street to Edith and Vance's to get Heather and bring her home.

I knocked on the door and asked Edith to tell me where Heather and Vance were so I could take her home. Edith explained, as she had done every day since the start of the school year, that Heather and Vance were someplace else, but today her answer wasn't sufficient. I had to get my sister and bring her home. Edith said maybe they were in the shed. I didn't like this answer. Why would Heather ever go into that awful shed?

The door was open to the first vehicle bay, just like so many times before. I stood just outside and tried to look in. I couldn't see anyone. Surely, they wouldn't have gone so far inside that I couldn't see them. I called my sister's name. I waited, but no one answered. I called again, and again. Finally, I heard something, shuffling and hushed voices like someone was trying to hide. I called louder. They were in there. I could hear them. Why would they pretend they couldn't hear me?

I was becoming increasingly anxious. I was afraid. I was terrified. I called out again. "You have to come out. Mother says you have to come home."

Vance's voice answered back. "Don't come in here."

I called for my sister again, "Please! You have to." I was pleading. I was trembling.

At some point I had stepped part way over the threshold. It was like walking into a pressure wall. An invisible force was fighting me, pushing me back and down. I couldn't move forward. I couldn't back away. There was a heavy weight pressing down on my shoulders. I could feel my knees giving out as it pushed me to the ground. What had happened to the air? Why couldn't I breathe? Why was everything around me going black?

How long? How long did I stand frozen in place, crying for my sister and unable to do anything more?

It took several minutes. Vance kept telling me not to come back there. Heather was saying something, but I couldn't tell what. They were in the one-time office where Vance had kept his records; routes, inventory, and pay records from his milkman days. I remembered the office with its writing stool and slanted table bolted to the wall.

How did I know this?

I had never been in there! Had I? The door to the office was just back and over to the left. I tried to look towards it, but I wasn't far enough inside to see around the corner. How did I know it was there?

They needed time and get all their clothes back on.

Why would they have their clothes off?

How did I know all these things?

I couldn't move. I couldn't breathe. I couldn't do anything other than stand there sobbing for them to come out.

It felt like forever. And then it was over. Heather came out from the office, and we walked across the street and got into our car and drove away with Mother. Like nothing ever happened.

I had never even seen Vance.

Heather Smelled Bad

Nothing changed. The school year continued on. Heather visited Vance every day and I was free to do whatever I pleased.

Heather became increasingly withdrawn and expressed a number of petty complaints. One was that her underwear hurt. She insisted it was too tight. If I had made such a complaint, I am sure I would have only been laughed at, but Mother treated Heather differently. She threw out all the old underwear and replaced them with a larger size. When Heather still complained she replaced them again. I was eleven, Heather was only seven and smaller than I had been at her age, but one day while folding laundry I noticed that her, new again, underwear was now larger than mine.

This only added to my bitter feelings of jealousy. Heather was getting all kinds of special, alone time with Edith and Vance. Heather only had to ask, and Mother got her new things even if the reason for the request didn't make any sense. It never worked that way for me. When Mother noticed that all my underwear and socks had holes worn through them, she chastised me for being too hard on my things, causing them to wear out too fast.

Her routine tirades on everything wrong with me; her evil, sinful child, became an endless monologue. She was a saint for putting up with such disrespectful, devious, ungrateful child. I was constantly "pushing her buttons" and causing her to lose her temper. She certainly wasn't going to buy me new things in the middle of the school year.

These might seem like petty little complaints, but they are the intimate details that shape our psyches. All Heather had to do was complain and whine. Mother would give her anything she asked for even if she didn't need it, or rather, even though the thing she asked for was not what she actually needed. I, on the other hand, was secretly, deviously, responsible for every little thing that went wrong in our household.

To this day it is hard for me to throw away obviously worn and threadbare socks and underwear. When my husband sees gaping holes in the bottom of my socks, or a waistband that is barely attached to tattered panties, he will tell me I really have to throw them out. In response I have to fight the desire to turn away and hide the offending item. Letting go is so very hard. Never mind the fact that I have enjoyed economic stability for most of my adult life. Never mind the fact that I keep a dresser drawer full of new socks and underwear just to ensure that I never run out. In some deep well of my psyche worn socks and underwear are a symbol of shame and unworthiness. Throwing that symbol away would be the healthy response, but I feel the need to keep them close and to continue wearing them as if doing so is some form of penance that will somehow, eventually, make me worthy.

There was one more element that drove a wedge between Heather and me. She smelled. She smelled bad! She smelled like musty, yeasty, poop!

I could smell her from ten feet away. I could smell her when she stepped across the hall from her room to the bathroom. She had to be doing something horribly sinful and awful to smell that way. Was she playing with her poo? Was she smearing it around like finger paint or mud pies?

So, what about Mother and Father? If I could smell something wrong from the next room, couldn't they smell it too? I know that Mother could. Her olfactory sense and her emotional state have always been closely linked. I know she smelled it. I know it had an impact. I just don't know what that impact was. At this point in her life her own experiences of sexual abuse were still buried beneath the surface. Who knows what her emotional reaction was to Heather's stench. Maybe it had something to do with her out of character willingness to buy set after set of bigger and bigger underwear for her seven-year-old daughter. Maybe, like me, she felt the need to hide her feelings of trauma. Or maybe, maybe she experienced a warped sense of nostalgia from the days before she had blossomed into woman hood only to be rejected by her special friend.

Murderous Intent

In the deep cold of Maine winters and the rapid inflation of gas and heating oil prices in the 1970's it made sense to have more than one means of heating the home. Our house had been built with a centrally positioned, triple flue chimney. Adding a couple of wood stoves seemed like the right move so we closed up the living room fireplace and placed a cast iron, Franklin stove in front of the hearth. The stove sat far enough out into the room to ensure all surfaces were exposed, allowing heat to radiate into the room rather than escape up the chimney. We added a second, smaller, not so pretty, stove in the basement near the laundry.

The addition of wood heat made the house feel warmer and cozier beyond its actual impact on inside temperatures. We discovered that cabinets on the side of the kitchen that backed the chimney remained warm. In response we flipped the kitchen organization. Warming our dry and canned goods didn't seem like a great plan but warm dishes on cold winter days were a very nice thing. On the second-floor blankets and towels stored in the linen closet and shelf that backed to the chimney were also gently warmed.

The living room stove was Fathers. The one in the basement was Mothers. On cold winter mornings I would take my turn in the shower while he was downstairs renewing the fire from remnants of overnight embers. Mother would wait until we all left the house before cleaning out last night's ashes and rebuilding her fire in the basement laundry and stoking her little stove with the contents of all the household waste cans. One day I returned home from school to find Mother shouting and yelling angry words at me before I even walked in the door. What had I done this time?

She was in the basement, in the corner with the laundry, some long-term food storage and our little box stove.

Apparently, I had tried to kill her.

It took several minutes of listening to a long list of what an evil, ungrateful, plotting, vengeful child I was before I got the story of my heinous deed. I had, supposedly, placed an empty aerosol deodorant can in the bathroom waste basket. I had done this with full knowledge and expectation that Mother would unknowingly empty the waste basket into the box stove, the can would then explode. Mother would be killed by the blast and then the house would burn down destroying evidence of my crime and making it all look like an accident.

I was a very calculating, devious, and spiteful child with evil, premeditated, murderous intent.

I tried to plead innocence. I did have a spray can of deodorant, but it wasn't empty, it wasn't even in the house. It was in my gym locker at school. If I had emptied it, why would I carry it home just to throw it away?

Nothing I said mattered. Mother was in such a rage that she barely seemed to realize I was there. Burning household waste was generally a morning task in her routine. She had probably been pacing and yelling at me for hours. The fact that I was home now didn't seem to register. There was no hope of talking her down.

Eventually I gave up and walked away. I could find a quieter, friendlier place to spend my after-school hours.

I couldn't help but wonder, how. How had she missed a spray can of deodorant when emptying a two- or three-quart waste basket, mostly filled with used tissue, into a small box stove? The fire in the box stove burned out overnight. In the mornings Mother would clean out yesterday's ashes and use the paper waste to build a new fire. How could she miss a deodorant can while picking through a small can of trash and selecting the best material to set the fire?

Even if for some reason she had dumped the waste basked into an active fire, how could she miss an aerosol can mixed in with a handful of used Kleenex?

The door at the front of the stove was about 10” by 12“. You could open it to place fuel, like firewood, inside, but to add trash you would have to reach in and deposit one handful at a time. How could she not notice a deodorant spray can?

There were a couple of round burners on top of the stove. These could be lifted off with a detachable handle, kind of like lifting up a manhole cover with a crowbar, but the openings were only about eight inches across. Again, how could she not notice a deodorant can?

If I had made such a mistake while feeding the fire, she would be more irate at me for my reckless lack of attention to detail than she was now for my supposedly, premeditated, murderous intent.

In the end I never learned the answer to any of my questions. The explosion in the box stove was just a one-off event in an otherwise hostile world. It was just another thing.

After I added this story to the list of events worth sharing in this book, I told it to my therapist. Part way through I paused. I realized that this was a story I had never shared. Having never told the story I never gave the reality of the accusation any consideration. I never questioned the existence of the can or whether or not there actually had been an explosion.

Was there a can? If there had been, surely, I would have been presented with the twisted, charred remains. Mother would have enjoyed showing off the evidence of my crime. But I never saw such a thing. No evidence no can. No can no crime. Was the whole thing a lie?

Could it have been something else, maybe a shampoo bottle. Could a plastic bottle have managed to explode before it melted? I will never know.

One day I came home from school to learn I was an attempted murderer but in the end, no one died, no evidence was offered, and, of course, no one ever apologized. Like so many things we never talked about it again.

Mother and Father take a Weekend Away

Early in the school year Mother and Father decided to take a mini vacation, a long weekend away, just the two of them.

Since they would be gone for multiple days, Mother arranged for Heather and me to stay across the street with Edith and Vance. I was excited. I was finally going to be let in on all the secrets. I was going to get to eat breakfast, lunch and dinner at their house. I was finally going to get a glimpse into all of the secret places and activities Heather and Vance had been getting up to without me.

We each put together a small bag of overnight items and walked across the street together. I remember my thoughts and emotions as I climbed the stairs in Edith and Vance's house. I had never been upstairs before. I wanted to know what was up there. I wanted to be included.

Heather was puffed up with the importance of being already in the know. Edith didn't need to show me the room we would sleep in. Heather was already at the end of the hall, claiming her side of a saggy full-sized bed with an orange and yellow flowered spread and showing off other items of interest. She gave particular interest to a colorful, cylindrical, trash can. On top of the can was a plastic mold of a lion's head. It was painted as a circus lion with bright colors and a mouth open wide in a roar. In order to place trash in the can you had to put your hand into the lion's open, roaring mouth.

For much of her life Heather suffered from an irrational fear of large cats. She has never expressed particulars. I am not sure she even knows them. I believe the fear began in that time and place and her only exposure to a large cat was proximity to a colorful trashcan with a roaring lions head for a cover, in the spare bedroom of the house across the street, the house of her abuser.

I should have all kinds of memories from that weekend. I walked in full of curiosity and questions.

Was it really true that the only plumbing in the house was limited to the cold-water kitchen tap and the flush toilet under the stairs? I absolutely expected to find a perfectly fine bathroom hidden up there.

What would Edith cook us for dinner? What about breakfast? She was a much better cook than mother. Maybe I would learn some new recipes.

What evening TV shows did they like?

What about the fun stories Mother and Father would share when they got home from their trip?

These are just samplings of the things I should remember. In a better world I would tell you about all the exciting activities we shared and how much fun we had.

In the real world I cannot tell you anything. I cannot tell you anything because I don't remember anything. I remember climbing the stairs. I remember Heather running ahead and taking full advantage of showing off that she had been there first. I remember stepping into the small bedroom at the front of the house. I saw a window, a bed with a flowered spread, and a colorful trash can with a lion's mouth...

And then there is nothing.

I have no recollection of battles over space in a shared bed, of the meals we shared, of conversations, of activities... I have no recollection of Mother and Father coming home. In fact, I don't have any memories for the entire rest of the school year!

It took me a full week to write the above passage. During that time I tried to remember other things from that year.

Whose farm did I work for Fall harvest?

What about school? It was my first year of Jr. High; the first year in a new school. There are so many things I should remember. It was the first year of different teachers for different subjects. My first experience of carrying books from class to class.

I can bring to mind a parade of schoolteachers starting with kindergarten and all the way through high school, except for sixth grade. I can see the faces of my English, Social Studies, Math and Science teachers from seventh and eighth grade, but sixth grade was the first year in that school. Those are the teachers who should have made the most impact. Why can't I remember them?

So much was new and different. It should have been exciting. I should have made so many memories. Until now I have shared stories of each school year. In my mind I can identify specific memories from kindergarten all the way to high school graduation, with the single glaring exception of sixth grade. Why can't I find them?

Much like the big black hole in my memories from the first year at Reunion in northern Michigan, all I have is an awareness of a gaping void. I don't even know how long this one lasted. There are no easy to date follow-on activities like my birthday, medical visits, or the county fair. All I know is that I walked into that room and my mind simply shut down.

Where did I go in those times of blackouts and how long did this one last?

Heather Tells

Maine winter was melting into spring and Heather was nearing her eighth birthday, time for her to be baptized.

Years later Heather would explain that she knew she had to tell before she was baptized because she understood that what Vance was making her do was a sin and she was afraid that if she allowed herself to be baptized when she was doing things she knew to be a sin, God would kill her!

Of course, none of this was on my radar. I still don't know what my focus was that year or where I was spending my time. I am pretty sure I wasn't spending time with Edith and Vance. Vance was focused on Heather so I was left to myself and I wasn't paying attention to what was going on in Heather's life.

I was alone in my room one afternoon and completely unprepared when Mother, sounding extremely irate, shouted for me to come downstairs "NOW!"

Mother and Heather were standing in the dining room. Odd. We never hung out in the dining room. Heather was tightlipped and on the verge of tears. Mother, holding herself with a dangerous stillness, turned to me and asked, "What have you done?"

"Huh?"

She continued. "Your sister tells me that Vance has been touching her!"

"Um?" I didn't understand. What was she complaining about? Heather visited Vance every day. Of course, there was touching. There were hello and goodbye hugs, occasional pats... what was wrong with touching?

She continued. *"Your sister says that Vance took her into the bathroom, took down her pants and rubbed himself against her!"*

I was still confused. My mind had nothing but questions. What? Why? What a bazaar thing to do!

His behavior, as she described it seemed wrong but to me it was wrong like strange, not wrong like bad. I was eleven. Sex was not my first thought. I had a confusing image in my mind of two people rubbing bare bellies together. It was a strange thing to do but not something to get so upset about.

Next, Mother demanded to know if he had ever behaved that way with me. My mind went immediately to the mysterious lump and how it was right there on his belly. I could feel him gripping my wrist and pressing my clenched knuckles into that rigid lump in his lap. Was there a connection between these? Could I get an explanation? Please? Please help me understand!

Mother's face was inches from mine. Her rage was all consuming. She insisted I tell her what I had done. I tried to explain that sometimes Vance did things I didn't understand. I wanted to tell her that I was afraid he had cancer and he was dying.

How could I explain? It seemed like anything I said would only make her angrier? Finally, I said "Sometimes he does strange things that I don't like and I don't understand, but I usually just pull away."

I didn't get to say anything more. I didn't get to ask any questions. Mothers screaming rage was at full boil and I was the only target. Heather was gone. She had obviously taken advantage of an opportunity to bolt out of the room. I tried to back towards the doorway, but she circled around and trapped me, one shoulder barely into the opening and my back pressed up against the solid frame of the door.

Once again everything was my fault.

Why hadn't I protected my sister? Maybe I was big enough and strong enough to pull away, but I should have known enough to protect my little sister. How could I let this happen? Didn't I understand what he had done to her?

No! No, I didn't.

Vance never acted strangely with me when Heather was around. He only did strange things when he and I were alone. How could I know what happened when the two of them were off doing something special, when I wasn't ever included and in fact I was literally told to go away?

Mother never seemed to care or worry that my daily visits had been reduced to a few seconds standing outside the screen door as Edith told me to go back home. If Mother didn't care about what we did at Vance and Edith's house how was I supposed to know that there was any reason to protect anyone?

I wanted to ask questions. What did his behavior mean? Didn't Mother understand that I hadn't been welcome at Edith and Vance's house for most of the year? Hadn't she seen me come back home day after day? Hadn't she heard me tell her that Vance and Heather were off by themselves, and they didn't want me there? How was I supposed to be there protecting her when I didn't know where she was or what they were doing?

To this day, Mother continues to insist on two things; one, she had no way of knowing what was happening between Heather and Vance, and two; I was the one responsible for protecting my sister. I am the one to blame.

I didn't understand anything. I begged for answers but all I got was rage. *Heather's life was RUINED! It was totally ruined!* This could never be fixed. She would never be okay again. *And it was absolutely all my fault!*

Much like the nine cents, this episode went on and on. I spent hours trapped, the hard edge of the doorway digging into my shoulder blades. Nothing I said or did mattered. At some point I think Mother stopped realizing I was still there. I wasn't her living breathing child, I was just an object, a focal point for her rage. She couldn't really see me or hear my sobs and questions.

Unlike the episode with the nine cents, this time she made it clear she *would* be telling Father when he came home.

Finally, his arrival imminent, I was told to go upstairs, think about what I had done, wash the tears off my face and wait until I was called to come back down.

After Father came home, I could hear the two of them talking for what seemed like a long time. Finally, they called for Heather and me.

Father was cold and grave. He wasn't the sort to erupt in fiery rage like Mother. His anger was cold and still or sometimes white and hot with righteous indignation.

He asked if we knew of any other children who visited Edith and Vance.

I thought this was a stupid question. Wasn't that the point? Edith and Vance supposedly didn't have any grandchildren to visit them (even though we all knew this wasn't true). Wasn't that why we went there every day? They were lonely. They were 'ostracized.' Wasn't that why we were told that visiting them and developing 'special relationships' was our 'ministry?' I had so many questions I wanted to ask but I wasn't allowed to say anything.

We were given new rules. We were told not to visit by ourselves anymore. We were to use a buddy method.

It was still my responsibility to keep my little sister safe. I was blamed again for not protecting her. None of this would have happened if I had protected her the way I was supposed to.

The buddy rule seemed to make Heather feel better, but I thought it was pretty stupid. It wasn't my fault that Heather got out of school before I did. It wasn't my fault that she never waited for me to get home before going to visit Edith and Vance. It certainly wasn't my fault that when I did get home Vance and Heather were always away doing something 'special' and Edith always turned me away. How could this be my fault when she was the one who told me to go home, day after day?

What was I supposed to do? How could I change any of this?

Father asked us if we knew of any other children who visited Edith and Vance. He made us promise to tell him if we ever saw other children visit them. He said this in his best grave and serious voice. He stressed it and repeated it several times. If we knew of any *other* children visiting them, we had to let him know, because if *other* children were at risk, he would have to call the police.

That was the end of it. Heather and I would use the buddy method and tell him if any other children ever went into the house. I remember staring at him for a moment. I feel like my mouth must have been hanging open. I still didn't understand what had happened, but one thing was clear, as long as the only children at risk were Heather and me, then my parents wouldn't do anything. If at any time any other child went to visit Edith and Vance, then we were supposed to tell Father so he could call the police and apparently make sure no bad things happened to other children.

In my mind I tried to understand. Whatever this was about, it was really bad. Except that since it only happened to us, it was actually not so bad after all. Still, it was important for us to keep watch and make sure it never happened to any other child because if that happened to anyone else, we would have to do things to protect *them*.

And, of course, all the old horror stories of what would happen if we ever told, still hung over our heads. People would think that we were a bad family and by extension our church and Father's mental health clinic were also bad. No one would get to know Jesus through us so the lives of those (theoretical) people, as well as the lives of all the theoretical people those people would share Jesus with, would be ruined. Father could lose his job, we could lose our home…

Again, as usual, there was no help or support for Heather or me. We weren't given any access to medical or emotional care. We weren't asked any more questions or allowed to even talk about what we had experienced, much less ask for explanations. Clearly the really bad thing didn't actually matter if it only happened to Heather or me. And even though I still didn't understand what I had done to ruin Heather's life (*her whole life*), now I was responsible for every other child who might ever go into that house!

My only solace was that I knew no other children went into that house, ever. Obviously, Father knew this too. He knew he didn't have to worry about other children. I was pretty sure he had just made that part up. It was a way to pretend he could be brave enough to talk to the police, but only if this thing that never, ever, happened actually did.

We were wrong. Of course we were wrong. Pedophilia is not for the faint of heart. Anyone willing to enter those waters will never be satisfied with a single victim, or two. I never saw any other children visit. When we were in public at school concerts or Christmas Eve services Edith never spoke to anyone outside my family. I was a child. I lived in the moment. I didn't know to wonder if other children visited when we were away for vacations, Reunions, and summer camps, or who used to visit before we moved in. I naively thought we were alone. It was only after I released the first draft of this book that I learned differently. It had been decades since I communicated with anyone from my hometown but sometimes news travels fast. It only took a few weeks. An old classmate reached out with her story of "Me too." then there was another, and another... I should have known. This story I am telling is not just mine. It never was.

The next day after school Heather stayed home. She looked at me and said she hadn't gone across the street because of the, "Ah. Well... You know."

"You know," became our code word. We never talked about what had happened between her and Vance. All we ever did was refer to the,"You know."

This was the first day since moving into town that Heather and I did not go directly across the street after school. Of course, for most of the last year I only went to the door and talked to Edith for a few minutes before being sent away, but both of us had remained faithful to the daily ritual.

On this day we set our books on the kitchen table and looked at each other not quite sure what our new routine would be.

A few minutes later the phone rang. Edith wanted to know if we were coming to visit. I did my best to politely say "No," we wouldn't be coming to visit. Then I hung up the phone.

A minute later the phone rang again. Was I sure?

"Yes" I was sure.

The phone rang again. Didn't I want an afternoon snack? She had fresh peanut butter cookies. (Yes, despite my peanut butter aversion I always enjoyed her homemade peanut butter cookies.

To this day her peanut butter cookie recipe is the best I have ever found.)

I said, "No. Thank-you." We could eat cookies at home.

After a couple more calls, she offered to teach me a new recipe I had been asking to learn. I tried to be as polite and firm as possible. It was all very stressful and difficult.

After half a dozen volleys, or more, Mother walked into the kitchen. I have no idea what she had been doing up until this point. She wanted to know what was going on. I did my best to explain that I knew we weren't supposed to visit Edith and Vance anymore, and I was trying to be polite about it, but every time I said we couldn't come, Edith just called back.

Mother erupted at my explanation. She launched right into one of her tirades. This time the subject was my rudeness. *How could I behave in such a way to this wonderful, lonely, old woman who had so little in her life and lived for the few hours each afternoon when Heather and I came to visit? How could I be so rude? She had brought me up to be better than that!*

I tried to remind her of the conversation the night before, but this only added fuel to her fire. I was more than just rude, now I was putting the whole family at risk! We absolutely could not afford to make any changes in our routine, that would be like telegraphing to the world that something bad had happened.

We had to keep visiting every day. We had to make it look to the rest of the world like nothing was wrong!

A few minutes later Heather and I walked across the street hand in hand. We stood in the kitchen, and I listened as Edith explained about the recipe she had promised. As soon as we possibly could we backed away and made our escape for home.

I am sure they were more frightened than we were, but they deserved it. We were just children fighting to survive an unimaginably hostile world with very little understanding of what it all meant.

There were plenty of other "buddy system" visits but they were all short and became more and more infrequent over time.

To my knowledge I was never alone with Vance again. I hope that Heather can say the same, but I don't think she can.

A thing that didn't change was outings to school concerts and to Christmas Eve services at Edith's church. These outings had only ever been with Edith. Vance never left their home except to go golfing with his buddies.

Taking Edith to school concerts was an activity that probably started during my lost year. Band practice began in the second semester of 5th grade and chorus was added in Jr High. Two or three times a year all the families would gather in the high school auditorium to hear our musical offerings.

It had been Mother's idea to bring Edith to our concerts. The tradition then expanded to include Christmas Eve service at her United Parish church. Of course, Edith's actual Grandchildren performed in band and chorus too; and attended the same church. On several occasions I made a point of waving to my classmate who was her Granddaughter. I thought maybe Edith would like to sit with them rather than us, but any time I tried to point them out, or suggest we approach them, everyone seemed to be looking the other way. No matter where we chose to sit for Christmas Eve service my classmate and her family always ended up on the other side of the Sanctuary. When I tried to explain my intent, everyone was suddenly looking in another direction or found someone else they had to talk to.

The Wizard of Oz

The last time we took a family trip to visit Father's family in Montana was summer of 1971, just before my ninth birthday. We spent one very long day detouring to a barren, high desert town where Father met with a man who worked for the local social services clinic. After father finished talking about work, we all toured the man's home as, apparently, it would be for sale soon.

The low, ranch house had been painted a rusty brown that blended in with the color of the dry earth and dust that surrounded it. It wasn't much to look at from the outside but on the inside, it was blessedly cool. I liked the large living room with floor to ceiling windows that looked out at mountains in the distance. I didn't yet understand that Father was looking for a new job, or the rest of the family and marital strain that was behind it. In those days, very few automobiles had air conditioning which was unfortunate as our visit coincided with the hottest part of the summer. Temperatures were in the triple digits with no shelter from the blazing sun. On the drive out of town I begged for something to drink but we hadn't packed any water. When I started to cry Mother hissed for me to shut up and told me that crying would only make me thirstier.

Mother was in a mood.

I do not remember much more of the trip or my interaction with my grandparents, but I came home with a wonderful, new, prized possession. It was an early edition of Frank Baum's "The Wonderful Wizard of Oz." The book had been passed from my grandmother's childhood home to my father's childhood home and now to me. It was not a preciously preserved, handle only with gloves, family heirloom. It was a well read, well worn, tattered book that had been loved by generations of children. The cover was worn through in the corners. The binding glue had long crumbled to dust, several sections of pages were not attached at all…

I was just the right age to love such a book and the knowledge that it was a precious family heirloom made me feel wonderfully special. I read it over and over again. It was my most prized possession.

One day during our first year or two in Maine we acquired a petite silver ring with a blue sapphire stone, from my father's, father's family. We were told it was a baby ring and also a family heirloom. The ring was declared to be for Heather as I already had the book. A rather big deal was made of having two precious heirloom items, one for each of us.

I felt a small pang of jealousy as I worked out that, even though it was very small, the ring was real jewelry made of precious metal and a gem. It was obviously more valuable than my grubby old book, but I wasn't willing to complain. I loved the book. I wouldn't ever trade it for a silly ring, especially one too small for anyone but a little baby to wear.

Sometime later I noted that "The Wonderful Wizard of Oz" was not in its usual place on my bookshelf. I looked for the book and eventually spied it in my sister's room. There were no rules to prevent anyone from looking at or reading it, but she didn't seem to be using it at the time, so I picked my beloved book up and returned it to its place in my bookcase.

A day two two later I found my book in her room again. I still didn't think she was reading it. She hadn't carried it around with her and there was no bookmark to save her place. I wondered why it kept migrating to her room, but no one was around to ask so I just returned it to its customary spot.

The third or fourth time I found my book in her room I asked questions. I was not prepared for my sister to look at me and simply say, "It's mine." This didn't make any sense at all, but in response to my questions of how, why, and when, she just answered, "Grandma said."

Eventually, Mother and Father joined the argument. Certainly, they would explain to Heather that you can't just walk into another person's room, take something of theirs, and then declare that it is yours now.

I cannot begin to explain my feelings of confusion and betrayal when my parents sided with my sister. Hadn't we just made a big fuss about giving Heather the ring? Didn't they remember? I had the book. She had the ring. Each of us had a thing. It was all fair…

When, why, and how had this changed? I stood in the doorway to my sister's room looking at the three faces of my family staring back at me like they were just sooo tired of my always having to make everything about me!

I tried to push back. "That's not true! Why would you say it is? "

No one answered. They just stared at me like they were wondering how long it would take for me to give up and go away.

I screamed and yelled and stamped my feet. I broke down into inconsolable tears. I could not understand why this was happening. But no one showed me any mercy of any kind. No one acknowledged the ring or the allocation of one item to each child or bothered to explain when or why things had changed.

I do not think they even understood how to explain about the book. Neither of my parents could articulate how the thing that made the book special was its chain of custody. No one knew to explain that the book had never belonged to anyone. The book was special because of its journey. The book had passed from child to child on a journey that spanned generations. For the book to remain special it had to continue traveling from child to child.

Somehow, Grandma had tried to pass this message, but my family was too socially inept to understand, let alone explain it. Unfortunately, the conversation had taken place without my knowledge, and no one had the presence of mind to explain anything to me.

How was I supposed to believe that Grandma had said my book was Heather's now when no one was willing to tell me when and how she had said this?

Why walk into my room when I was not there and take my book without even bothering to tell me? Wasn't it polite, wouldn't it have been appropriate to let me know what was happening before taking something precious out of my room?

How about reminding Grandma that passing the book to Heather meant she now had both family mementos. Grandma's house had plenty of interesting old things. If there was communication between my parents and Grandma, why not ask for something else that could be mine?

Why were we so incapable of even the most basic of civil human interaction?

I looked at the three of them and screamed out the agony in my soul. *"Why do I get nothing? Why did you tell me that we each got one thing and then take my thing away? How is this fair? How can you just take away something that was mine? Why does she get everything, and I get nothing?"*

After all these years I still do not understand that day. We were always a mess of a family. I do not have any memories of compassion from my family, but one could usually count on basic fairness and logic. We were all present when the ring was declared Heather's because the book was, and had been, mine.

No one was willing to deny that fact. No one knew how to explain, so they just stared at me, faces blank and unblinking.

I will always remember the feeling of abandonment. I remember looking at those heartless faces and realizing there was no point. Why show them how badly my heart was broken? *No one cared, not even a little bit. I wasn't a real person. I obviously didn't have, or deserve to have, feelings. Why let them know that they could hurt me?*

Fort Kent and the Grand Jury

Two other things occurred in the months or years following Heather's cry for help. I do not know the order in which they occurred or how closely they followed the revelation of my sister's sexual assault but both events are significant in understanding our family story.

One is related to Father's job. The county mental health clinic where he was director of the inpatient ward had a satellite office in a town about 40 miles north. The director of that facility was leaving his position and the job was offered to Father if he wanted it.

Wow! What a miracle! Here we were as a family, all of us reeling in one way or another from the realization that we lived across the street from a pedophile and the opportunity to relocate simply dropped into our lap.

At least they thought about it. We all drove up together to visit the outgoing director and his family. We toured the big red, farm style house they were preparing to sell. Wasn't this wonderful? Wasn't it amazing how all the pieces were ready to fall into place? An unsolicited job offer for Father; a bit of a promotion really. It was a smaller clinic, but he would be director of the whole place, not just the inpatient ward. And a perfectly suitable house as well!

I liked the town. It was slightly larger than the one we lived in and where I was used to being adjacent to the US – Canada border this town was a true international community with an American and a Canadian side bisected by the St. John River. I was enticed by the opportunity to move there.

Mother and Father felt differently. It was too far north (as if 40 miles was enough to impact the climate). The French influence was greater. (Exposing us children to a bilingual community would obviously be a terrible thing, they would never put their children in such a position.)

The answer was no. We would stay right where we were, with the devil we knew.

When the outgoing director finally left, and no one had been chosen to fill the position, Father was tapped as interim director for both locations. He spent the better part of a year managing two facilities and commuting between them, but there was no more talk of permanently accepting the job and actually moving there.

The second event was a jury summons for Mother. She was selected to serve on a Grand Jury, in the county seat, a town about an hour's drive south. During her three-or four-weeks of service she claimed to be strongly affected by the case of a sexually abused child. To her the abuse itself was nothing compared to the ordeal of testifying in court and being grilled by a defense attorney. For the rest of her life, she would insist that covering up our sexual abuse was a kindness, necessary to protect Heather and me from the horrific experiences of prosecuting child rape. She would exclaim again and again how grateful we should be that she and Father protected us from having to endure such a thing.

Winniaugwamauk

A precious lifeline.

Winniaugwamauk (Whinny-aug-wa-mock), the Community of Christ reunion grounds in Maine sits on the north end of Walker Pond, outside a little town called Blue Hill. The name is supposedly from the Passamaquoddy language and translates as "Walk on the Water."

I do not believe we attended Reunion during the first two years we were in Maine. Reunion '72 would have occurred within a week or two of moving into the house. In '73 we were traveling elsewhere. I was in Montana with my grandparents and Heather and my parents were making a slow trek home from the trip back to Michigan.

I first visited Winniaugwamauk in the summer of 74, just before my 12th birthday.

The Reunion grounds in Michigan was lovely but Winniaugwamauk was to become my home away from home. One difference had to do with lodging options. We weren't limited to just tents or trailers. There were cabins, "motels" and dorm rooms. Each included real walls and bunks or cots. Or you could just rent a tent, one that was set up and waiting for your arrival. That first summer Mother and Father paid $6.00 for Heather and me to share an 8' X 8', sturdy, straight walled tent that came with two cots. It was standing ready when we got there and it smelled much better than our well-worn, musty, heavy canvass one.

Oh, the joy of taking my bags out of the jeep and walking away to set up my own tidy, quiet space, free of the hours-long battle that was somehow always necessary in order to sloppily erect our slightly cattywampus, slope shouldered, family tent. (The instructions that came with the tent clearly said it could be erected in ten minutes, yet somehow it always took my family at least 60 and as long as 90 minutes of rage, frustration, and recrimination, to mostly get all of the walls sort of upright.)

On this year the rage had to be tempered. We were not alone. We were meeting the Maine community of Saints for the first time, and we were accompanied by guests. Mother's younger sister Jeannie who lived in England was visiting and had brought a traveling companion, a true English lady! All that negative energy had to be somehow suppressed. It hovered just below the surface like a tired pressure cooker about to explode, but I didn't care because Heather and I had our own tent, safely distant and protected by other people's canvass walled campsites.

A little bit of freedom, like so many other things, breeds more of the same. I wasn't just out of my parents' tent, I was out of sight and out of mind. Classes and activities were separated by age. There was plenty for me to do and lots of new people for me to meet. We crossed paths during meals and other activities but for the most part, I had a whole week of freedom and safety. There was so much to explore.

In addition to multiple lodging options the 40-acre property included a large dining hall, two chapels, a couple of campfire rings, woodland paths, a cove for swimming and another for boating, complete with a supply of canoes and half a dozen single mast, two-person sail boats we called bathtubs.

Separate from all the other lodging options was a one room building with a large, covered porch. Inside was furnished much like army barracks in the movies, two rows of bunk beds, one against the front wall and the other against the back. It was called the Girls' Dorm and shared by young women from Jr. High to college age, usually with at least one older adult female as chaperone. I wasn't old enough for the girls' dorm that first year but I would thoroughly enjoy my time there in years to come.

I made friends. I sang songs. One warm night when the air was just humid enough, and the breeze just soft enough, to feel like it was caressing your skin, a friend and I got ahold of a couple of glass jars. We skipped campfire and spent the hour running back and forth in the twilight catching fireflies. Later that evening I tried to explain to a random adult how magical the experience had been. She looked at me with the air of superiority too many adults use when they think they don't have time to be bothered by children, she said the campfire had been special and I had missed out by choosing not to be there. I will never forget the fabulous night of fireflies. Every time I think of it, I wonder if the woman who chastised me so rudely has any recollection of that one particular, special, campfire.

Winniaugwamauk and I were off to a wonderful start!

Twelve

I was awake and aware again. The pain was still present, but it had gone from constant to intermittent and the mist that stole all recollection of the previous year lifted. I was once again a willing participant in my own life.

I wasn't expected to visit with Edith and Vance any longer. I do not know if Heather was still making daily visits, but I feel like she was beginning to make more friends and spend at least some of her after school time in other places.

We still interacted with Edith and Vance a couple of times a week. Edith still accompanied us to school concerts, and we still took her to her church for Christmas eve services. These interactions never stopped. They continued until the day we moved back to Michigan.

Seventh Grade

School started. It was my middle year of Jr. High. It wasn't all good, but it wasn't all bad either.

Seventh grade English was taught by the father of one of my classmates. He had a reputation as a bully. According to the stories that circulated (and obviously grew with each retelling) he once threw a boy down a flight of steps. I believed these stories. I walked into his classroom with great trepidation. I was always on my best behavior in his room.

He introduced me to Ray Bradbury. He taught me to look for deeper meanings in what I read. He helped me see books as windows into other people's lives, beliefs, and experiences. But I was still afraid of him.

One day I managed to get on his bad side. I do not remember what my infraction was but if I had to guess I would say talking out of turn. I heard him say my name and it felt like a stone falling into my gut. I stopped breathing. I had done it now. I can still feel the fear of that moment. The silent pause was endless. His eyes locked on mine, and he said, "You have been batting 1000 all year. It would be a shame for you to ruin that now."

I had no idea what the phrase "batting 1000" meant but I knew the moment was over. I had crossed him, and no bones were broken. I had survived!

I don't think it was actually the first time in my life that someone in authority became angry with me and expressed it in a mature, measured way. But it may have been the first time that I was aware of being treated that way. I couldn't have expressed at the time how I felt, but I think it gave me one little block of stability, one glimmer of understanding that I deserved to be treated with dignity. Sometimes lifelines come in unexpected ways, from unexpected allies.

As the year went on, school became more and more fun. Seventh grade seemed to be all about projects, and they were wonderful.

I teamed up with my two best friends to build a diorama of a woolly mammoth. Two of us worked together with a balloon, Paper Mache, and poster paint to build a surprisingly good model. Sadly, as we got caught up in the joy of building our Mammoth, we were not very nice to the third member of the group, leaving her out of the fun of crafting and sticking her with the whole job of writing the report. Again, I must express my gratitude for my two dear friends who stuck with me through all the challenges and missteps of youth.

We were given a research project on local history. It was to be not just a report, but packaged as a presentation with a folder, cover page, and references. I chose to write about local Native American Tribes. My Native American roots were from Michigan, not Maine, but I studied the people who had thrived in the north woods around our little Maine town. I included hand-drawn illustrations and penned my report so neatly and carefully it would have looked good framed. I found two thin sheets of wood to use as front and back covers. I stained the wood and split the margin of the front sheet and added two small hinges. The result was far more than what we had been assigned, but I had so enjoyed the assignment that I just kept adding to it. It became my masterpiece. My teacher's response was simply, "Wow! I guess you enjoyed this."

In Social Studies we drew detailed maps of the local region, including undeveloped parcels that were only identified by grid notations; A7,B8 and so on.

In Science we drew diagrams of single celled plants and animals, labeling the individual parts such as the nucleus, membrane, and cell walls in the plants. There was one lovely afternoon when a group of adolescent girls met at the public library and took over all of the tables near the Encyclopedia Americana with our pencils and drawing paper. Who knew homework could be so much fun!

More Winniaugwamauk

Near the start of the school year, we took another trip to Winniaugwamauk. A Men's Retreat was scheduled for Labor Day weekend. My Father, a cerebral sort, who loved in-depth scriptural study and considered himself a theologian, was looking forward to it. I think Mother joined the trip to help in the kitchen. Since both of them were going away, they decided Heather and I had to come along. Maybe my parents acknowledged enough of what had happened when they left us alone for a long weekend the year before that they didn't want to risk the same thing again. Whatever the reason, Father's trip to a men's retreat was accompanied by his wife and two little girls.

The final member of our party was a young man named Jason from one of the two other church families in our region. This was the nineteen-seventies. There was no Facebook or other online means of connecting people with shared background or interest. When we moved into the area, Father visited the nearby Air Force base and used his ministerial credentials to identify military families who had recorded affiliation with Community of Christ (then the Reorganized Church of Jesus Christ of Latter Day Saints (RLDS)). He found two church affiliated families in the region, and we had been holding weekly Sunday services in our home since shortly after moving in. Jason was the teenage son of one of these families.

I was happy to take the trip. Two whole days at camp. No classes, no church services. Just the freedom to do whatever I wanted.

The blackberries were ripe and bountiful. I loved picking berries, any kind of berries. I was still small and agile enough to avoid most of the thorns and took pride in braving my way deeply into the thickets.

I didn't find Jason particularly interesting, but I was happy for the opportunity to show off the wild and special parts of the campgrounds.

The first place I wanted to show off was the big flat rock that created a warm sunny glen in otherwise deep woods. All the young people knew where this rock was. It was large enough to serve as an outdoor classroom for groups of 20 or 30, and far enough away from the heart of the camp to feel secure and intimate. I naturally offered to take Jason there.

We were less than halfway up the path when he asked me to stop for a moment. I was a couple of steps ahead, so I stopped, turned around and waited for him to catch up.

Before I could take another step up the trail, he placed a hand on my hip and another behind my neck.

I was twelve, still closer to childhood than adolescence. Boys were not yet on my radar. He was fifteen.

Before I realized what was happening, he pressed his lips against mine then forced his big, slimy, muscular tongue into my mouth.

I tried to back away and close my mouth, but he was bigger and stronger than I was.

He was almost a man. I had been taught to treat men with respect and obedience. I had also been taught that my virginity was my most precious attribute. (I know. I have never actually been a virgin but there is no point in trying to apply facts or logic to the extreme dysfunction of my upbringing.)

This almost man, who was supposed to see me as a righteous, shining example of chastity and purity had just forced his fat, slimy, serpent-like tongue into my mouth and was quickly working his way into my clothing.

He pulled his tongue back for just an instant, probably to take a breath, and I clenched my teeth, tightly. Maybe he would get the point. But instead of giving up, he pushed and he pried. His hold on the back of my neck became even more forceful. He wedged his tongue into the gaps between my teeth, the places where my overbite prevented me from forming a solid wall. He forced my mouth back open and pushed his tongue so far down my throat that I thought I would choke.

Did he think this was something I wanted? How was this something anyone wanted, ever? What had I done to make him think I was okay with this? What could I do or say to communicate respect for his authority as an older male and also get him to stop?

Saying "No" was not an option. He was male. He was older. He was the authority figure. Women were supposed to be obedient and so obviously pure that no man could see them as a target of lust. Yet here I was with this young man tugging furiously and fruitlessly at my sweater.

Despite my history of previous abuse, I was still sexually naive. Because of my history of past abuse my emotional response was to shut down rather than to call for help or run away. I was the same child that had spent an afternoon curled into a ball in the back of my closet while my mother kicked, slapped and screamed. How could I have run? There was no place to run to. Who could I have cried to for help? The only person who could have heard me was too busy slapping, kicking and screaming to notice my bruises and tears. How could I possibly expect a different response this time?

We don't always behave logically in moments like this. With neither fight or flight as an option my next move was to try and placate my assailant. I managed to free my mouth from his tongue again only to say, "You can't untuck it. It's a body suit." (Popular in the 70's, body suits always stayed tucked in because they fit like a one-piece swimsuit, fastened by snaps, or sometimes just continuous under the crotch.)

In some innocent, unworldly part of my soul I expected him to say, “Oh, I’m sorry. I guess that won’t work, will it.” This little part of me hoped we could both laugh at the silliness of trying to pull up a body suit and then go on with our day.

Of course, that’s not what happened. He simply shoved his hand further down into my crotch looking for the snaps that would free the body suit while my panicked brain desperately searched for a way to distract him. This led me to my second outrageous statement, “Don’t you want to keep going and see the cool place I told you about?”

This shouldn’t have worked either. I would never suggest to a young woman that the way to get an oversexed boy to stop mauling her is to propose moving to a more secluded location. Thankfully, this young man, crude and forceful as he may have been, was not intent on rape. We walked the rest of the way to the big rock, me keeping carefully out of arms reach the whole time. As we stepped into the sun-warmed glade he reached out and pulled me towards him again. I held my body as stiff and rigid as I possibly could. How could anyone ever mistake this tonic immobility for an invitation?

I still believed I could not say “No.” If this man misunderstood my intentions, it was my fault, it was because I had misled him in some way. I was responsible. I had to give him a face-saving opportunity to step away without being told he had done anything wrong. My mind searched for the right excuse. I finally settled on suggesting we should get back to the group. We had been gone long enough. We didn’t want anyone to come looking for us. After another moment or two of continued pawing at my unresponsive body, he turned his back and walked away.

I never told anyone about that day. I didn't even realize that I had never told anyone until a week ago in my therapy session. I was catching my counselor up on where I was in writing this memoir and what part I needed to address next. Halfway through relating the scene I stopped. I just stopped and looked at her as I realized I had never said these words out loud.

It occurred to me that I never wanted to tell the story because I was so ashamed. Deep in my soul I was still carrying the belief that this child, barely twelve years old, was responsible for what happened that day. I believed the child had committed some sin, some unknown but horrible transgression, that I had failed to protect an otherwise righteous young man from temptation and carnal lust. Yet again, I believed regardless of the situation or transgression, any time anyone hurt me for any reason the fault was always mine.

I have known better for a very long time. I recognize that no child should ever bear the burden of believing he or she is ever responsible for sexual acts perpetrated against them, but I was still carrying the burden of this shame because I had never addressed it. I had not bothered to open this compartment in the depths of my soul to clean it out.

I am working on this now. I am walking through all my memories and trying to help that child within me to understand that she is not, was not, ever, evil.

In the process of working to absolve my inner self of sin and responsibility for the sins of those around me my view of God and religion have changed. I have taken to describing myself as a religious pragmatist and a monotheist. I have come to understand that if there is one God, one Creator of all mankind, then all of mankind is equally precious. This belief creates a deceivingly simple and incredibly specific litmus test. *Any religious practice, tenant, belief... any thought or act that denigrates another of God's children, is not of God.* It doesn't matter how beloved a tradition is or how different and therefore perceived as underserving the other person is. God is Love. God is Peace. God is harmony for all mankind. God is not, ever, harmful or dysfunctional. This is the truth I now choose to cling to and measure my life by.

Father

There were a number of other significant interactions that year. I do not think I can put them all in order, but I will list them as they each have meaning.

I started learning to cook at six. Our Marquette kitchen had a built-in stove top and wall oven. Mother had bought a new stove a year or so before. It was big purchase. She was pleased they could afford it. She picked out just the one she wanted, and she wasn't willing to leave it behind when we sold the house in Detroit even though our new kitchen in Marquette came with built-ins. There was just enough room to squeeze one additional appliance into our rather small kitchen so she upgraded the wiring and installed her beloved stove across from the built-ins. As a result, the unused oven and stovetop became mine and of course, now that I had my very own stove, I had to learn to cook!

At first my minimal menu included canned soup and Jell-O brand pudding. It wasn't much but I was very proud of my ability to cook a whole meal (soup and dessert) even if I did need a chair to reach the stove. By the time I was 10 or 12 the kitchen was my domain. I was cooking most of our family meals as well as keeping us supplied with homemade bread and cookies.

One Saturday afternoon, shortly after my twelfth birthday, Father joined me in the kitchen. He said he would like to talk to me and suggested we take a walk. This was interesting. I rarely spent one on one time with Father, and when we did I was either receiving instruction or we were merely existing in the same space. He had never before shown any interest in just spending time with me.

He led me out of the house, up to the corner and down along Main Street. He told me that I was growing into a woman now, that things would change for me and that he and I would have a different relationship.

I tried to understand what he meant. The conversation was not unlike the one between Vance and me a year earlier only Vance had tried to explain that as I grew into a woman I would not be spending as much time with him. Father seemed to be saying the opposite. He wanted us to spend more time together. He wanted to guide me and teach me things.

I was bothered by his statements. I didn't think I had changed all that much in recent weeks. Why was it that despite being totally beneath his notice a mere month ago now he wanted do develop a relationship with me? My Spidey sense told me not to trust him.

We walked to the one pizzeria in town. He ordered a pizza, paid for a couple of cans of soda, and set us down at the single table in what was otherwise a take-out business.

He spent money on me! This had literally never happened before. Family restaurant meals were a once or twice a year event. The only exceptions were while traveling and then we were limited to the children's menu only, preferably to items that cost $0.99 or less.

I still didn't trust him. The whole situation was very out of character, but it did feel pretty special to have a pizza date with my father.

Sadly, my father's plan was not to take me on a pizza date once a week, or even once a month but he did begin to engage with me with more regularity and at a deeper level.

He had lots to say. He talked about religious theology, politics, his job... He spent a lot of time expressing his expectations for me. I was expected to be mature and proper. I was to be pious, chaste and virginal. I was to be focused first and always on God and his righteousness. I was to be mindful of my status as a representative of our family, our church, and his place of business...

He seemed to have made a list of every possible adolescent challenge and wanted me to be very clear on his stance. Basically "no child of his" would ever do ___ or _____ or _____ ...

He explained that "Preachers' kids" had a general reputation for being wild and rebellious. I had never bothered to consider how my life was affected by my status as the oldest child of a minister from a church that no one had ever heard of, most people didn't care about, and others thought was just made up. But he outlined a long list of potential pitfalls and insisted with every one that "no child of his" would ever do x, y or z, or anything else for which they could be seen as a "Preachers' kid."

He explained how unhappy children who struggled to fit in with their peers commonly blamed their parents for placing them in untenable positions, trying to balance conflicting expectations of family and the wider world. Again, '"no child of his" would ever blame either of our parents for our own failings at being perfectly adjusted, happy, capable, and mature.

He talked about adolescents who failed at achieving maturity and how many of them considered suicide. I was to understand that there was absolutely nothing romantic or tragic about suicide. I was subjected to detailed descriptions of hideously bloated bodies and explanations of how varying methods of suicide resulted in scarred, ugly death scenes that did absolutely nothing to make those left behind feel sympathetic or sorry for the obviously inadequate person who had killed themselves. He added detail to this story telling me about how a patient in his mental health ward had recently walked out of the hospital and drowned herself in the river that ran through our town. He expressed his disrespect for this woman and her behavior and provided detailed descriptions on the condition of her body, as well as where and how it had been found. "No child of his" would ever consider such an act.

He talked about his work as director of the small mental health inpatient ward in our local hospital. I never heard him express any compassion for his patients. They were manipulative, they were needy, they were incompetent, incapable, and inadequate. He expanded this judgement to anyone seeking any kind of mental or emotional health care.

Because he worked for a mental health facility, Heather and I could have had access to off-the-books, and cost free, emotional counseling and support. However, disclosure of sexual abuse would have necessitated reporting. Instead of being given assistance and support, we were specifically barred from seeking help. "No child of his" would ever air our personal, family, dirty laundry to the local community. And, of course, we wouldn't want to anyway. All of his colleagues lacked some degree of professional skill or were inadequate in some personal way. He recited a list of co-workers and described specific failings of each one of them.

To me it seemed that he anticipated whatever struggle I was feeling and contrived to block any possible avenue of support. I felt like I had when I tried to say no to Vance and his response was "Go ahead and tell. No one will hear you. No one will believe you." With my father I didn't even have to make the threat. He was always one step ahead of me, predicting how I was feeling and what I might try to make it better. He managed to cut me off at every turn until there was no way left to go.

A month or so after the pizza dinner Father decided it was time for me to have a real steak dinner.

I knew one of the date places he took my mother was a steakhouse. I had no idea where it was and the only steak I had ever eaten was part of a large, inexpensive, cut of beef cooked in a frying pan and shared with the family.

Father drove us across the border into Canada and north, for almost an hour. I enjoyed the trip and filled the car with trivial twelve-year-old chatter for the entirety of the ride. We finally pulled up in front of a large, 'V' shaped motel and restaurant. For some reason the motel surprised me. Apparently, my parents steak dates had always been overnight trips. I just hadn't realized.

In the end they had not stopped taking overnight trips after the weekend Heather and I spent with Edith and Vance, they simply left Heather and me at home with me in charge of the household.

The hostess sat us at a small window table in a crowded dining room. The room was mostly filled with older couples. Almost all the other patrons were what I would call Grandma and Grandpa aged. Father ordered two T-Bone dinners medium rare. He didn't bother looking at a menu.

Dinner arrived in multiple courses. First was an appetizer, a corn fritter, kind of a gooey corn cake glazed with maple syrup. Then came a breadbasket and salad. The main course included a T-bone, rather thinly cut and definitely overdone. Of course, I didn't know it was overcooked, having never before been asked how I wanted my steak. At the end of the meal there was a small portion of dessert. It might have been a single scoop of ice cream, but I do not remember for sure.

To me the whole experience was new and interesting. The steak itself wasn't inspiring, and I could only take Father's word for it when he explained that I would have liked it better if we had received the medium-rare preparation he requested. What impressed me the most were the separate courses and the service. It felt so gracious to be served a little plate of food, followed by another course and then another one again. I would be lying if I said it didn't make me feel special.

I cannot tell you what happened next. Did we simply go home? Why do I feel disquiet in my gut whenever I picture that motel? I have absolutely no memory of the drive home. I have asked myself many times if there was more to that visit than a simple father daughter dinner. In the end my answer is no. We did not go to that motel, and he did not take advantage of me in that way. I arrive at this conclusion not because of any specific memory or lack thereof. My father was many things, but he did not sexually abuse his own children. If he had there would be many more events and much more evidence. Sexual abuse is a compulsion. No one who gives into such temptation can walk away after only one incident.

I have no memory of the drive home because it just wasn't as interesting and exciting as the drive out.

The final outing with my father was rabbit hunting. It was early winter in northern Maine, but the snowpack was already deep and the daytime temperature was somewhere in the single digits. Even to a child of the north it was too cold to be simply walking or standing outside, but Father wanted to hunt rabbits, so we drove off down empty forest roads and into the woods.

There were moose tracks near where we parked our little yellow Volkswagen but that was the extent of the wildlife we found on that too cold day.

After walking around for an hour or so without spotting any other trails in the fresh snow, Father decided I should help him scare rabbits out of the brush. He indicated a sizable blackberry thicket with most of the canes bent down to the ground under heavy snow. He told me to go stomp around and rustle the thicket while making noise. He was sure there were rabbits under the bramble, and he wanted me to scare them out.

The lack of any tracks going in or out made me doubt his tactics would be successful. The day was too cold. Even the birds were absent. If there were rabbits under the bramble, I expected they were snugly tucked into their underground burrows trying to stay warm. Stomping on top of their home would more likely send them deeper into the burrow rather than out onto the cold, open snowpack.

And then there was the matter of the gun. My father was carrying a double-barreled shotgun. I had never been hunting before and never seen him fire this weapon, but I was pretty sure I didn't want to be downrange of him when he did. I asked him, "Isn't there a rule about not being in front of you when you fire the gun?"

He replied that he wouldn't be shooting at me. When I complained again, he pointed out that the rabbits would try to run away from me so he would shoot in the direction they were running, not where I was stomping on the bramble. I was not convinced, but he was my father, and we were a long way from home. We were miles from the nearest house or even hunting shed. I didn't see any chance of getting back into the warm car until I proved that there weren't any rabbits dumb enough to run towards the man with the gun when I stomped on their bramble.

I walked toward the bramble. When I got there, I turned and looked back at him and at the gun that I didn't want to be in front of. He jerked his head, gestured with the gun and said something about not being a chicken.

I sullenly stomped my way a few feet into the bramble but only far enough to reasonably say, "It's too deep here. If I go any further, I will get caught by the thorns." Then I backed out of the bramble and looked back at him, and the gun. He clearly wasn't satisfied so I walked a bit further around the edge of the bramble and tried from a different approach. Once again, I was quickly waist deep in snow covered, thorny blackberry canes. I backed out again, circled further around the bramble and made a third approach but I was not hoping or trying to scare out any rabbits, I was only interested in satisfying the minimal amount of effort required by my father before we could give up.

Even if I had the stomping power of an elephant, I did not want to rouse any rabbits. I didn't want to give my father any excuse to fire at anything. It wasn't possible to stomp on top of the bramble. All I could do was carefully wade in trying not to tear myself or my winter coat on the sharp thorns. If my having to move carefully meant I didn't scare any rabbits, I was quite okay with that. My father may have been the ultimate authority in my life at that point, but it was not okay for him to insist that I walk in front of him while he carried a loaded gun.

I didn't feel *too* threatened by him. I don't think it was his intent to actually harm me, but I do think he was demonstrating his position of authority. He clearly did not have any concern for my comfort. He wanted me to understand that he was the one in control. I did not have the right to say, "No. I don't want to walk in front of your gun." And I certainly didn't have the right to say, "I'd rather not watch you shoot and skin a bunny rabbit," either. Had anyone else been holding the gun Father would have called it a "power play." He didn't want to physically hurt me, but he did want to demonstrate his authority, ability, and willingness to control my life.

Anniversary Dinner

My parents' wedding anniversary was two days after Christmas. I always felt a bit bad about this. I thought that anniversaries should be special, like birthdays, and it seemed to me that people with birthdays too close to Christmas were too easily overlooked on their special day. Mother and Father didn't always commemorate their wedding anniversary. To my mind this was because the anniversary got lost in the general business of Christmas, so I thought it would be nice if I prepared a celebration for them. I had really enjoyed the steak dinner at a restaurant with Father and I knew it was a place they had gone to together on multiple occasions, so I decided to recreate that meal at home, just for the two of them.

I wasn't able to get steak. I didn't have enough money to buy steak and I would not have known what to choose if I did. I was stuck with selecting a cut of meat out of our freezer. I think I settled for pork chops or pork steak. It wasn't the same, but it was still a nice cut of meat that I could plate individually and serve I like they had done at the steak house. I didn't know how to make the apple fritters from the restaurant, but I saved a couple of apple muffins I had made a day or so earlier. I split and buttered the muffins warming them in the oven and finally topping each one with berry jam. I served them on the small salad bowls from our good China. Then I brought out two individual salads, also served in China, as I plated the main course and dessert. I was proud of myself. I thought it was a nice gift and my plan included executing it well.

Mother was furious. She wouldn't explain why. All I could learn was that she didn't want me to serve the meal, she was angry at Father for taking me to the steakhouse and therefore angry at me for trying to recreate the event.

Mother trying to hold in her fury was something I had never seen before, and I didn't know how to react. Mother was always explosive in her anger. She always told anyone within range exactly what she was angry about, who was at fault and, in general, how terrible everyone was to her, how amazing it was that she could put up with any of us at all, and so on...but not this time. This time I could see how rigidly she was holding her body, trying to contain the anger. When I walked out of the room, I could hear her spitting comments to Father between tightly clenched teeth. She was obviously angry at me too but for some reason she wouldn't tell me why.

I didn't know what to do. I had planned and prepared this nice event and I didn't understand what was wrong. It wasn't about me usurping her place in the kitchen. The kitchen had been more mine than hers for years. She seemed to be angry because I had gone to the steakhouse with Father. I thought I overheard something like, "It's bad enough that you took her there, but now I have to sit here and pretend to smile while you rub my face in it!"

I tried to explain that I thought it would be nice to treat them like they were out on a date, but my input wasn't making anything better. When I brought out the salads she threatened to get up and leave. By the time the main course was ready I gave up. She insisted she was tired of being 'isolated' in the dining room she wasn't going to tolerate this a minute longer, and she absolutely wouldn't eat anything else if it was served by me!

I gave in and brought two extra plates to the table for Heather and me, then I and threw the meat and potatoes on a platter family style. The four of us finished our meal in stony silence unable to pretend there was anything nice or special about the event.

I never learned why Mother was so angry at my attempt to create a date night for them. I know it was related to Father having taken me to the Steak House, but why did that upset her so? Was she simply jealous? She seemed too angry for just the cost of a few hours and a meal.

I have to remind myself that she was also a sexually abused child. Did she think Father had taken me to their date place to sleep with me? I do not believe he abused me on that outing, but something about the event triggered memories and emotions for her. I just don't know what they were.

We never had another father-daughter outing again.

More About Father

The weird era of father-daughter dating was over but the oversharing was not. It was as if he saw that I was getting closer to adulthood and thought now was the time for him to step in and help me understand the world.

He talked. He talked a lot. He talked about his patients. He explained how they were inadequate, manipulative, and sinful women (he never had much to say about male patients) and how their behavior had robbed them of a full and satisfying life. He told me they were "loose women." He demonstrated their loose behavior by telling stories of therapy sessions in which these women declared their love for him. He properly named this behavior as transference, an understood process in which patients will project emotions onto the therapist, but to hear him tell it, they couldn't help but be attracted to him because he was just that desirable. Of course all the women he treated wanted to be his lovers. He told me what they said, supposedly word for word, as they declared their infatuation. Then he described the women themselves focusing on physicality and how attractive he found them to be.

He was consistently derisive when referring to his patients. I never heard him express compassion or respect of any kind. The message was consistent. Seeking therapeutic help was a clear indicator of irresponsible, immoral, and sinful behavior. People who sought therapy were sinners who had messed up their lives beyond any hope of recovery. No child of his would ever blacken the reputation of our family by requesting such support.

I only remember one reference to a male patient. This man was dying of syphilis. My father transferred him to the state mental hospital because the disease, which had progressed beyond the ability to treat it, was destroying his brain. He was unquestionably a sinner who was being punished for his own actions and iniquity.

The story, according to Father, began when the man had an affair. In her anger, the man's wife sought out the most disreputable partner she could find and had her own affair as a way of getting revenge on her philandering spouse. It was her act of revenge which brought home the disease that was now destroying this man's brain and would eventually take his life. To my father this was the perfect morality play. It was an example of one momentary sin and the consequences which destroyed the lives of everyone involved. It was not a tragedy. It was an example of righteous judgement. There was no need for mercy.

Despite, or perhaps due to, his persistent judgement of other's sexual behavior my father also paid close attention to all of the women in his life. Women, all women, were judged on the quality of their figure, which my father liked to pronounce as figger. Any new woman we met would be qualified based on her figger and my father would share this evaluation with me including specific attributes and detriments that factored into his judgement.

I remember one woman in particular. She was the young wife of a new employee. They had moved from out of state, and we interacted with them as a family while they looked for housing and settled in. To me this woman was beautiful. She was young, vivacious, stylish, self-confidant and outgoing. I wanted to be near her. I wanted to be her.

Father disapproved. He explained that I was being misled. This woman did not meet his expectations. She was skinny. She had no figger. He considered her a perfect example of the kind of woman who used hair, makeup, clothing, and attitude to appear attractive when in reality she was scrawny and ugly. She was a lie! She tried to deceive people into finding her attractive when she clearly was not. To hear my father describe it, her sense of style was a hostile act of deception aimed specifically at him. I was strongly cautioned to beware of this woman. In fact, after our conversation all social interaction with this new couple came to an abrupt end. I never saw her again.

There were other ways that my father displayed misogynistic attitudes. Playboy and Penthouse magazines were still in the house. The collection had grown too large to remain in his nightstand and there was notable friction between Mother and Father about the where, or if, of overflow storage.

As director of a hospital ward Father was also a hiring manager. He explained that it was his prerogative to hire young attractive women and again, went into detail about the qualities that made one woman more attractive than another. He also shared stories of employees who were engaging in intercourse during overnight shifts. He told me who was sleeping with who, including details such as where their trysts occurred and how they were caught.

The list of misogynistic attitudes kept growing. He didn’t believe in marital rape. I am not sure why this mattered, why he felt the need to explain this to me, but he did. When a woman married, she surrendered her right to decline sexual activity.

When a colleague had an affair, he insisted all fault lay with the woman. His friend had been seduced. He deserved compassion, she did not…

I knew his attitudes were wrong. I could feel it in every cell of my body. I tried to explain but I was a child, and he was a skilled debater who wanted to see things his way. He was also a preacher and pastor. His word was the word of God and he believed he wielded that authority to seek and call out the sins of everyone around him.

Both of my parents enjoyed pointing out flaws and insecurities of the people around us.

Everyone we knew was deficient in some notable way. As I young person on the cusp of adulthood I was expected to learn how to similarly judge the people around me. It was like a macabre test. We would meet a new person and as soon as they were out of sight I would be quizzed on their deficiencies.

Smoking and drinking were the easiest to identify. If the behavior wasn't immediately visible, I had to learn to look for secondary clues like beer-bellies (which were, apparently, distinctly different than your average doughboy love handles) for drinkers, or crow's feet to indicate smoking. Other unacceptable behaviors included immaturity, insecurity, brash behavior… No matter the person or the action there was always something wrong with them and their iniquities were held up to be measured against the perfectly righteous behavior of my family.

I didn't like this game. I tried to explain that I knew no one was perfect but most people were kind and likeable. They had qualities I enjoyed. I would rather appreciate someone for who they were than constantly focus on what was wrong with them.

Mother and Father refused to accept my way of thinking. They considered it terribly important for me to understand how blessed I was to have been born to people so beloved of God. I had to learn to see and appreciate the difference between the Godly environment I was privileged to inhabit and the rest of the world. Nothing I could ever do would make me worthy of such a gift. Nothing could be more important than carrying on my family's spiritual legacy. How could I be worthy of this legacy or the blessings that would come with it if I couldn't identify sin when it was right in front of me?

One day I tried to explain the challenge of learning to be so judgmental. I was listening as my parents ticked off their lists of what was wrong with the people we had just been to visit. I interrupted and said, "But I liked them. Why can't we just like people and enjoy them sometimes?" Conversation stopped for a couple of precious seconds, and I stared into their unblinking eyes, until they decided to just ignore my question and continue their assessment of perceived shortcomings.

Sadly, I picked up too much of the judgementalism my family practiced. I developed reflexive judgmental attitudes that took years for me to identify and root out. I believe I did a good job of getting past this early training, but I know there were periods in my life when my own attitudes were the cause of my feeling unliked and alone. I am genuinely sorry for any people who were hurt by my attitudes.

The differences between Community of Christ and Mormonism are many and of course those differences are far more significant to members of my small denomination than they are to the Mormon church, or to the outside world. I am sure I have spent much more of my life explaining who we, as a faith, are not, rather than who we are not.

There was one Mormon family in our small town. They moved in a year or so after we did and bought a large house on Main Street around the corner from ours. When they decided to host Mormon Missionaries, our house became the obvious first stop.

Fathers' response was to welcome them. He believed it was his ministerial role to guide these young men, to confound them with his wisdom and help them see the light. Night after night he invited them into our home. He prayed with them. He asked for blessing on their discourse and then proceeded to prove that he could theologically best these young men. He could outmaneuver these earnest eighteen-year-olds who had never experienced anyone speaking up or challenging their faith and back them into corners.

He was twice their age. He was a skilled and well-practiced preacher. And he was so very proud of himself. He was proud when they begged to leave in order to look up some of the things he discussed. He was proud when they returned with their Bishop and even prouder when the Bishop and Missionaries finally tucked tail and left, after promising to consider my father's opinions.

I disagreed. I knew I would never win an argument with my father, but I trusted the feeling of shame in my heart at watching a grown man theologically batter a couple of sincere young men, practically children, children who were trying to find their way through their own mix of supportive and simultaneously soul crushing spiritual legacy.

Another thing our rural location close to the Canadian border provided was unique television choices. With no cable and only minimal broadcasting the physical age and location of the television determined what we could watch. We had a black and white television in the kitchen that only picked up local American channels, one network and local PBS. The color television in the family room only played Canadian channels, one in English and one in French.

Canadian television was different. It was not at all restrictive about things like nudity, language, or violence. In 1974, only two years after its release, Canadian television aired the movie "The Godfather," full length and unedited. Father decided he and I should watch it together. He said he wanted me to understand the types of things that really went on "out there in the world." Mother didn't think this was a good idea, but she was overruled.

At first, I was intrigued. Every child is eager to see their first R rated movie. What amazing things were there in this grown-up movie that Father thought I should know about? I felt grown up and excited as we settled ourselves into the family room. I watched the wedding scene with feelings of joy and envy. The bride was so pretty, and did people really give out that much money at weddings? Wow!

The plot didn't turn dark until after I was relaxed and enjoying myself. This was when the guns came out, and the piano wire... People talk about the horses' head as the darkest scene. I have a couple of others more deeply etched into my psyche.

I spent most of the movie sitting on the floor, behind an armchair with my hands over my eyes and/or ears. I would have loved to run out of the room and never come back, but father kept encouraging me to uncover my eyes and watch. He said it was important for me to understand how hostile the world was so I could fully appreciate how safe and sheltered my life was, under the protective care of Godly parents and a spiritual legacy. So, I stayed. I did as I was told and once it was over, I never talked about it again, at least not for several decades.

Piano

Ever since Mother's ill-fated attempt to teach me piano I was considered to be the only non-musical member of the family. Mother played piano. Father had won a state-wide vocal competition in High School. Heather had been taking piano lessons since first grade.

Piano still wasn't an option for me. It wasn't something we talked about it was just something I knew. I wasn't musical. I was reminded of this every time I hummed or sang around the house. It was so widely known in our family that I had no musical talent that one day when Father caught me alone in the kitchen, singing on key he spent several minutes theorizing how this could happen, finally settling on the theory that the song was written in a minor key and obviously, there must be something about the minor key that made it possible for me to carry a tune in this one instance.

I never stopped wanting to learn piano, but I knew it was expensive. Sometimes I was allowed to spend $2.00 on various art and/or craft classes at our local community center, but piano lessons cost $6.00! I couldn't imagine asking for that much money. I was surprised and anxious about my parents spending that much on just one child. Six dollars a week was so much I literally worried that it put us at risk of losing the house.

Heather did well at piano. She moved through a new book every year. By now the books for years one and two were sitting unused in the piano bench. One day I took out her old books and tried my hand at what I could teach myself. No one seemed to notice or care so I began to regularly practice simple pieces from her beginners' books. After a few weeks I was feeling proud of the few songs I had learned.

One night, when everyone was at home, I decided to show off a couple of pieces I had taught myself. With everyone in the room I played one of the first two-handed pieces in the beginner's book. The piece was named "Up in the Sky" I still remember the tune and the illustration of a girl on a swing that accompanied the title.

When I was done Father asked if I wanted to learn to play. I had no idea how to respond. I knew better than to say "Yes! Yes please. Yes!" I knew that doing so would make Mother angry and that if I said "Yes" I would be walking into a trap because no matter how hard I tried I would never, ever, do well enough to satisfy her, and when I failed to live up to her impossible standards she would use my failure to hurt me. I knew she would find a way to make me pay.

But I couldn't say "No." Saying "no" was a lie that was just too big for me to swallow. I tried to say something, but my mouth just hung open. Nothing would come out.

It was Heather who broke the silence. Her struggle to find respect and value in our home was at least as difficult as mine. Here was a moment for her to shine. She said, "I could teach her! Please. Please let me teach her. I know I can do it!"

Any flicker of hope in my heart died then and there. For a moment I had allowed myself to feel a little spark of hope. But even then, I knew it wasn't true. Mother had tried to teach me herself and had failed. It didn't matter that I was so small and her expectations were more than my little child's hands could manage. I had begged to learn and when I couldn't live up to her standards, I had showed her to be a failure. She would never forgive me. From that moment on I was the non-musical member of the family. She had taken piano away from me, and I could never be allowed to have anything again once she had taken it away. And, of course, there was the cost. Six dollars a week, times two children. We would be out on the street.

Now Heather was on her feet, literally jumping up and down at the idea of being so much better than me that she could be teacher to a sister nearly four years older! My soul curled into a tight little ball just thinking about it.

I muttered something under my breath, something like "Forget about it." Or "I didn't really mean it." The moment passed. Maybe, just maybe, we could all step away and forget that it had ever happened.

The next afternoon, I came home from school and sat down at the piano, but the books I had been using were gone. I looked in the piano bench and through the various stacks on the piano and end table, but they were not anywhere. Mother walked by and I asked if she knew where the books were. She looked me in the eye and said, "Oh. You said you didn't want them, so I gave them away."

I could try to describe the rest of the scene but it wouldn't matter. I couldn't possibly express how shattering the experience was, and there is no reason for me to put you through it. The books were gone forever. We couldn't possibly ask to get them back. What would people think of us? We couldn't buy new books. Obviously, I couldn't be trusted to follow through with using them. If I had wanted to keep them, I should have said so, but I hadn't. This was just another example of how I was the passive aggressive child who manipulated every situation to cause as much drama as possible. According to Mother I had insisted I did not want the books. Of course, I had said no such thing, but the truth never really mattered in our home. She knew how I operated. I had pretended not to want the books just so I could create a scene after she gave them away. It didn't matter that the books had been in the house for years. It wasn't at all suspicious that after showing off my one little song Mother managed to give the books away on the very next day.

It wasn't ever her. It was me. It was always me. I was the one who caused all the drama.

I had been right to believe that piano was a thing Mother would never allow me, the only thing I underestimated was her cruelty.

Not the Only One

I “became a woman” partway through seventh grade. In my mind I think I saw menarche, and thus ‘adulthood’, as a magical portal. I believed I was always doing everything wrong, always causing drama at home because I was just a child and regardless of how hard I tried to be good and worthy of love and support, I was still “just a little girl.” I wasn’t important to anyone. I was always in the way and distracting from the important work, the God Ordained work, of the adults in my family. But now I was a woman. Didn’t that finally make me a person who mattered? Didn’t it make me real?

I tried to explain this one day to a classmate that I occasionally interacted with. I tried to explain that I was sooo happy. I tried to explain the confusing concept that menstruation meant entry into adulthood and entry into adulthood made me significant, made me real, made me feel like my life would be better from now on. She looked at me for a minute and then said, “But aren’t you worried? I mean, now. What if you get pregnant?”

I was stunned. I could tell she wasn’t just being dramatic. She was genuinely worried. I didn’t know how to respond. I hadn’t been alone with Vance in two years. I felt grown up. I had so much more autonomy over my own body. I didn’t have any worries about pregnancy. I hadn’t ever had to worry about pregnancy. Vance had given me the brush off the moment I sprouted my first body hair. I wasn’t even thinking about boys yet. Pregnancy was no more of a concern for me than waking up in an alternate reality.

But my friend was worried. My friend’s world was not safe.

I understood this immediately and it only took another moment for me to realize who.

Her abuser wasn't Vance. There wasn't any connection between my abuser and hers. We were such a little, itty bitty, town. How could there be so much evil and how did it all manage to hide just below the surface, always there, but just out of sight?

My heart broke for her. I felt totally helpless. I couldn't protect myself, or my sister. What could I possibly do to help her?

Mother

It shouldn't be a surprise that the changes in my relationship with Father sparked a different set of changes in my relationship with Mother.

From my adolescent perspective, she just got weirder and weirder every day. A lifetime later I can pick out the fear underlying everything she said and did, but as a child I didn't know our family history. I didn't know that my mother was a sexually abused child a generation before I was. I didn't know how many second chances my family had squandered.

I didn't know about the events at church in her hometown that left me so traumatized I couldn't eat peanut butter for over 50 years; so traumatized they couldn't even take me back into the building. I didn't know that this was the reason we moved off the farm suddenly, leaving her hometown and family, vacating a home my parents owned and leaving it empty for years.

I didn't know that my only sibling was the progeny of an extramarital affair.

I didn't know that the man, Mr. Special Relationship, who raped me as a five-year-old was the same man who abused me at the age of two, and the man who had abused my mother a generation before.

I didn't understand that the plan to adopt five abandoned children, the plan to show the world how amazingly altruistic and saintly my parents were, fell apart as the result of that rape, or how the shine of my father's promising career was irrevocably tarnished.

I didn't know that Mother was the one who hit my sister in the back of the head with a rock. None of us know how close we came to losing Heather that day.

I didn't know that the move to Maine was a Hail-Mary pass, an attempt to reestablish Father's professional reputation by moving 1000 miles in hope that none of the rumors and stories about our family could follow. I can only imagine the feeling of doom my parents felt on learning that we had moved all the way to Maine only to end up living directly across the street from a known pedophile.

I say all of this not to absolve my mother of responsibility for the harm my sister and I endured, only to recognize that neurosis is not a surprising outcome for someone with her experience. She grew up with the same dysfunctional religious messages as I did. She was taught that those who are Godly and righteous will be blessed and sinners will be punished. Every negative event in her life, including sexual abuse, was therefore a direct consequence of her own sinful and unworthy behavior.

Her way of coping was to revise history. She did this constantly. A simple example occurred many years later one day in at the Grand Canyon. We were waiting in a very long restroom line because some of the pipes had frozen overnight. When I reached the front of the line, I looked at the thin layer of dodgy water that had run across the concrete floor. I looked at the long line behind me, at unused stalls beyond the water stain, and at my thick soled sturdy hiking boots. I made a decision and braved a single step on the wet floor in order to move the line along. Mother was next to me in line. I told her what I was going to do, and she watched me do it, but as we left the restroom, she carefully explained how the middle toilet must have flooded while I was in the end stall because she knew I would never have willingly walked across that puddle. This behavior was common for her. It is hard to spend any length of time with her without witnessing a blatant revision of whatever reality, no matter how insignificant, she finds unacceptable. History just isn't history until she assesses it and revises any element or nuance that might not meet her approval.

She was a neglected and sexually abused child long before I was. She needed someone to make her feel special. She was an easy mark; easy to groom. Her abuser made her feel special; he made her feel seen. He would meet her in the movie theatre that was within walking distance of home and school, in her little hometown. He wanted to be with her, to spend time with her. He would save a seat in the very back row. So what if he liked to put his hand up her skirt during the show? He bought her candy. He made her feel important.

Like me she was the daughter of a prolific preacher, a man who claimed to speak with the authority of the holy spirit. Mr. Special Relationship was from her church, so she framed the relationship in the language of her religion, spending time with him was her gift of ministry to a lonely older person.

No one ever stepped in. No one helped her understand the relationship for what it was. No one gave her healthy emotional support, or the time and attention needed to break her dependence on him.

How could she not see this man as someone special in her life?

I think he may have been the most important person in her life; until the day she showed her first signs of womanhood and he lost all interest. I do not know the specifics, the when or how of the "you're not a little girl anymore" brushoff but I can imagine how it impacted her.

I remember my own experience. I remember Vance explaining that I was growing and changing, and that it was time for me to leave our relationship behind. I remember how confusing and hurtful the conversation was, but it wasn't the end of my world. I had other activities and friends enough to fill the void. I missed our after-school card games, but I didn't miss having to put up with his strange behavior or the lump in his pants and I still had regular occasions to be in and out of their home even if only to interact with Edith.

Mother's life was different. I have never heard her speak of childhood friends, only other little girls who taunted her or told her not to spend time with the one person in her life who made her feel special and wanted. I have only heard her talk of that relationship a few times, but her tone of voice speaks volumes. Her voice is wistful when she talks about him. The sounds of pain, loss and betrayal are reserved for the other children in her life, the ones who tried to explain why she shouldn't spend time with this older man who made her feel like she was special, like she mattered.

How could she understand the harm to her children, how could she protect us while seeing her own abuser as the only person who ever really cared for her?

It is simple really. In order to make sense of her life, she revised the relationship with her abuser as something righteous and holy. Those who tried to tell her otherwise were the enemy. When God blessed her with a daughter, she saw me as the longed-for opportunity to renew her relationship with this man. Is it any surprise she saw me as a means of vicariously claiming attention from this man who had given her the brush off not so many years before? Is it any surprise she taught me to frame my relationship with him as 'special' and as 'ministry?'

He was the man she sent me to every Sunday during adult fellowship after service. He was the man I was supposed to ask for candy. He was the man who smeared himself with peanut butter to entice me to lick it off. He was the man who took me into his trailer at Reunion after our tent flooded. But she couldn't see any of that. He was the man who meant so very much to her that she would do anything to have him speak to her, or just to see and acknowledge her again.

Then we moved to Maine. We moved across the country to a place this man would never find us, and directly across the street from a man with the very same predilection. Is it any surprise Mother framed his presence as a miracle? Is it any wonder she taught us that our relationship with Edith and Vance was our opportunity for us to demonstrate the sanctity of our family and religious beliefs? Is it any wonder she targeted me, the oldest and most independent, to take the blame when things fell apart?

Me

I grew up in a world where every bad thing that happened, no matter how trivial, ridiculous, or out of my control, was somehow my doing; this was reinforced by both parents.

Mother's frequent and violent temper tantrums were always my doing. It didn't matter if I had no idea what I had done to set her off, or even if I was present when it happened. If I pointed out that there was no rational link between whatever she was angry about and me. Her explanation was that this was because I was 'passive aggressive.' I was also a master manipulator. Any lack of evidence as to how I set up the events that triggered her rage were just examples of how skilled I was and the lengths I would go to in order to make her life difficult. I was skilled at what we would now label micro aggressions. I was told that if I honestly considered my behavior, I would see how I constantly needled her, constantly pushed her buttons until, with no other outlet for her anger and frustration my mother finally blew her stack.

The thing was that I wasn't needling her. I didn't secretly enjoy setting her off. I lived my life walking on eggshells while always, desperately trying to keep everything together.

I did search my soul. I knew that the accusations that I passive aggressively wanted to push her past the limits of her control were false. So I found a different explanation. I knew I didn't cause these things because I wanted to, but I still saw myself as the center point and thus the cause of all the dysfunctional behavior around me. I did my best to make things better but nothing in my power was enough to break the pattern.

The only explanation I could conceive of was sin. Somehow there was sin within me. I was so full of sin that I could not control when and how it leaked out. This sin that emanated from within me was the true cause of all the evil in my life. This sin caused Mothers tantrums. It caused the evil behavior of Vance and Mr. Special Relationship. If I could just find a way to exorcise the well of sin in the depths of my soul, then everyone and everything would be better.

I tried and I tried. I never stopped believing that if I tried just a little harder, I could find a way to be good enough that all the bad stuff would stop. I was a smart kid and a good student. I did more than my share of chores. My friends were the best and smartest kids in my class. I didn't ever do anything I knew was bad. I was better, I was kinder, I was more polite and more helpful than anyone

I knew. I was always careful to follow any and all of the rules I knew about. I didn't dare cheat in even the smallest of rules. I read the scriptures. I said my daily prayers. I made my bed. I folded the laundry. I brushed my teeth. I brushed my teeth a lot. Toothbrushing became an obsession. The dentist said I should brush twice a day. I brushed at least four times a day. I brushed when I got up in the morning, after every meal, and even after snacks. I brushed more often than my friends with braces. Other children asked me why I brushed my teeth all the time, but I never knew how to answer. How could I explain that I was brushing my teeth in a vain attempt to make my soul clean and pure. How could I explain that I was trying to brush away the evil that I was afraid emanated from the depths of my soul?

None of it mattered. Mother was a dry drunk who could literally lose control for days at a time and I was always the trigger.

I lived in a perpetual state of anxiety that followed me beyond my parents' home and into adulthood. My first marriage was to a man whose temper and willingness to blame me for whatever set him off was just as bad as hers. When the marriage failed (spectacularly) I knew that the evil of my childhood was still within me. Every relationship of my life was doomed, and I was the only common denominator.

A therapist (not my favorite one) once tried to point out that much of my anxiety was unfounded. She asked me, "So what? What if you make a mistake? What if you break a rule? What will happen? What are the consequences?"

She thought she could guide me to the realization that my fears were unfounded, that people get away with careless and even malicious acts all the time. She thought that when I couldn't name a specific consequence, I would understand that there were none.

We were so far apart in that moment I literally couldn't speak. I couldn't answer her. I couldn't find the words to explain. I just looked at her unable to express the reality of the world I lived in. It wasn't until weeks, or maybe months, later that I found the words. The answer wasn't about the one thing that would happen, it was that anything could happen.

Something always happens. In the world of my mother, and the world that she passed on to me, the consequence was that when the bad thing happened, no matter what the bad thing was, it was attributed to my general sinfulness and lack of worth.

If not for my sin, none of the bad things in life would happen. If not for me, all of our lives would be blessed and free of struggle.

Because Mother lived in a world of no mercy, she passed that life's perspective on to me. Mercy, grace, compassion; none of these applied to us. We were not beloved Children of God. Worthiness was a carrot dangling just out of reach and every failed attempt to reach it reinforced the truth, that we could never cleanse ourselves of the horrible sins that emanated from our souls and entrapped the otherwise Godly people around us.

Mother's denial was a trap of circular reasoning. There was no sexual abuse. It was just a story her unworthy children made up. If I were truly pure and righteous, the spirit of God within me would be so strong that no one would be able to harm either me or my innocent sister in this way. By choosing to interpret our accusations as lies, she was giving me the gift of pretending that I was a pure souled child of God rather than the cradle of sin we both knew me to be. By denying my accusations of sexual abuse, she was giving me a gift of infinite kindness.

She had to believe this because her own life story was a web of denial from the days of her own sexual abuse. As long as she could not face her own past, she remained unable to see the abuse we, her children, were living with.

Because she existed in this fragile globe of lies, she also lived in a perpetual state of fear; fear of the one uncontrollable event that could bring it all down. Her fear expressed itself in stories of good people who made one little mistake and lost everything. There was a story for every circumstance, and they were all the same; a good person (ironically a Godly person who should have been protected by their righteousness) made one well intentioned, miniscule mistake and their life was ruined forever.

There was the family who let a neighbor child play in the back yard. The child stepped in a hole and injured her ankle. The child's parents sued. This poor family lost everything! Their only sin was to let a neighbor child play in their yard and now they would be paying for this one little mistake for the rest of their lives.

There was a well-behaved young person who was in a store with a friend when the friend was caught shoplifting. The well-behaved young person did not shoplift and was unaware of what the friend did, but they were both arrested, they both ended up with police records. The good child had not done anything wrong but because of the friends she kept, she had a record. She would never get into any good schools, no nice boy would ever marry her, no one would ever give her a job… Her life was ruined!

I heard this second story a lot. Mother was always intimidated by my friends. She was intimidated by the little girl who lived up the street when I was three. She was intimidated by my grade school friends in Marquette and again by my friends in Maine. My friends! Somehow, despite all the dysfunction in my life I had the most wonderful friends! I am alive today because I was somehow privileged to team up with amazingly smart, compassionate, responsible friends. Of my three best friends in Maine, one became a teacher, another went to MIT, and the third became a literal beauty queen. These amazing young women kept me safe and grounded in a very harsh world.

So Lucky

One afternoon, while the house was quiet and I was alone puttering in the kitchen, Mother walked in. She looked at me like she had something on her mind and said, "You are so lucky. You don't have any idea how lucky you are." I looked back at her and waited for more. I knew there was more. Finally, she added, "Don't you understand that in countries like India a young woman can be stoned if people know she is not a virgin?"

I didn't understand. In my generation 'stoned' had something to do with illicit drugs but it wasn't a term I ever used so I had to ask what she meant. She explained, in detail. She referenced the scripture from John where Christ protects the woman caught in adultery by challenging the crowd and saying, "Let he who is without sin cast the first stone." Except that Mother left the role of Jesus out altogether. She described the woman and her sin, the ritualized punishment, enforced by a community, and surrounded by all the men in her life, standing as accusers, judges, jury and executioners.

I just stood there for a minute, trying to take in her message and the meaning behind it. Is my mother threatening to kill me? Finally, I asked, "What if it wasn't her fault? What if someone older and stronger made her do those things?"

I thought, what about the man? Why doesn't anyone accuse him of being a sinner? Is he the same man who raises the accusation, who incites the other men with him to carry out the sentence?

I also asked how a person could be stoned to death. I was a child. When I heard biblical references to throwing stones, I always thought of the phrase that people who lived in glass houses shouldn't throw stones (not that people in wooden or brick houses should throw stones either) but in my mind I always saw a literal glass house on a hill with a person inside so intent on throwing stones they threw an actual rock through their own glass wall. To me the phrase meant, "don't be so eager to point out someone else's failing that you damage your own life." I did not relate to throwing stones as a way to kill someone.

I also didn't really understand how it would work. I said if someone started throwing rocks at me, I would simply run away. Mother explained that if there were enough men, they could surround the woman and keep her from running away.

As I tried to conceive of a situation where all the men in a young woman's life would be willing to get together and do such a horrible thing, Mother assured me the law was real and it only applied to women. Adultery wasn't the same sin for men, especially if the woman was a virgin. It didn't matter if the man took part in the act, or even if the sexual act had been rape. She went on to explain that once a young woman was no longer a virgin, her life was ruined anyway. As long as she lived, she would only be an example of shame for her family. No one would ever want her.

The men throwing stones were doing so to protect the reputation of the family and the whole community. It didn't matter if the woman knew the men, if she had gone to school with them or been friends with them. If a woman was accused of being a sinner none of the men would be her friend anymore. No one would help her. They would all band together to follow the law to cleanse their community of her sin by stoning her until she was dead. She wanted me to know that this wasn't just a long-ago story from the bible. There were plenty of places in the world where women were still stoned today, and I should be very glad we didn't live in such a place because if we did, she would not do anything to protect me.

I watched her face as these thoughts settled into my soul. I swear I saw her emotions shift from manipulative anticipation to malice, glee, and finally triumph. Then she turned around and walked away, leaving me alone to catch my emotional balance and wonder about the fragile layer of ice I trod every day of my life. How thin was it? How close was I to falling through at any time? Her message was clear. When that thin layer of ice finally broke no one would be there to pull me out.

As bad luck would have it, a little while later I came across a melancholy, artsy movie on our Canadian television channel. The movie was about an awkward, adolescent girl, who didn't fit in and didn't have any friends. The girl finds and rescues a beautiful white dove with a broken wing. The girl cares for the bird until it heals but the bird still cannot fly. There are mean girls in the movie who taunt the girl with the bird. One of them convinces her that her bird really can fly but doesn't want to because it likes having the girl to care for it and feed it. The mean girls convince our protagonist that all she has to do is throw a pebble or two at the bird and the bird will be startled into flying away. Because the girl wants to have friends, she agrees to this and joins a circle of other girls throwing pebbles at her bird. This simple plot plays out over two-and-a-half excruciating hours and ends with a dead bird all but buried under a pile of pebbles. It was exactly the wrong movie for me to come across at that moment in my life. The final image of the beautiful white dove dead and broken under a pile of pebbles will be with me forever.

Odds and Ends

There are a couple of other events of note from that year.

First, Mother decided we should add a Sunday school hour to our weekly church schedule. Each of the two other families in our little church group had four or five children and one had a set of local grandparents. All in all, there were almost twenty people attending weekly services in our home and most of us were children or youth. It made sense for Mother to initiate Sunday School.

At first Sunday School materials consisted of a children's bible, along with crayons and construction paper. But a few weeks later other materials arrived.

One Sunday, as I sat with other children around our kitchen table, she passed out a stack of biblical graphic novels. They were all the same, twenty or so pages long, telling the story of Shadrach, Meshach, and Abednego.

Shadrach, Meshach, and Abednego were the three young men who refused to bow down to a false God. The King insisted that all of his subjects bow to his God. Any who did not would be thrown into a fiery furnace, but Shadrach, Meshach, and Abednego were steadfast. They would not bow to the Kings false God even under threat of being bound and thrown into the flames, in fact they allowed themselves to be taken, bound, and thrown into the heart of the fire.

Because Shadrach, Meshach, and Abednego were so brave and so loyal to the One True God the flames of the furnace could not burn them. Their bonds fell away and they were unharmed.

There it was, an actual bible story proving the point that God would always protect the righteous, that we had only to be faithful and pure of heart and we would be safe and protected from any bad and evil thing, no matter how powerful. Proof that if I insisted bad things did happen to me, I was also confessing to being horribly sinful and therefore I deserved to be punished by God.

I would like to believe this was a coincidence. I would like to believe that Mother was not intent on reinforcing the message that our accusations of sexual abuse had to be lies because of course her children were too pure for any such harm to come to us. I would like to believe this was not a deliberate, premeditated message on the importance of covering up evidence of my innate sinful nature, but Sunday School only lasted for a few weeks and the only materials we were ever given was a graphic novel of Shadrach, Meshach, and Abednego.

Her point was clear. She would do us the honor of believing us liars rather than acknowledge that I was so consumed with sin that my very presence tempted a poor old man, not to mention everyone else around me, into committing unspeakable sin. If I knew what was good for me, I would accept this little bit of grace and keep my stories to myself.

The second incident occurred at a school concert. Our small-town music program included both chorus and band and we performed at least two concerts a year. My parents always attended school concerts and always brought Edith with them.

Edith was happy to accompany my parents to school concerts. She claimed to enjoy watching me sing with the choir. Mother took great pride in being the wonderful person who could coax this otherwise shut-in out of her house. No one ever mentioned the fact that Edith's grandchildren all played in the band. Sitting safely next to my parents, Edith could at least see the grandchildren that never came near her on any other occasion.

The one time visit of grandchildren playing in their yard while Heather and I watched from across the street had never been repeated.

The only other time Edith saw her grandchildren was on Christmas Eve when as a family we took her to the church her children and grandchildren attended. Even then Edith never approached her grandchildren or their parents, she never spoke a word to or about them, and even though I saw her grandchildren in school every day, they did not speak to me at all.

But this story isn't about Edith and her grandchildren. This story is about my father and a school bully. I had wonderful classmates but, as with any school, we also had bullies. On this day my assigned seat on the choir risers was directly in front of one of the worst bullies among the girls in my grade.

I was wearing my best dress, a powder blue skirt and top with part gingham check and part sailor suit styling. Because I only sang with the choir, I had to sit on the risers for the whole concert including while the band played. The classmate and bully behind me also had to sit still with nothing interesting to fill her time while listening to the band, so she decided to try to make me cry. For about 40 minutes she poked me in the kidneys, pulled my hair, pinched me, and otherwise did everything she could think of to make me miserable. I tried desperately not to make a scene and didn't think anyone was aware. I didn't know that Father was watching every malicious act, identifying with my plight and becoming angrier by the moment.

When the concert was finally over, I grabbed my coat and stepped into the hall behind the auditorium to find my father physically holding the class bully against the wall. His face was purple and blotchy and barely two inches away from hers as he spit out his message presumably threatening unspeakable vengeance if he ever caught wind of her tormenting me again.

I had no idea how to react.

My father stepped away from her as I approached and neither of us spoke a word as we walked away.

The girl who bullied me spoke to me once in the days that followed. She tried to sound tough, but she was obviously nervous.

For my part, I never believed my father's actions had any meaning. This was a one-time experience. Nothing else in my life changed. Mother could still scream at me for days on end and he would simply raise an eyebrow as if to say, "You bring this on yourself." Heather and I still performed our awkward dance around Edith and Vance spending just enough time at their house to look like we cared about the 'special ministry' our presence brought them, all the while trying to stay within arm's reach of each other and bolting for the door as soon as we possibly could.

Father and I did not talk about that day for almost twenty-five years. When we did, he was the one who brought it up. It was the day he chose to discuss how I owed him 'atonement' for all the times I "fornicated against him," including 'touching' myself as a very small child. He started this conversation by reminding me how he had protected me by threatening a 13-year-old child.

As *if!*

As if he bothered to ask about or even look at the two columns of bruised pinch marks running up the sides of my back.

As if he ever once asked me if I had any more trouble from her.

As if that one day was the only time I ever dealt with bullies!

As if he ever cared any other time!

As if anything that he did on that day was in any way about me!

His actions were simply that of a once bullied little boy using my life as an outlet for his own baggage. And now here he was, detailing the various times I had "fornicated against" him; whether as a battered and raped child or as an independent and grown woman who had lived most of my life outside his home, and holding up this one meaningless moment in time as the shining example of his perfect parenting.

Summer and Camp

Summer came. If you have never experienced a northern summer then I am sad. There is so much glory in a climate where the growing season is forced into a window of a couple short months, and the sun shines long into the night.

For me, summers in Maine were all about Reunion and camps.

This summer, 1975 I spent three whole weeks at Winniaugwamauk, one for Reunion and then a week of Junior High camp, and a week at Junior Camp as a counselor. Being a counselor was made even better by the fact that I did not have to pay for the camp. There was no need to beg my parents for another weeks' worth of camp fees. In fact, they benefited as they did not have to provide room and board while I was away.

This was the year I drove down with the H's, one of the two other church families in The County, who comprised our little group of Northern Saints.

There were at least four of us smaller people packed into the back seat of their old sedan and lots of salty crunchy road food. I was used to bringing books and toys along to pass the time on road trips. My family didn't do junk food. I could swear the plastic bag of generic cheese puffs that joined us in the back of that car started out as big as I was. I am sure that by the time we arrived copious amounts of cheese dust adorned all our persons as well as the upholstery.

This glorious arrival was followed by a full week of all the wonderful camp activities minus the daily church services and stodgy adults. And so many more children my own age!

I believe this was the first year I made my own way home by bus. Bus service was available from the town a few miles away and could take me on a straight, albeit slow, ride to or from

Bangor, which itself was a little over fifty miles from camp. The bus took the back roads and stopped at every little hamlet along the way, taking a little over five hours to cover the 250-mile trek home. In the coming years this was my primary mode of transportation to and from camp.

I would arrive at camp with a single $20 bill tucked inside my bags to purchase the ride home. One of my best summer friends lived outside of Bangor so her family was a good source of transportation between camp and the bus depot. One year her father erected a set of bunks in the back of their old VW van. Not only were there no seatbelt laws in those days, no one looked twice at a battered van driving down the highway with happy children stretched out on totally unsecured bunk beds in the back of it. Risky or no, it was a joyous experience that still puts a smile on my face.

Mother and Father knew that camp ended on Saturday but depending on what transportation arrangements I made the trip home could take place on either Saturday or Sunday. When I broke the $20 to pay for the ticket, I would get enough change to use the pay phone, call home and let them know when to pick me up. The bus stopped for about half an hour in one of the larger towns along the way. I waited until then to call home, so as to save the long-distance charges. If I didn't get a chance to call from there, I would wait until I got off the bus, call home, and then wait 30 minutes or so until someone arrived to pick me up.

The hotel where we took our one 20-minute break had a lunch counter. I looked wistfully at the menu on that first trip home before realizing I could purchase a grilled cheese sandwich for only $.20. From that point on I saved back enough of my own money to treat myself to a hot grilled cheese. The ritual made me feel grown-up, off in the world having my own adventures. I didn't understand about tipping. I hope the man behind the counter understood.

A year later I managed four weeks at camp! The rules were a bit fuzzy as to whether one qualified for a new camp the summer you moved up to a new school or if you had to have graduated your first year of Junior or Senior High before attending the camp for that group. Naturally, I chose to interpret them in my favor. I attended Sr. High camp after completing eighth grade, shortly before my 14th birthday. I also attended both Jr High and Junior camp as a counselor. Of course, I was there for Reunion too.

Mother took me to the bus station for the trip down. She had also arranged for someone to pick me up in Bangor and drive me the rest of the way to camp. The rest was up to me. I always managed to find someone. Parents of a friend or one of the adults who had a role in running the camp. Sometimes I made it to the bus on Saturday other times I arranged to spend the night with someone and rode home on Sunday. Regardless, I was surrounded by good friends and responsible adults who got me safely to the next stop on my journey. I was surprised that fall, a week or so after returning home from camp when Mother made a point to say she missed me when I was gone for so many weeks. I think I responded, “You do?” She seemed to think that it was only natural for her to miss me when I was away. I looked at her as she said this and remembered the conversation from a few years before, when she insisted that the only reason my friend Paula spent so many weeks at summer camp was because then her parents didn’t want to have to deal with her being around all the time. Mother might have been telling the truth, but at the time I was certain she was lying and wondered what her motivation was.

A Bus Story

Sometimes I boarded the bus in Bangor, other times I started the trip in Ellsworth, twenty-five miles further south. Boarding in Ellsworth was a bit tiresome as it left me with a four-hour layover in Bangor before boarding the next bus for the five-hour trip north. Sometimes I found interesting things to do in Bangor, but there was one year when this created a challenge.

I was prepared to enjoy my time in Bangor, which to me was a big city. I had a little bit of money in my pocket and a plan for the afternoon. I got off the bus from Ellsworth and as I stashed my bags in a coin operated locker, a large man approached me. To my best adolescent assessment, he was a middle-aged adult, heavy set and appeared to be mentally slow. If you have ever seen the movie "Of Mice and Men" think of Lennie. This man looked and acted just like Lennie, as if he'd walked right off the movie set.

"Lennie" clearly wanted to talk to me. I wasn't exactly afraid of him; I just got the impression that with every polite response he became more and more attached. If I didn't break away, he was going to stick to me like glue for the whole afternoon, so I excused myself. I said I had some other things to do and walked away towards downtown.

I visited a favorite craft store but after browsing for just a few minutes "Lennie" walked in and headed towards me. I managed to circle around some of the displays and exit the store without coming face to face with him. There was also a music store on my list. I tried to duck behind a group of people on the sidewalk but within a few minutes he had tracked me again. The same thing happened at the sandwich shop. I was tired of trying to shake him off my trail. By now it was late enough that my bus would be waiting outside the terminal so I hurried back to the bus station, retrieved my bags, gave them to the driver who stashed them in the cargo hold, then I boarded the bus and found a seat near the back. I still had about an hour before we were scheduled to leave but as long as Lennie didn't have a ticket for this route, I thought I was in a safe place.

I probably shouldn't have been looking out the window, but it is human nature to want to look and see if the coast is clear. Other passengers were boarding before Lennie figured out where I was. I heard the driver ask for his ticket as he stepped onto the bus. Thankfully, Lennie didn't have a ticket. He muttered something about the "Girl" and pushed past the driver. There were a couple of people standing in the aisle between me and the front of the bus, but Lennie had seen me and was pushing his way back. There wasn't a back door, no other way out. Nothing I could do except pray for someone, anyone, to get between Lennie and me.

The driver did not know a thing about this little drama he just knew that someone without a ticket had forced his way onto the bus. I watched the driver walk up behind Lennie and grab him by the back of his jacket. Lennie was almost a foot taller and much beefier than this man. Lennie turned around and said "I just gotta talk to the girl." I hunched down further in my seat, as if that would do any good. I don't think the driver had any idea who I was or what girl Lennie was talking about. He had an attempted stow-away and was not going to allow it. What followed was a battle of wills.

The Driver said, "If you don't have a ticket, you need to get off of my bus."

Lennie responded, "I just want to talk to the girl."

The Driver said, "Show me your ticket."

Lennie said, "There she is. There's the girl. I want to talk to the girl.

They stared each other down. I wasn't sure which way this was going to go but Lennie wasn't the sort to challenge authority. After a moment he backed down, hung his head, and allowed himself to be pushed off the bus. I breathed a sigh of relief and pushed back against the headrest. When the time finally came, I was very happy to pull away from the terminal.

A Boy

I think it was the month before I turned fourteen when a new young man joined us at Reunion. No one had met him before. He was polite, charming, and easy to look at. It made me feel good just to be around him.

Since he was new to our campgrounds, I offered to show him some of the best places. Maybe I should have considered what happened the last time I showed a boy around camp, but I was still young and not wise to the secret language of intimacy and invitations.

We started talking to each other during a morning group activity. He said he had come to Reunion with an uncle who lived near Boston. He also claimed his uncle was a member of the Playboy club and had taken him there a couple of times. This sounded like a warning flag. I asked why he would go to such a place, and beyond that why he would choose to tell me about it. He insisted it was not what I thought. He said it was just a nice place to have a drink and spend some time. I was still put off. I thought maybe he was just trying to sound worldly because he thought I might be impressed. I wanted to show him the boat dock and the trail to the Point. I figured that once I showed him some of my favorite camp places, he might realize why this beautiful campground was so much more interesting than a club were women walk around with fake bunny tails.

We didn't get to either of my favorite places before he asked me to stop and wait for him to catch up. I stopped, he stepped close, put a hand on my shoulder and kissed me. It wasn't like Jason at all. This kiss was soft, friendly and gentil. His tongue lightly touched mine. His breath was sweet and fresh. He was holding me lightly, not controlling me.

I felt something warm and looked down to see that he had pushed my blouse down and his hand was lightly cupping my breast.

Um?

I didn't say he could do this. Was I okay with it? This was very different from my last experience. I didn't feel at all like I was being run over by a serpent tongued, handsy tractor. This was nice. Maybe I was okay with it.

He kissed me again and asked if I would like to sit down in the grass. Okay. I was good with that. We were not on a secluded trail away from the camp. We were along a quiet but well-traveled route. We were at the edge of the campfire pit, near the children's chapel and along a path that led to campers and tents. We were alone at the moment, but anyone could happen along at any time. I knew that. I knew the patterns of life in this place. What could it hurt to sit here on the grass with this engaging young man who actually seemed interested in talking to me?

Of course, maybe he didn't realize that this quiet place was not actually so private. I turned to look at the ground behind me before sitting on the grass.

Penis.

Penis!

PENIS!!!!

Penispenispenispenispenispenispenispenispenispenispenispeni
spenispenispenispenispenispenispenispenispenispenispenispen

ispenispenispenispenispenispenispenispenispenispenispenispe nispenispenispenisNo!no!no!no!no!no!no!no!no!no!no!no!*no!* *no!no!no!no!no!no!no!no***no!no!no!no!no!no!no!no!no!no!**

He was stretched out on the green grass next to me with his pants down and his manhood beautifully displayed on a perfect mound of curly brown pubic hair!

When had he taken off his pants?

How did I even know what that was?!

When had I seen one before?

It all happened so fast! I felt like everything had jumped forward by a few seconds. I was confused, disoriented.

Then he was on his feet, stammering apologies and stuffing himself back into his jeans while backing away. He said he didn't know. He didn't mean to upset me.

What had happened? Why was I looking up at him? He suggested sitting down on the grass, but I didn't remember doing so.

Someone was crying. Who? It wasn't him. He stumbled backwards one last step then turned and ran. I

was sitting on the grass. I was alone.

Was I the one crying?

I was sitting with my knees pulled up to my chin, my arms wrapped tightly around my shins, rocking back and forth. All my clothes were in place. My shorts were still buttoned and zipped but I was rocking and shaking.

Those sounds. Those soul shattering gasps and cries. Was that me?

I couldn't remember. I couldn't remember sitting down. I couldn't remember him sitting down either. I certainly didn't remember him opening his pants. *How had this happened?*

Vance! Vance and the lump in his stomach that I never understood. The lump that I thought was cancer! Obviously, it wasn't! The lump in his stomach. The place that was just soft tummy on me.

I just saw a boy's penis! *It was exactly where Vance's lump was;* the lump he wanted me to touch; the place he wanted me to sit; the lump he wanted to show me; the lump I was supposed to be so impressed by!

What had I done?

There is a behavioral pattern among trauma survivors that doesn't always make sense to people around them. It is the habit of putting ourselves into similarly risky situations again and again. Therapists refer to this as attempting to normalize the situation. In this case I think I can offer a reasonable explanation.

I believed I had made a mistake. Somehow my innocent intentions, which initially started to become something unexpected but pleasant, had gone all wrong. I didn't understand exactly where or how things had gone wrong, but I wanted to make it better. I wanted a do-over.

Surely if I tried a second time, I could avoid making such a mess of things.

I went back to my bunk in the Girls Dorm. I changed into long pants and a more substantial shirt then joined the line for lunch. I filled my tray, found a seat right next to this beautiful boy and sat down like we were old friends. Of course, I hadn't thought to ask him if he wanted a do-over. He looked at me like he had seen a ghost, wolfed his last couple bites of lunch and bolted!

The next day I learned that he had left the campgrounds. The story that filtered back to me was that he had been overly forward with a young woman and upset her badly. No one would tell me who the young woman was but apparently, several adults had been up much of the night trying to calm her down and determine how to deal with the situation. In the end the young man and his uncle were both asked to leave.

My father had been one of the men involved. One of the men who issued the verdict, "Go. Go now and never come here again." Mother said that I would understand if I had any idea what he had done. She insisted she couldn't tell me, but that if I knew I would be horrified.

I was surprised and confused. He had certainly been overly forward with me, but not forceful in any way. I didn't understand. Compared to Jason's advances, this young man was the definition of courtesy.

How was it that a young man who didn't grip so tightly a girl couldn't pull free, who didn't force his serpent tongue down her throat, who didn't force his hands down inside her pants, was forced to leave? Who was the girl whose sensibilities were so fragile that this eager but not forceful young man had left her "truly traumatized?"

The young woman was not me. I never said a word to anyone. I don't think I have ever told this story before today. Who would I have talked to? What would I have said? All I could expect in return would be more of the same old advice, "Stop being a sinner and the bad things will quit happening to you."

Yes, he was waaay too forward, but he owned his mistake. A young man who backs off, literally runs away at the very first sign of crossed signals. The world should always be so safe.

Why tell anyone that once again my sinful nature had gotten me in trouble and threatened the reputation of our pristine and Godly family?

Tricia

That fall there was a new student in my class. Her name was Tricia. She was from the next town over, but her parents had divorced and she moved to our town with her mother and brothers. She was super smart, funny, musically talented, and more worldly than me. We both fell headlong into one of those adolescent friendships that feels more important than anything else in the world.

Tricia was several months older than me. She read teenage heartthrob magazines and spun ongoing, soap opera fantasies about the boys in them. When we were together we would build on each other's stories almost to the point of believing they were real.

We didn't want anyone to know the embarrassing truth, that all our exciting tales were just fancies in our minds, so we gave our characters numbers to use in place of names. That would keep people from catching on, wouldn't it?

Tricia's mother got angry with us one day. She didn't understand that our stories were nothing more than make-believe. She thought we were gossiping about real people in our lives and considered our behavior to be terribly rude. We couldn't do anything to defend ourselves without making things worse so we took the tongue lashing and tried to remain out of ear shot from then on.

I enjoyed talking about boys. I was developing all the right parts to attract boys and wanted them to pay attention to me, but my interest and expectations, including the stories I made up, aligned nicely with the chastity message I received from church and family. All evidence to the contrary, I thought I lived in a world where we all operated by the same code. I dreamed of a boyfriend who would hold my hand, swap funny stories, enjoy my company, sometimes hold me close, and kiss me sweetly before saying goodbye. Wasn't that what everyone wanted?

Near the end of our freshman year Tricia started dating a boy in our high school who was a Junior. I didn't think he was good enough for her and I was hurt by no longer being the most important person in her life, but summer was coming, and I would be away enjoying five full weeks of camp so there wasn't much I could do to shift the dynamics of her relationship.

A Long Glorious Summer

Me, second from right with Heather and my parents at Winniaugwamak. Summer 1977.

Summer came and I was scheduled for more glorious weeks on the Maine coast than ever before. This year after Reunion, I was scheduled as counselor at the Junior and Junior High camps and I could attend both Senior High and Adventure camp!

Adventure camp did not take place at Winniaugwamauk. Instead, a group of older youth and young adults loaded our gear and found some place, a different place every year, only accessible by canoe. I couldn't cheat on Adventure camp like I had with Senior High camp the year before. To attend Adventure Camp, I had to be at least fifteen and have completed my freshman year of High School. Of course, my birthday was in August, so I bent the rules just a little. The first day of camp was one day before my fifteenth birthday.

I don't know if anyone would have quibbled about the one day, but I had an extra factor to weigh the scales in my favor. My father had developed a diverticulum pouch at the back of his throat, behind his larynx. He had suffered through a couple of frightening episodes when food lodged in the pouch closing off his windpipe. The Heimlich maneuver would not be widely used until the early 80's but after a choking episode that was only relieved by ramming his chest on the back of a kitchen chair, we all learned how to respond to such emergencies. The only permanent solution was surgery, and this was a delicate and complicated procedure in the 1970's. The closest hospital and surgeon with experience in this procedure were in Boston. My father expected to be inpatient for several days. Overall, my parents planned to spend about three weeks in Boston. The plan was for everyone to attend Reunion together than Heather would stay with church friends and I would be left to joyously jump from one camping experience to another.

Five whole weeks! Six if you counted the gap between camp time!

Adventure Camp

I had camped in one way or another almost every year of my life, but Adventure Camp demonstrated a level of skill I had never considered. The site that year had long ago been set up as a wilderness picnic area. It included a couple of old wooden picnic tables and an outhouse with a mostly watertight roof. The nearest approach by road was a couple miles away.

One of the adults who supported the camp every year was a big rig truck driver. He had converted a flatbed trailer into a custom-built canoe rack and hauled it behind his pickup with a fifth-wheel hitch. The canoe frame held two canoes side by side and two front to back, stacked four rows high for a total of sixteen canoes in all. Plywood sides at the base of the trailer provided room for gear.

I had been farmed out to a family who lived on a barely paved dead-end road. I watched in astonishment as the camp trailer arrived and the driver pulled this huge rig past the house then gently backed it down the two-lane rutted drive, positioning it perfectly in front of a tired, freestanding garage.

Seatbelt laws were not what they are today. I found a place in the back of the pick-up, slightly cramped by the fifth-wheel hitch. We drove for a couple of hours while the warm wind whipped at my hair, before arriving at our landing place, offloading our canoes, filling them with gear and paddlers and heading out into wild, untamed lake country.

We barely banked our canoes before the young men set out to build the kitchen. They cut saplings, two to four inches in diameter and attached them as crossbeams between standing trees, surrounding the two picnic tables. Once the walls were framed, plastic sheeting was added to form two sides and a roof.

Someone pulled out a small oil drum that had been converted into a camp oven. The oven was laid on its side over a bed of coals with a few well-placed rocks to keep it stable. A hinged door had been cut into one end and a rack placed inside the barrel kept pans of food upright. There was even a thermometer to watch the temperature. In a few short hours we had tables, shelves for prep and storage, a working oven, and a cast iron pot for cooking.

Another group of experienced campers roamed the nearby woods looking for a spring. They located a damp depression where the water bubbled up from below. A few minutes with a shovel and more carefully placed rocks gave us access to fresh groundwater.

By the end of our first full day of camp, we were huddled in our smokey, but cozy kitchen, safely out of the rain.

There was one more camper on his way, not a boy, a young man several years older than me. He was going to school out of state and hadn't been able to join us on our first day. I knew his name and had a vague memory of interacting with him once or twice. He was coming in his own canoe and had directions to our campsite, but finding one's way through a myriad of lakes and peninsulas on a dark rainy night was challenging. We were deep in the wilderness. There were no lakeshore houses or cabins. It was raining hard. The moon and stars were hidden by clouds. There was not a single point of light, just a young man alone in his canoe paddling a handful of miles across an inky black lake.

One of the older campers left the group to guide our straggler in. He walked out to the tip of the peninsula with a flashlight and waited in the dark and pouring rain flashing the light on and off, on and off, a beacon in the darkness.

The rest of us were crammed into our dry but smokey kitchen. It was late and we were getting a bit anxious. In a world before cell phones, we had no way of knowing if our missing camper was lost or just delayed, and no way of calling for help or effectively starting a search before daylight. It was a relief to hear that he had spotted the light and shouted from out in the water that he saw us and was coming in.

A while later, after the canoe was safely beached and unloaded, a tall young man in a dripping yellow rain slicker joined our huddled group. I was sitting on top of one of the picnic tables with my legs dangling over the end. Our new arrival worked his way into the crowd finding a warm spot between the firepit and the table where I sat. As the crowd repositioned, I met his eyes for just an instant. I looked up at his face and said "Hello Paul." There was a pause, just the space of a heartbeat, but something unexpected and precious passed between us.

His response was a simple, "Well, Hello!"

It was August of 1977; it was my fifteenth birthday, and I was in love.

There wasn't any time to explore this newfound attachment, at least not right away. I had made plans to join a smaller group of campers on an overnight trip to explore a different part of the wild lake-lands. Paul hadn't been included in the planning of this trip and wanted to spend time with the larger group. We were not in a relationship. We had exchanged one 15 second greeting. We were years apart in age, had never been part of the same group, and hadn't laid eyes on each other in two or three years. It was just that something, something indescribable and unmistakable, had passed between us.

After breakfast with the main group, I joined the campers who were heading out. We left in four canoes and paddled off on our adventure.

If you have never spent time in a region of connected lakes it is a bit difficult to describe the environment. The Grand Lakes region of Maine is not a single lake or even a chain of lakes. There are few simple shorelines and even less road access. I think we were in the area of Big Lake Township, but I could be mistaken. We were in a place with more water than land, where it is difficult to know where one body of water becomes another. As I have said there were no roads, no cabins, no powerlines, no signs of human habitation. We canoed across the open water away from our base camp, past countless islands, peninsulas, channels and through marshy areas that were not exactly open water, swamp, or land. Towards late afternoon we pulled up on a small stretch of beach along what appeared to be an island of several acres.

We had brought our sleeping bags and a couple of small tents. The plan was for the girls to sleep in the tents while the boys camped out on the beach, under the stars. The small area of sandy beached sloped uphill and was quickly overtaken by heavy forest dense with undergrowth and tamarack trees. The ground was rugged. After canvassing most of the island we determined there was no single open space large enough for even our smallest two-person pup tent. In the end we laid all our sleeping bags side by side on the little beach, heads upslope and feet towards the water.

I had never slept in the open air before. Tents may not provide much privacy, but they are helpful for changing clothes and allowing one to feel like they have at least a little personal space. I didn't think there was any chance of rain but I wondered how bad the mosquitos might be. I thought the sand would be soft but it was slightly damp and packed hard as cement. I had to wriggle furiously in my bag to carve out a slight depression molded to my body, but it still felt weird having my head so much higher than my feet and nothing to do about that.

We were three girls and six boys, and everyone was at least a year older than me. It felt funny to say goodnight to a young man less than a hands width away from me. I had to remind myself that we were each in our own sleeping bag. I had often slept just as close to strangers on the opposite side of a plywood or canvas wall. There was nothing wrong with the arrangement. It was just different.

Despite all my anxieties, sleep found me and It was deep and restful. Someone woke with the first pale light of dawn and looked out over the water at the pink and orange sunrise. This was followed by a domino chain of jostling elbows and foot nudges until we were all awake. The slope was steep enough that no one even had to raise their head, just open their eyes and take in the beauty of the sun rising above the smooth still surface of the water. It is a moment I will remember all my life.

We breakfasted on eggs and potatoes fried in a big cast iron skillet over an open fire, splashed around in the lake and spent the rest of the day exploring nearby coves before heading home to base camp.

Our canoes glided through a garden of marsh grass and water lilies. Brightly colored dragonflies darted and hovered above the lily pads. I can still feel the sunlight, smell the freshness of the air and water, and see the whirlpool drip patterns left by our paddles as we stroked our way through one of the most beautiful places on earth.

I sat in the back of the canoe, behind a boy and girl who were a couple. As I paddled, I watched the interaction between them. They traded positions between stops. The person in the front paddling and guiding the canoe while the person behind them, the middle seat, merely a passenger, reached out lightly touching, rubbing stiff back and shoulder muscles. Those gentle touches created a longing in me that I did not understand. Many years later I would hear it defined as “skin hunger,” a physical longing for the touch of another human being.

In my family we did not touch. We did not hug or snuggle. We never said, "I love you." Occasionally my stiff, aloof, Mother would reach out to hold hands with an attitude of desperation that I recognized but didn't understand. It was confusing, emotionally charged, behavior from a woman who would otherwise cringe and pull away from her own children if we sat too close or accidentally brushed against her as we passed.

I didn't know I was craving human touch until that day, in the back of that canoe, where every caress I witnessed was mapped on my own body as a void of longing that I did not understand.

The sun was setting as we wound our way through the maze of channels, marshes, and lakes back toward base camp. We were clustered together in our canoes, comparing notes, trying to identify which direction was home as the twilight deepened into darkness and then we saw it, a single flashlight blinking on and off, on and off, from the far side of the lake. We were still a long way out. It was an hour or more before we reached home shore. I expressed concern more than once. "They will give up and decide we are not coming. How will we find the right landing place without the light?"

My fellow campers were surprised by this concern they tried to explain, "They are lighting the way for us. They know we are coming. They won't walk away. Why would they leave the beach before we are safely back?"

I heard the words, but they didn't help. I heard the unspoken question, "Why are you worried? This is how we take care of each other." How could I explain that I didn't understand? No one had ever taken such care of me.

The light never died. When we came close enough, we called to let them know we were on our way in. Once our canoes were safely beached there were hugs all around and then food, the portion of dinner that had been saved for us. We were home.

We were welcomed. We were family. We had been briefly lost, but searched for, cared for, and gathered safely back into the fold. Didn't everyone care for one another in this way?

Paul

By breakfast the next morning I was clearly the center of Paul's attention. I should have felt strange being shadowed by a young man literally one-an-a-half times my age. If not strange, it should have been an intoxicating, heady, experience. It was neither. It simply felt right. We were side-by-side at any and all activities. We swapped stories and bantered like friends who had been together all our lives.

After breakfast I brought out the piece of wood I had been given on the first day of camp. It was a 1X6 plank about six feet long. Our craft for the week was to carve these planks into handmade canoe paddles. There is an old adage, to me a joke, about what it takes to carve something. The statement goes like this, "It's easy. Just remove everything that isn't a paddle" (or whatever else it is you intend to create).

I can do many things, but I do not have the vision for carving.

I found a seat with a few other campers and pulled out my penknife and began ineffectively chipping away slivers of wood. No way was this going to look anything like a paddle by the end of the week. At first Paul tried to offer suggestions and encouragement but it didn't take long before he offered to take over the task of carving.

That night we all gathered at the end of the point for a campfire. Campfires are a long evolved, well-loved tradition within Community of Christ. We sang songs, told jokes, sang more songs, told stories…

At some point as we were sitting around our fire, in a half circle, so everyone could look out over the water, a flickering blue light appeared above the lake. It was irregular in shape but large enough to be interpreted as the glowing image of a man standing in a small boat.

Our songs and chatter died down as we watched this light that we did not understand. It seemed as if the light came closer until it looked to be sitting on the water no more than 30 or so yards away, where it stopped, and stayed.

Our conversation was hushed. What was it? Some unknown phenomena of moonlight and water? Someone suggested it was an angelic form watching over us. (We were a church camp after all.)

(I considered leaving this mysterious light out of my narrative. It is hard to maintain credibility while describing seemingly mystic phenomena. I may never know what the light was, but it was there. It was a thing that happened in that place and at that time. It was part of an experience that was significant in so many ways. I cannot bring myself to leave it out.)

We sat quietly on the beach as our fire died with the blue light shining just offshore. A few people got up as if to leave but couldn't drag themselves away. So they remained standing, hushed, staring out at the shimmering luminescence. After half an hour or so, one of the adults suggested we should head back to our tents and bed. We reluctantly began to trickle back towards the heart of our camp. Paul and I filtered towards the side of the crowd making us among the last to leave the beach.

In this magical moment, before we turned our back on the shining lake, we wrapped our arms around each other. There was no awkwardness, no mixed signals. A warm friendly hug naturally transitioned into a gentil, mutual, loving kiss. No forceful serpent tongue. No shocking moment of exposure accompanied by disorienting flashbacks. Just a boy and a girl, drawn to one another, in perfect harmony, embracing the moment.

That night my dreams were filled with love, comfort, and acceptance. My skin hunger was aroused head to toe. I dreamed of that embrace over and over. My subconscious reveled in it, the feel of another body against mine finally satisfying a longing I had not known existed.

I was sleeping in a tent with two other young women. Three sleeping bags on the ground. Mine was in the middle. I was dreaming of the evenings embrace, relishing the feel of another body against mine. Then I was being shaken awake by one of my tent mates. “Wake up! What’s wrong with you? Stop rolling over into me!”

This happened several times during the night. When morning finally came the young woman on my right shook me awake again and said, “Look! Look at this! Look at how far you pushed me.” Her sleeping bag was pushed so far to the side it was bulging out the wall of the tent, not to mention straining the stakes on the other side.

I apologized profusely. What else could I do? I was horribly embarrassed but I didn’t want to explain. How could I tell her that in my dreams I had confused her sleeping form with that of a beautiful young man who was one-and-a-half times my age?

By Friday my plank looked a lot like a canoe paddle, and we swapped carving tools for sandpaper. We also had paints and varnish. I decorated the blade with a daisy and Paul signed his work. Then we sealed it all under a coat of varnish.

On Saturday morning we packed out. Our last group activity was lunch at McDonald’s where we each grabbed helium balloons and were rowdy enough for the manager to ask us to quiet down. Then someone drove me to the bus depot. Summer was over.

The Trip Home

My heart was heavy, made even more so by the bus radio playing nothing but Elvis singing heavy-hearted love ballads. They suited my mood so perfectly I didn't even think to ask why the station was all Elvis, all day. I had been in the deep woods, away from civilization all week. I had no idea Elvis had passed. His next live performance was to have been in Portland. I still feel sorry for the friend who had tickets for a show he never played. She had been soooo excited.

Jason and his younger brother were also heading home on the same bus. I don't recall what they had been doing on the coast, but this was the last weekend before school started so we were all headed home together.

I had called home before boarding in Bangor, but no one answered. This didn't worry me. Phones were still physically wired. No one even had answering machines in 1977.

I called again when the bus stopped in Houlton. Still no answer. I deboarded at the downtown hotel in Presque Isle and dragged my stuff into a corner of the lobby, near the payphone. Me, smelling strongly of campfire, two tightly stuffed army duffel bags, a handmade canoe paddle, and a McDonalds helium balloon. There was still no answer to the home phone, so I began calling back-up contacts. When the first round yielded no results, I waited for 20 minutes or so then tried again.

There was a party going on in the adjoining ball room. Apparently, many of the local schoolteachers had come together for a "Before the School Year Starts," event. The room was full of smoke and music, and I recognized many of my teachers from both Jr and Sr High. I had been in the lobby for almost an hour before one of them not so casually walked past, obviously checking up on me.

By now I was expanding the number of people on my call list. Eventually I called my friend Tricia's house and reached her mother. Tricia's mother answered "Yes. Yes, I will come get you. Just give me a few minutes to find someone to watch the younger children. Can I call you back?" I gave her the number for the front desk at the hotel and sat back down to wait.

A few minutes later the desk clerk waved me over, wrinkled his nose and passed me the house phone. The caller wasn't Tricia's mom, it was Jason. He said "Stay where you are, we will come get you."

Apparently, my father's recovery had taken longer than expected. My parents were headed home but would arrive a day behind me. The plan had been for me to stay on the bus until it reached the town where Jason and his family lived, an hour or so further north. I do not know who was supposed to pass the message, but it had not reached me, Jason, or his brother.

There was a plan for me to spend the night at Jason's house?? No! No, no, no, no! I'd had a second run in with him a year ago or so earlier. I would not be sleeping and bathing in the home of Mr. Handsy Serpent Tongue! I gratefully explained that I had resolved the situation on my own and a friend's mother was on her way to pick me up.

Another one of my schoolteachers, not so casually walked across the lobby.

The desk clerk waved me over again. Tricia's mom was on her way.

The next call was from Jason's father. Was I sure? Yes! I insisted I was okay.

Yet another teacher wandered through.

A final call came in from one of my Father's co-workers. Presumably, messages had travelled from Jason's family to mine and then to Father's colleague. The hotel clerk was clearly tired of taking calls for me.

By the time Tricia's Mom arrived I was grateful to retreat from a hotel lobby where I had become the center of everyone's attention.

Tricia's mom had news. Tricia was pregnant. They had moved Tricia to her father's home, one town over. It was a, not so effective, attempt to separate her from the boyfriend. Her parents decided to end the pregnancy. Tricia, at fifteen, didn't have any say in the matter.

My family had never appreciated my friendship with Tricia. Her parents were divorced. She and her family weren't the "right kind of people." I noted the irony. None of the "right kind of people" were available to drive me home from the bus depot. None of the "right kind of people" had even managed to get a message to me to let me know there was a change in plans.

I was extremely grateful the not so well thought out plan to have me stay on the bus with Jason didn't work out. Tricia's mom dropped what she had been doing and rushed out to rescue me even though she had to break sad news in the car as we drove away.

We got to my house late at night. It was locked and empty. I hadn't expected to come home to an empty house and didn't have a key. After deciding there was no easy way in, Tricia's mom took me home with her. One of Tricia's brothers had moved into her room so the only available place to sleep was with Tricia's mom. I spent the night less than comfortable, on the far side of a king-sized bed.

In the morning Tricia's mom took me to my still locked and empty house.

I walked across the street and knocked on Vance and Edith's door. They had lived across the street from our house for decades. Did they have any keys? Our house had five exterior doors, but we only had a key to one of them. Edith sorted through a bowl of hard candy, coins, buttons... and found a key she thought might work. It did. It opened a side porch we had never had a key to. The key was old and the metal was soft. There was a small tear between the shoulder and the blade. The key only had one turn left in it and I had to take care to prevent tearing the blade off in the lock. I succeeded and safely entered the house. Tricia's mom drove away. Summer was, now, really over.

A few months later Tricia with her mother and brothers moved to Detroit, hopefully it would be far enough to keep her away from the boyfriend.

I still have the canoe paddle. I have since lived in Michigan, California, Texas, Hawaii, Maryland, Arizona Germany... Many things get left behind in cross country, sometimes cross oceanic moves. Paul's paddle is still with me.

Another Boy

It's funny to look back and realize how insecure I felt around boys. I didn't think I would ever find a boy to like me. I suppose that I was so used to a family that did not like me, that only ever engaged to chastise me or tell me how I failed to live up to what they wanted me to be, that I didn't recognize the signs from people who genuinely enjoyed my company. Even in my group of long-term girlfriends I felt like I was only included as a sort of charity case. I felt like they tolerated having me around because they felt sorry for me.

I continued to feel this way despite juggling three young men, Jason, Paul, and one I will call Bobby, who were clearly, unquestionably, interested in me.

Bobby was a kid from the other side of the tracks. He was in my grade at school but two levels below me in our structured curriculum tracks.

Let me take a minute to explain the level system my school district used. In elementary school we had reading groups, one through four. Beginning in Jr High the reading groups became levels. All of our classes were segregated by level. Expectations and even curriculum varied according to the level a student was assigned. If asked what grade we were in a child in my town would answer with both grade and level. It was not enough to say one was in sixth grade. The expected answer was 6-1, 2, 3 or 4. Level one students were on a college prep track, level four were the kids whose education would end with High School, two and three fell in between. These expectations were established in elementary school reading groups, followed us through the rest of our public schooling, and were closely aligned with social economic status.

I literally silenced my parents once when they complained that my grades, as a level one student, were not as good as those of a level three student and son of one of my father's co-workers. I explained that they could not legitimately compare grades across the gap in levels and when they accused me of making up excuses, I turned over my report card and had them read the printed statement to that effect.

Bobby and I were in the same year in school and shared the same homeroom, but I was level one and he was level three. We had absolutely no classes together. We should have known who each other was, no more.

Our paths crossed early in the summer of 1977, before I left for my six weeks of glorious summer. I was still a wild child. I wandered at will and enjoyed exploring new places on my own. On this day I was appreciating the summer foliage surrounding the town snow dump.

You might recall the snow dump in the town we first moved to in Maine which yielded a wealth of returnable bottles. In our second Maine home the snow dump was a low-lying meadow with a stream running along one side. This generally damp basin produced choke cherries and high bush cranberries. I liked the choke cherries best. My grandmother in Montana made a pancake syrup from them that she called larrup. The larrup was bright red. It might have made my breakfast plate look like a crime scene, but it gave me warm fuzzies, nonetheless.

There was a small dam across the stream that ran along the snow dump, and below the dam a pool of water just deep enough for jumping into. I was wading across the top of the dam when I ran into Bobby. We spent half the day splashing in the water, talking while sitting hip deep on top of the dam with our legs splashing in the down flow, and learning about each other.

He was the oldest of a gaggle of half and step siblings. The family had nothing. I do not think there were enough plates in the cupboard or places in the beds to allocate one for each member of the household.

Bobby didn't tell me stories about himself. He told stories about his siblings, who were struggling in school, who were being taunted by classmates, why, and the steps Bobby took to make their lives better.

Because of the social differences between us, I didn't see Bobby as boyfriend material. He, however, saw me as a catch. He placed himself in my path at every opportunity. I didn't mind. He was an amazing young man. Spending time with someone who cared so much for the people around him touched my soul in places and ways I didn't know I needed.

Once, when we were alone, he suggested a game of strip poker. I thought for a moment and mentally inventoried how many things I could take off before actually exposing myself. He was down to his skivvies before I lost a hand. I removed an earring. He was clearly disappointed, but we were comfortable enough in each other's presence that he just shrugged and gave up.

Bobby was the first person to ask me on a real date. By then his family had moved to the next town over and we were both still too young to drive, so his mother drove him to pick me up. I could feel her joy in sharing this moment with him. She dropped us off in front of the movie theatre in Presque Isle. After the movie we wandered around town. It was mid-winter; very cold and dark. We stopped into McDonalds for hot tea and time to warm up before walking back to his house.

It was spring before our mis-matched level of interest came to a head. We were bowling; the two of us with his mother and a handful of his siblings. After a good throw he pumped his fist in the air, jumped for joy, then wrapped his arms around me and planted a close-mouthed kiss directly on my lips.

I didn't kiss back.

Kissing and cuddling weren't things I thought about with Bobby. I could see the disappointment in his face. I still regret that I hurt him. One could argue that I used him. He was the safe boyfriend. The relationship worked for me because I wasn't ready for anything else.

Bobby stopped calling after that day. My family moved out of Maine the next summer. I hope he had a good life. I think about him often. He was a genuine person who deserved many good things.

Correspondence

Paul was a safe boyfriend too.

I thought about snuggling and kissing him a lot, but it was only in my head. We had only kissed the one time. Now I was home and back at High School while he was attending Graduate School in Chicago. Long-distance phone calls were expensive. Email did not exist yet. We wrote letters.

I wrote long rambling, dreamy teen-age girl letters. I bought a spiral bound notebook with brightly colored pages and scrawled the details of my life across them. Every letter was answered.

I knew it didn't make sense. As much as I enjoyed the memory of sitting, walking, talking, side by side with this beautiful young man, despite the fact that every silly, girlish letter I sent was answered with an equivalent note, sharing the details of his life and confirming how he missed my physical presence, I reserved a space in my heart for protection. He was fantasy. I didn't dare count on him to be reality.

Strangely, my parents barely seemed to notice. Mail delivery occurred before the end of my school day. Mother sorted through it every day, setting aside the letters for me. She never commented, never asked, never really seemed to care.

Allow me to back up a bit and explain why her behavior was so surprising.

A year or so earlier I had been invited to join a group of friends to see a 'Christian' movie. It was an offer of an outing to the next town over and a free movie in a theatre. I enjoyed the company of the other girls who were invited, so I said yes.

After the show there was some Christian music with a bit of a light show and a group of people walked out on stage. The speaker warmed up the crowd for a few minutes then asked everyone who wanted to be a good person to stand up. Pretty much everyone did.

Then the speaker asked everyone who believed in Jesus to remain standing. We did.

Finally, the speaker asked those of us who believed in Jesus and who wanted to be good people but also believed we could be better people than we currently were, to remain standing.

It was about this time that I looked around and noticed the people who were not standing. The parent who had driven us to the event was firmly seated, as were pretty much all the other adults in the packed theatre.

Before I could form the question in my mind the speaker on stage closed the latch on his little trap. "Thank you! Bless you! You have just accepted Jesus Christ as your personal Lord and Savior!"

"No! I hadn't!" I had agreed that I wasn't a perfect person. I was angry. That was not what I had agreed to when I remained standing. This was a dirty trick!

This was bad. I felt like I had been punched in the stomach. I lived in a home of religious elitists who would view my accepting an alter call as unfaithful to our Christian tradition. (Community of Christ today would not disapprove of any genuine spiritual experience but in that decade and especially in my family attitudes were different.)

Every alter call is unique. This one broke all the records for being contrived and forceful, and I was still a young person who found it very difficult to say no to adults.

If I had worked this out even one second earlier, I might have been able to sit back down, but now it was too late. Ushers had appeared at the end of every row and were guiding people towards a side room for one-on-one prayer with other volunteers. The youth behind me were pushing the line along. I was trapped. I tried to look for an opportunity to step away only to witness another person being literally grabbed by the arm and pushed back into the line while the speaker, still on stage with a microphone, admonished us not to walk away.

By the end of the evening, I had prayed for my soul and filled out a form, giving up my name and address.

I did not hide this experience from my parents. I told them what had happened, and how. I told them I didn't want to. I tried to explain that I had been tricked and trapped. I endured their cold, disapproving stares and backed away from the conversation as soon as I could.

A few weeks later I received a letter from the volunteer who had greeted and prayed with me. I was still angry and embarrassed, not only because the alter call had been contrived, but also because I had to deal with hostility at home.

As always, Mother had retrieved and sorted the mail. She had passed the letter to me with a look of distaste so palpable one could believe it was evidence of a mortal crime.

I took the letter to my room, read it once, then tore it to small pieces before dumping it into the trash can. What was supposed to be an enjoyable evening had turned into weeks of tension and I wanted it to be behind me.

Mother stopped me before I could get to the back door. "What was in the letter?" I told her it was nothing. She asked to see it. I told her she couldn't as I had torn it up. She tried to press further but I pushed my way past into the blessed outside. When I came home a couple of hours later the carefully reassembled letter was sitting in the middle of the kitchen table along with notes and specific questions. It didn't matter that I had not willingly accepted the alter call. It didn't matter that I had demonstrated my lack of complicity by tearing up and throwing away the letter. There was no sympathy or commiseration for having been unwittingly trapped in a situation I knew they would not approve of. I was one small step into the house, and she was waiting for me; no chance to stop in the restroom; no pause for a glass of water. I would pass her inquisition before anything else.

This was my mother. This was also the woman who did not make any comment, ever, about my year long correspondence with a young man eight years older than me, a boy they never met. I was grateful, don't get me wrong, but I was also confused.

Jason Again

At some point in the year Father decided it was time to look for a new job again. I do not know what the trigger was this time. He had been in the same position for six years, maybe he felt ready to move on to new and better things, maybe it was just wanderlust.

Father claimed the move was for me. He said it was time I had the opportunity to meet more young men from our church. He talked a bit too graphically about how I should be able to find men who would hold me, kiss me, and cherish me.

This job search was much like the time before. He scoured want ads in professional journals. Mother prepared beautifully crafted resumes on high quality paper and Father flew across the country for various interviews. He was quite excited about a job in Rapid City, South Dakota but in the end he was hired into a position in central Michigan.

It had been ten years since his career stalled because of my suspected rape. The people he had previously worked with in Michigan, the ones with knowledge and suspicions, were likely retired. This new job was in a different region; and it was funded by the County rather than the State. By early summer he had a start date. He would leave in a few weeks, after Reunion. The rest of us would follow once we packed up and sold the house. It was to be my last glorious summer in Maine.

The first event of the summer was the local Potato Blossom Festival, a weeklong annual event we often missed because it coincided with Reunion. This year they fell in separate weeks.

It was mid-morning on Potato Festival Saturday. There was a knock on the door. Jason was here. Surprise!

Jason lived over 40 miles away. He had never showed up unannounced. Never. Jason claimed he had a spur of the moment desire to come attend Festival activities. Father looked smug.

I went into panic mode. I had never told my parents about the run ins with Jason, how experience had taught me to never be within arm's reach of him. Why would I tell them this? They would only blame it on my sinful nature.

I contemplated various escape tactics in my head, eventually settling on my sister.

"Heather, do you want to come with us to check out the festival?" (Please, please, please, please. Pretty, pretty please! Forgive me for all the times I refused to let my kid sister tag along. Please!)

We looked over the schedule of activities (which had somehow been conveniently left in plain sight) and decided to wander down Main Street, little sister in tow. We wandered around, looked at some exhibits, listened to some live music, ate a little street food, and made our way back home.

I tried to escape back to my room, but the schedule was still sitting out with suggestions for the rest of the day. There was another live band behind the Jr High and sky diving behind the High School. "Heather, please come with us to watch the sky diving?"

A few hours later we were back at the house again. It was dinner time. Surely, he would leave now.

Sadly, Father wasn't done. He suggested a movie. A movie? Movies required driving to another town. "Heather, do you want to come see a movie?" This time Father said no. He directed his response to Heather as if she had been the one insisting on tagging along all day.

How could he not see this? She was barely twelve. I was almost sixteen. I was at an age where I never wanted to be burdened by my kid sister, now I was the one insisting she come with. What part of "Please don't send me off alone with this guy," was he not seeing?

I tried to come up with another excuse. School was out for the summer so I couldn't fall back on homework. I needed to clean my room. I needed to pack for Reunion next week... Nothing was good enough. I was getting into Jason's car, alone with him. There was no getting around it.

Jason drove an old sedan with a bench seat. I sat waaay over on my side, literally smashed against the passenger door. He was a gentleman all the way to Presque Isle. He asked what music I liked and tuned the radio away from his Country station to my Rock one. We saw a movie. I have no idea what. He kept his hands to himself.

On the drive home we got caught in a torrential downpour, literally the heaviest I have ever encountered. We had to pull off the road because the rain blocked all visibility.

I was still smashed against the passenger door. He stayed in the driver's seat. The Rolling Stones played "Miss You" on the radio. He looked at me and said, "You listen to that? That's not music. What the hell is that?" I laughed, not because I agreed with him, I laughed because my anxiety level was too high to keep it inside.

When the rain let up, we drove the rest of the way to my house. As we pulled into the drive, I was still smashed against the passenger door, a couple of precious feet separating us. I made it all the way home. I could not believe it. I was safe!

And then I wasn't.

Then he was all the way across that bench seat and my back was pressed against the door, the same door I thought was my safety point. The serpent tongue was down my throat. His hands were up inside my shirt, down inside my pants. How many hands did he have?

I don't know how to explain what happened next. I have written that I froze, but that isn't exactly right. I didn't stiffen. I want to say I went limp but that isn't right either. I didn't freeze solid like a board. I didn't go limp like a rag doll, I just went away. Somehow, I threw my consciousness out of my body. It was as if my psyche floated somewhere about four feet above myself. I drifted outside and above the windshield. I wasn't a part of my body anymore, just a witness looking down at the scene. I was still aware of what was happening to my body I just wasn't a part of it.

How could he possibly think I wanted him to do this? How could he not realize that he was mauling a dead, lifeless thing? I waited, I prayed for him to figure it out, but the mauling went on and on. My mind was racing, trying to find a way out.

"No" still wasn't an option. He wasn't a boy he was a man, eighteen, out of High School, with a job. I was a child. I was not allowed to say no to a man. Hadn't I tried to say no earlier? Hadn't I made it obvious again and again that I didn't want to be alone with this man? Why had Father insisted? Why had he pushed me to get into this car, alone with this young man that was not my friend and who had never been safe?

After what seemed forever, I managed to pull my face away from his and forced out a few shaky words. "I should go inside. They probably heard the car. They are probably watching." He backed off then. Grunted. Didn't say anything else, just freed his grip so I could open the door and climb out. Then he drove off as I got to the side door. He didn't wait to see that I got in the house, didn't smile or wave, just looked away and drove off.

I hoped I would never see him again.

The next morning, Sunday, Jason and the rest of his family showed up for our regular church service. I didn't realize until later, after everyone else was gone, that Jason had arrived in his own car. I asked why he hadn't left with the rest of his family and was told that Father had invited him to stay for Sunday dinner and a game of chess.

Father was fond of chess. He considered it intellectual and manly. He had a sizable collection of hand carved chess sets.

I wasn't happy with this development but hoped, at least, I wouldn't have to be alone with Jason again. Surely, I would be safe here, in our kitchen, with the rest of the family all within arm's reach. I turned my back to the room and busied myself at the stove.

I was a skinny fifteen-year-old wearing a pair of boy's jeans that stretched taunt across my protruding hip bones.

Jason stepped up behind me. He placed his hand on my right hip and asked what I was cooking.

I felt a slight tickle of his breath disturbing the hairs on the on top of my head and the warmth of his body standing too close behind mine. I could feel his breath in my right ear as he asked the question.

I held my body still, frozen, unwilling to offer any reason to believe I welcomed his presence. Even my breath was still. My only movement was the continued back and forth of a wooden spoon as I pushed a tab of melting butter across the bottom of the pan. I looked at the items sitting out on the stove with disdain and uttered a single syllable, "Peas."

One syllable, expending as little air as possible. I ignored the other items on the stove, premeasured flour, and milk.

Mother hated cooking, at least that was my understanding. Years later I would see photos of her gleefully showing off a homemade, heart shaped cake to her then fiancé and wonder about the parts of her life she chose to deny.

In our home food was prepared to the minimal level required. I was the only one who chose to spend a few minutes to make food preparation an art, or a joy, rather than simple drudgery. Sunday dinner should have at least a small nod to gratitude and celebration, hence the milk and flour, a quick béchamel, a small sign of respect for the bag of peas we had grown in our own garden.

I did not explain any of this to the unwanted, overly forward dinner guest, shifting his stance so that his chest pressed against my back.

I uttered one single syllable, unfroze my body just enough for that tiny puff of air.

"Peas."

One syllable,

Half a heartbeat,

One minute contraction of my diaphragm,

In an instant his hand slid forward and down. One swift, obviously well practiced move. Inside my jeans, between my hip bones, inside my underwear, between my legs, between my labia, two fingers down, in, and up, all the way inside my vagina!

I froze stiff, then I started to shake. I pulled away and turned to face him. Without bothering to think I said, "We need to talk." He smiled in agreement, and we stepped out onto the back porch together.

The bravado of the moment before began to leave me. I opened my mouth, but nothing came out, I just started to shake a little harder. I gulped air, paused, and tried again, "Please." It was all I could say. I sucked more air and tried again. "Please. Please. Can we just, just... slow down? Please."

He looked me in the eyes for half a second, shrugged his shoulders as if to say that I literally meant nothing at all to him, and answered, "Yeah. Whatever."

We both stepped back into the house. I turned away from him and faced the stove again. He started a conversation with Father. When the meal was ready, we ate. He sat beside me at the table, not so close I had to feel him and not across the table where I had to look at him.

After dinner he and Father set up their chess game. I helped pick up the kitchen and retreated to my room as soon as I possibly could, grateful to be all the way upstairs and at the far end of the hall.

Sometime later I heard the house door close. He was gone. I breathed a sigh of relief and realized he had not spoken another word to me. "Yeah. Whatever," was the end of it all. The next week we were at Reunion, then Father flew off to Michigan. I never saw Jason or any other member of his family again.

No one ever bothered to ask me about any of it. No one asked if I had enjoyed the movie the night before or how I felt about being sent on a date with someone I never would have chosen to be alone with. No one seemed to notice that I had run to my room at the earliest possible moment or that Jason left without saying goodbye. No one wanted to know what had happened or check to see if I was okay.

That was our family. When I got suckered, deceived, into an Alter Call, I had to face a full-on inquisition. But when my own father set me up with an uncontrollable, serpent tongued, handsy ape, it was up to me to sink or swim. They didn't even want to know.

Good-Bye to Maine

Maine was coming to an end. I had one last glorious summer, Reunion, Junior, Jr. High, Senior High and Adventure camp. Then back home for my sixteenth birthday with all of my friends in attendance, all the wonderful girls who stayed friends with me throughout six and a half years despite the times that I was a messed-up kid who couldn't have been the easiest to get along with.

I spent a surprising amount of time of time at Mrs S's house, she of the pea soup, my Sophomore English teacher. I felt safe at her house, and she never seemed to mind if I showed up unannounced. (Thank you, Mrs S. Even I didn't know how much I needed that.)

One more Adventure Camp, one more week with Paul. We picked up just where we had left off, but it was also sad. I tried to believe I would find my way back to that place, but I knew it was a fool's hope.

The house didn't sell right away. We were still in Maine for the start of the school year and the potato harvest but then it was time to go. The moving truck came and went. We packed what was left into our old Jeep. I only had my drivers permit but Mother claimed she was too stressed to do the driving. Surely my permit was good enough to let me drive for four days through New Brunswick, Quebec and Ontario. Surely a sixteen-year-old who had never driven on a highway could handle a twelve-hundred-mile trip. Surely Canada would honor a teen-age American who didn't even have a license, just a Maine drivers permit… but those are stories for another day.

Acknowledgements

First, always, thank you to my dear husband Wesley. You have taught me so much about how to love. You have taught me what it feels like to be safe, cherished, supported, and trusted. I cannot imagine writing this book without your steadfast encouragement. You gave me the foundation to become fearless. Thank you for choosing to share this earthly adventure with me.

To Stephanie, my therapist of many years. You have been my guide, my cheerleader and friend. Without you this book would not be possible.

To the family I have found along the way.

> To Damon, my son: I am awed by your strength and spirit. I cannot express the gratitude I feel to you for choosing me.
>
> To Joshua: are you son, nephew, brother? Does it matter? My life is infinitely richer for having you in it.
>
> To Iryna, Dima, Anna, and Alisa: Our journey is just beginning. I treasure having you in my life and home and look forward to everything still to come.

A Note to Readers About Community of Christ

I was born into the little-known Restoration denomination Community of Christ, as were my parents, their parents, and generations before them. Sadly, my worship family is also a primary player in my story, which includes sexually abusive acts committed by members of my denomination and at church sponsored activities.

While I understand it is tempting for the reader to see our small denomination as the source of dysfunction, abuse, and isolation, I ask them to please withhold judgement. I ask the reader to remember that dysfunction, abuse, even sexual abuse, are not unique to my worship family. Sexual abuse is endemic across religious and social institutions. The values we cherish; trust, acceptance, repentance, forgiveness… are easily exploited by manipulative, predatory people.

Failure to compassionately respond to the needs of the sexually abused is also common. People who do not know what to do, or are afraid of what they might learn, choose silence over action. At times my church has been silent. Individuals within my church have chosen not to hear my cries for help. But others, including those in leadership positions, have listened as I have tried to explain that silence is not the answer, and have supported me in writing this book.

Community of Christ remains my spiritual home even as I struggle with the wounds and challenges of my abusive history. My church is filled with people who have nourished and supported me throughout my lifetime, even when they did not understand the challenges I was facing. My church is filled with people whom I love and who love me deeply.

Community of Christ is not a just a place to sing hymns and spend a couple of hours on a Sunday morning. In Community of Christ, we support and care for each other like family. I am deeply grateful for the many members of my church family who have loved and cared for me and brought me to this place where I can reach out, Face the Storm, and Tell the Truth!